Christ in Perspective

CHRISTOLOGICAL PERSPECTIVES
IN THE THEOLOGY OF KARL BARTH

Christ in Perspective

CHRISTOLOGICAL PERSPECTIVES IN THE THEOLOGY OF KARL BARTH

John Thompson

THE SAINT ANDREW PRESS
EDINBURGH

First published in 1978 by
THE SAINT ANDREW PRESS
121 George Street, Edinburgh

ISBN 0 7152 0372 X

Printed and bound in Great Britain by
Morrison & Gibb Ltd, London and Edinburgh

Contents

Preface

In his splendid biography (*Karl Barth*, English Translation, SCM Press, London, 1976) Eberhard Busch has succeeded in letting Barth speak largely for himself in his own words. The present work does not aim exactly at this but is rather an attempt to let Barth be heard on a central (indeed *the* central) theme of his theology—the name and reality of the living Lord Jesus Christ. For, Karl Barth—the greatest theologian of our time (he himself did not like this kind of statement)—centred his life and his thinking on Jesus Christ who fully and alone reveals God to us. Therefore theology must deal at every point with Jesus Christ in perspective, i.e. in relation to God, the universe and man. Jesus Christ is, therefore, to be seen as a whole and not in the separation of the various aspects of his being and work or in the relative isolation in which traditional Christology placed him. On the contrary, he is to be viewed in the totality of his being and work and in relation to every aspect of theology as its focus and determining centre.

This book is an attempt to expound this central theme which runs like a golden thread throughout the massive tomes of the *Church Dogmatics*. Aspects of this work have been touched on before but the whole has not previously been expounded. This work is largely a straightforward exposition of Barth's thought on this central theme of his theology. Critical questions have been dealt with by others so that the writer has limited himself to dealing both with exposition and with some of these criticisms. This limitation has been necessary for two reasons. First, this is a shortened form of an original thesis. Secondly, the writer finds himself more in agreement with Barth than his critics and has himself only rarely and briefly entered a critical caveat. It is his belief that Karl Barth's contribution to this central theme and so to the whole of theology has been outstanding and is most relevant to the current debate on who Jesus really was and is. Barth follows the mainline of Christological thinking in the Church though with a refreshing new rethinking and modifications. There can be little doubt that he would be completely against the idea that Jesus Christ is simply the best man who ever lived. It is my hope that this book will offer some contribution not only to making Barth's mature thought more widely known to

English-speaking readers but also to clarifying and deepening our thinking on the current debate on Christology.

References to the *Church Dogmatics I/1* are to the G. T. Thomson translation and those referring to Jüngel: *Gottes Sein ist im Werden* are to the original German with my own translation. This is because the script was in the hands of the publishers before the new translation of *Church Dogmatics I/1* became available and also before the translation of Jüngel's book.

Anyone who produces a book, of whatever nature, owes a great deal to many others—and I am no exception. I am grateful to Professor J. L. M. Haire who supervised my thesis and to the Very Rev. Dr Austin Fulton who read the present script. Most valuable of all, from the theological point of view, were my contacts and conversations with Professor Eberhard Jüngel of Tübingen in the Summer Semester of 1972. He is one of the finest living expositors of Karl Barth. The book would probably never have seen the light of day had it not been for the fact that Professor J. K. S. Reid (then of Aberdeen University and my extern examiner) thought it fit for publication. The Saint Andrew Press willingly undertook the onerous task of publication, together with Wm Eerdmans of Michigan, USA. I am most grateful to Mr T. B. Honeyman and Mr Maurice Berrill of the Saint Andrew Press for their help and advice.

My thanks are also due to those who typed the script; to Mrs Rosa Martin, Librarian of the Presbyterian College, Belfast and to the staff of the Inter-Library Loans in Queen's University for their courtesy and assistance. My chief thanks, however, must be reserved for my wife Ann and the family who made it possible for me to toil long hours at my tasks without interruption. Their willing selflessness and support I gratefully acknowledge and commend.

Belfast, August 1977   JOHN THOMPSON

CHAPTER ONE

Christological Perspectives

This chapter is an introduction to the basic christological perspectives of Karl Barth's theology. It will seek to show some of the issues involved in these perspectives and will also try to indicate Barth's approach to them. Here several main themes will be discussed.

I. THE PLACE OF CHRISTOLOGY

The position of Barth in this respect can be put in the following paradoxical way. In his theology there is no Christology as such;[1] on the other hand, it is all Christology. By this we mean the following. It is an interesting but a significant fact that there is no such thing as a section on Christology as such in the whole of Karl Barth's writings. Yet it is christological through and through. This is due to the fact that Barth's theology as a whole and in every part is determined by its relation to Jesus Christ, his being and action, so that one cannot detach any aspect of it from its christological basis. At the same time the person of Christ is never considered in isolation, i.e., apart from his work. It is the fact of this inter-relation and interaction of 'his active person or his personal work',[2] as Barth calls it, that leads to no Christology in isolation and it is the fact that the person of Christ is central to all his theology that makes the christological emphasis so important and significant for Barth.

This does not mean that the themes and subject matter traditionally associated with Christology are abandoned, i.e., that Christology in this limited sense is not dealt with. Quite the contrary is the case. It means rather that the themes of Christology are set within the context of God's revelation and reconciliation as a whole.[3] It is for this reason that we speak less of Karl Barth's Christology and more of the title of this work, the christological perspectives—perspectives which are definitive for the whole of the *Church Dogmatics*.

Since Jesus Christ is the Word of God spoken to man, the content of the revelation of God, and since Christology has to do with Jesus Christ clearly christological thinking is central and paramount. This

Barth defines as follows. 'For me thinking is christological only when it consists in the perception, comprehension, understanding and estimation of the living person of Jesus Christ as attested by Holy Scripture, in attentiveness to the range and significance of his existence, in openness to his self-disclosure, in consistency in following him as is demanded . . . We are not dealing with a Christ-principle, but with Jesus Christ himself as attested by Holy Scripture.'[4] The living person of Jesus Christ is, however, not a vague but a distinct person, 'the crucified and risen Son of God and Son of Man, as the one almighty Mediator between God and man'.[5] He is God and man in their union, distinctness and communion.

Because Jesus Christ has this priority, centrality and normative position for faith and theology, all theology has this christological basis and perspective. Hence, '*per definitionem* christological thinking forms the basis for all other theological thinking'.[6] It is, therefore, out of the question to start with other prior decisions about God and man, sin and evil, and then support them christologically. Hermann Volk writes, 'from the beginning Christ is the main content and presupposition of theology. In Christ, revelation has its high water mark. Theology is in every part christological. Christology is therefore not one treatise alongside others . . . its [theology's] starting point is Christology.'[7]

Again, it should be clear what this does and does not mean. It does not mean that there is no theology except Christology, that all other theology is absorbed and assumed into it. Barth's *Church Dogmatics* is a massive proof to the contrary. It means rather that all aspects of theology and dogmatics must be dynamically related to this living and concrete centre and be determined throughout by it. So while 'the decisive word must be spoken in Christology',[8] it is not the only word. To isolate it or leave it out of any area of theology is to cut loose from one's moorings and to drift. Barth constantly seeks to avoid this danger; he vividly describes the relation of Christology to the rest of theology in this way. 'If Christology in particular insists upon this truth and its recognition, it thereby describes as it were an inner circle surrounded by a host of other concentric circles in each of which it is repeated, and in which its truth and recognition must be maintained and expounded.'[9] While Christology is central it is not all but it does pervade every other aspect of theology as its determining centre without which it would cease to be Christian theology in any real sense of the term.[10]

H. Hartwell has seen and emphasised this point clearly. He writes, 'The *Church Dogmatics* is wholly *christological* in the sense that in it, generally speaking, every theological proposition has as its point of departure Jesus Christ, the Son of God and the Son of Man, in the unity of his person and work. This christological concentration of the

Church Dogmatics and indeed of Barth's theology as a whole, is "unparalleled in the history of Christian thought".[11] This christological concentration does not mean, however, that the work of the triune God is neglected or that the Father and the Holy Spirit within the Trinity are unimportant. 'It does not contradict the asserted concentration on the Word of God since in Barth's view . . . Jesus Christ is himself the Word of God . . . in view of Barth's teaching on the triune God, creation and the Holy Spirit, it may even be doubted whether his theology can be classified as wholly christocentric, seeing that to both the Father and the Holy Spirit a prominent place is assigned in it.'[12]

2. THE THEME OF CHRISTOLOGY

For Barth, the reality and name of Jesus Christ are almost synonymous concepts. The name is, however, not the Reality as such but is a symbol or sign of it. It is 'a name indicating a person'.[13] Therefore, when Barth speaks of the name of Jesus Christ he is using it in this sense and not as a simple nomenclature.

The reality of Jesus Christ is the theme of Christology. However, when the New Testament speaks about this reality it always speaks of the name of Jesus Christ.[14] This name is the name of the Lord equivalent to Yahweh in the Old Testament. This is simply another way of saying that we are here speaking of the reality of revelation and 'that Jesus Christ is this reality' which is 'utterly simple, as simple as anything else in the world, as simple as only God is'.[15] Barth can put it also in this way. 'This name is God's revelation, or to be more exact, the definition of revelation arising out of revelation itself, taken from it and answering to it.'[16] Barth is saying that in this person Jesus Christ who is true man we meet with the one true God, the God-man in his unity and totality; we see the union and communion of God and man in him.[17] It is this which gives content and meaning to this simple reality. This reality of revelation has thus a two-sided expression which is summed up by Barth in this way: 'That God's Son or Word is the man Jesus of Nazareth, is the one christological thesis of the New Testament; that the man Jesus of Nazareth is God's Son or Word is the other.'[18]

Friedmann puts it in this way 'The name of Jesus Christ is the ultimate Word of which the New Testament writers speak. He is first and in relation to him the christological confession is secondary; this has a twin aspect and already has a refracted light.'[19] Two things follow from this as Friedmann points out. (*a*) There can be no systematizing of it.[20] 'The sentences about God and man, about Jesus and Christ, stand in a relative antithesis to each other and point beyond themselves to the ultimate Word, Jesus Christ.'[21] That thinking in this form should take place is self-evident but its relation to Jesus Christ reveals its relative character. (*b*) 'The completely comprehensive meaning which the name of Jesus Christ receives, it does so not as a principle, name, symbol, sign and cypher as such but because it points concretely to the being of Jesus Christ, the reality of his person and work.'[22] Hence, in Christology we are dealing with 'penultimate sayings . . . in their position of relative antithesis' and so they 'point beyond themselves . . . to Jesus Christ'.[23] We must, therefore, look to Christ and to him alone. 'The Church must be severely vigilant to see that it expects everything from *Jesus Christ*, and from Jesus Christ *everything*; that he is unceasingly recognised as the way, the truth and the life.'[24] It is because he is such that no other truth or reality is to be the object of faith or the content of theology. This christological concentration[25] is a necessary deduction from the nature and reality of Jesus Christ as he is attested in Holy Scripture. 'The name of Jesus Christ covers the whole power of the Christian message because it indicates the whole of its content, because at its heart, which is normative for the whole, it is a message about him.'[26] In him is the fulness of the divine life and love, and there is no necessity to go to any other source for the knowledge of God. In fact no other source can give it. This automatically excludes all 'natural' knowledge of God, all natural theology.

Barth expresses this truth otherwise when he speaks of Jesus Christ as the 'light of life' and says that this is summed up in the affirmation, 'Jesus Christ lives'. He continues: 'This is at once the simplest, and the most difficult christological statement.'[27] It means that he exists in the manner of God and in the manner of man but in their unity and this is the basis and the possibility of the co-existence of God and the world. This life has a formal and a material side. The formal is that he lives 'as very God and very man, as Lord and servant, in all the singularity of the act of his existence'.[28] The material is that his life is reconciliation, the overcoming of man's contradiction. 'It takes place as . . . the history of salvation; as the occurrence of the coming and eventuation of the salvation of the whole world and all men.'[29] This is the glory of the Mediator. In this life of reconciling grace as God and man Jesus Christ does not leave his testimony to another but is 'his own authentic witness'.[30] 'In so doing he declares and expresses his inward self. By it he makes known no more and no less than his very being. He gives us to understand who and what he is, his person, will and work.'[31] Put otherwise, he makes known his name, the reality of the living Word, of God himself in this man Jesus of Nazareth. It is this whole content of the self-revelation of Jesus Christ that is the theme and object of Christology.

There have been many criticisms made of this so-called christological concentration of Barth's, of his repeated emphasis on the name of

Jesus Christ. The chief one is that, in stating it in this way, it becomes a Christ-principle. Friedmann, while not expressly making this criticism himself, quotes a thesis by W. Günther[32] and summarises as follows: 'Because Barth uses the name of Jesus Christ so frequently and so comprehensively it has been objected that he deduces it from a principle. The name Jesus Christ expresses the unity of person and work and prevents it from being a mere concept. In this way Barth is free to dispense with the individual details of the historical life of Jesus and at the same time make Christ a principle of his theology.[33] The objection here is that the Christ-principle to some extent takes the place of the historical Jesus. Similarly Colin Brown objects to Jesus Christ being made the complete centre of Barth's theology and argues that in so doing Barth is using 'a key idea' to interpret everything. 'All along the line Barth has attempted to reinterpret Christian theology in accordance with this *single* Christ-principle.'[34] If this is in any sense true it is far from Barth's own intention. Indeed, as we have seen, it is the complete opposite. Not even 'grace'[35] is such a principle. What we are here concerned with is the living reality of Jesus Christ in his revelation.

Moreover, Barth repeatedly warns against seeing this person as in any sense the embodiment of a form, principle, idea or general truth.[36] The repetition of the name at various places in the *Church Dogmatics* does not imply subservience to a principle but is a pointer to the centrality of the person of Jesus Christ, to the truth that he is God and man, in their unity. The name is a sign of the person and the person has this content, significance and meaning and the two are one.

Further proof that Barth is not dealing with a Christ-principle but the very opposite is the use he makes of the term 'history' to describe what happens in Jesus Christ. History is at the opposite pole from a principle or idea since it tells a concrete story of particular events associated with a person, indeed the history of that person himself; whereas a principle is used to utter abstract or general truths. Jesus Christ is God's once for all action in atonement—for us men and for our salvation. When we speak of the name of Jesus Christ we are speaking of this history with this concrete content and meaning. 'We must realize that the Christian message does not at its heart express a concept or an idea, nor does it recount an anonymous history to be taken as truth and reality only in concepts and ideas.'[37] It does recount history but the very particular history of Jesus Christ and of God's dealings with man in him. 'For he is the history of God with man and the history of man with God.'[38] So that 'all the concepts and ideas used in this report . . . derive their significance only from the bearer of this name and from his history, and not the reverse'.[39] Moreover, Barth repeatedly emphasises the 'event' character of the history of Jesus Christ. It is something which no principle, idea or concept can embody, the action of God in reconciliation in the cross of Jesus Christ. All this the name of Jesus Christ includes and all this is meant when we speak of Barth's christological concentration.

Though Friedmann does not actually accuse Barth of adopting a Christ-principle he does believe that by repeated emphasis on and use of 'the *living* person of Jesus Christ he is ultimately unable sufficiently to guard against it. The reason is this: so long as Barth speaks of the living person of Jesus Christ without a closer definition he remains in the abstract sphere of life. . . . It is obvious that consistent christological thinking can only be convincing in so far as it includes a correct doctrine of the *reality* of Jesus Christ. It does not help much to overplay the systematic difficulties of such thinking by a mere reference to the name and person of Jesus Christ. . . . If the reference to Jesus Christ is to be a true antidote to misunderstandings it must continually be related to the full meaning of the *divine-human reality* of Jesus Christ, i.e. the life of Jesus Christ must be further defined as a divine-human one.'[40] Friedmann has not only correctly seen what is here necessary but has also clearly stated what Barth means and has himself already expressed. For it is in this precise way that he has defined and given content and meaning to the *life* of Jesus Christ. 'That Jesus Christ lives means quite simply that he exists in the manner of God . . . but it also means quite simply that he exists in the manner of a man'[41]—exactly as Friedmann prescribed. However, Friedmann shows in the next sentences that this is not his real concern. His criticism is that of many Roman Catholic theologians and the point where they differ fundamentally from Barth, namely, that the latter does not give a relative independence to the humanity of Jesus Christ and so fails to preserve a proper tension and polarity between the divine and human. In other words the anthropological factor as itself partially determining the nature of the relation of God and man is not fully observed. This is a matter for later comment. Here it is enough to say that it is completely contrary to Barth's understanding of the human nature in the person of Christ.

H. Volk[42] believes that in Barth 'Christology is so much a principle (Prinzip) that there is the danger of systematizing over a wide field . . . The danger of the use of a principle in a forced way is not far distant. For even in Christian theology Christology can be used as a principle in such a powerful way that it results in a narrowing of the theological basis and contents.'[43] This is a well known and oft-repeated criticism; and the answer has been given by Barth himself in the whole of his *Church Dogmatics*. Where the christological concentration has in fact led is not to a lessening but to a very great enrichment of the whole of theology. For if Jesus Christ is *the* truth[44] then to follow him in faith and theology is the one way to true understanding.

Barth in turn puts a question to his critics and particularly to his Roman Catholic ones. If one refuses to give sole place to Jesus Christ, *solo Christo*, and gives a place to others, does this not at once jeopardise and undermine the sole lordship of Jesus Christ? He writes: 'I now have an inkling of something which at first I could not understand: what is meant by the "christological constriction" which my expositor and critic urged against me in terms of mild rebuke. But we must bring against him the counter-question, whether in all the spiritual splendour of the saints who are supposed to represent and repeat him Jesus Christ has not ceased—not in theory but in practice—to be the object and origin of the Christian faith.'[45] On this point Colm O'Grady comments 'undoubtedly, we see here the really basic difference between Karl Barth's christocentrism and Catholic christocentrism. . . . The problem concerns the reconciliation of an objectively and perfectly accomplished unique redemption of Jesus Christ with a salvific activity on the part of the individual Christian, the Church, our Lady, etc.'[46] Barth rightly denies that the second part is true.

It is a further elaboration of the same basic objection when many theologians accuse Barth of what has come to be known as Christo-monism (Christ alone).[47] The same answer may be given as above—there is nothing wrong in speaking of *solus Christus* if he is the one and only revelation of God—as he is. Barth's only desire is not to give to man a part which is not his in the Gospel and not to undermine the sole sovereignty of Christ.

W. Schlichting[48] strongly rejects both the charges of a systematizing of theology by Barth on the basis of a principle and that of Christo-monism. So to interpret Barth is completely to misunderstand him. He points out that Barth consistently refers all theology to its centre in the living Lord Jesus Christ and sees it as a form of discipleship, i.e. following after him and his way,[49] in life and thought. Schlichting quotes E. W. Wendebourg in approval of Barth. 'The whole of the Church Dogmatics, the further one goes into it, is an attempt to illumine the centre of Holy Scripture and of all true Christian preach-ing, viz., the person and work of Jesus Christ and to let this centre be perceptible and relevant in every dimension of Christian theological thinking.'[50] Again as Wendebourg says[51] 'The way of evangelical theology will only be full of promise if it does not fall back again behind the *solus Christus* which Barth demands.'

3. CHRISTOLOGY AND RECONCILIATION

(a) *Starting-Point and Method in Christology*

In his christological perspectives Barth questions the validity of the procedure in the older Dogmatics whereby there was a 'single, complete and self-contained chapter on Jesus Christ, the so-called "Christology",[52] followed by others on the work of Christ, the atonement, the two states of humiliation and exaltation and the three offices of Christ as prophet, priest and king. The reason is simple. Jesus Christ as he is witnessed to in the Scriptures is true God and true man in the unity of reconciliation. 'In him both are in this order, the one whole of the event of reconciliation.'[53] To study Jesus Christ in isolation from this event and its unity is to fail to see him whole and to be in danger of abstracting him, as it were, from his proper context. Barth argues that by treating each aspect as a self-contained unit the older Dogmatics tended towards such an abstraction with the result that too often Christ could be understood nominalistically rather than realistically. This means that he could be understood as a symbol or name for something else rather than himself being the subject and content of God's reconciling act. 'An abstract doctrine of the person of Christ may have its own apparent importance, but it is always an empty form, in which what we have to say concerning Jesus Christ can never be said. Again, it is almost inevitable that a doctrine of the work of Christ separated from that of his person will sooner or later give rise to the question, and perhaps even impose it, whether this work cannot be understood as that of someone other than that divine-human person.'[54] The New Testament, on the contrary, always sees Jesus Christ in the totality of his being and action. It is, therefore, only for the sake of our thinking out and stating the doctrines that we must distinguish these aspects and so deal specifically in the more limited sense with Christology.

While, therefore, the person and work of Christ can be distinguished they must not be separated. Indeed it is not even correct to speak of them in this simple way as if we were dealing with the older doctrines of Christology and soteriology. Christology, in Barth's sense, includes the work and reconciliation presupposes, involves and includes the person. 'What is needed in this matter is nothing more or less than the removal of the distinction between the two basic sections of classical Christology, or positively, the restoration of the hyphen which always connects them and makes them one in the New Testament. Not to the detriment of either the one or the other . . . Not to cause the doctrine of the person of Christ to be absorbed or dissolved in that of his work, or vice versa. But to give a proper place to them both.'[55] Barth's position in this matter is admirably summarized in these words: 'Jesus Christ exists in the totality of his work as the Mediator. He alone is the One who fulfills it, but he does completely fulfill it, so that in and with what we have to say about *him in particular* we necessarily speak about that *comprehensive whole* which constitutes its particularity.'[56] The particular aspects of the person and work can only be rightly understood and interpreted in the light of the whole (i.e. reconciliation) which gives to each its real content and meaning. In speaking of one aspect for all its particularity one speaks of the whole; the whole must be manifest in each part. While, therefore, we must deal with Christology in the narrower sense, it is the whole Jesus Christ in reconciling being and action that is meant, and it is he who controls and determines this whole. 'What is said about Jesus Christ himself, the christological propositions as such, are constitutive, essential, necessary and central in the Christian doctrine of reconciliation. In them we have to do with that one whole. They cannot, therefore, bear that respectful isolation with which they have been and are so often treated . . . Rather they must be represented and thought of as the statement from which all truth derives, which control the whole nexus, which themselves constitute and reveal this nexus. Self-evidently they have to be made, they cannot simply disappear . . . Otherwise we would be well on the way to asserting the autonomy of the event of atonement in relation to the One who must be regarded and understood as the subject, executor and Lord.'[57] So, while the more limited christological propositions have this constitutive character for reconciliation and show us who Jesus Christ is, we must always see this being of Jesus Christ as a being not in and for himself but for us and for our salvation. This is in fact a central and crucial point in Barth's understanding of Jesus Christ and of God. He is Who he is but he is known in what he is for us and this is understood in no merely functional way but as pointing back to the reality of his being and nature.

If, then, we are to describe who Jesus Christ is we must see him in the context of the atonement while, at the same time, in this light affirming the truths and insights of the traditional dogmas. We must not, however, see the person first and the work as a follow-on or consequence. 'Jesus Christ is not what he is—very God, very man, very God-man—in order as such to mean and do and accomplish something else which is atonement. But his being as God and man and God-man consists in the completed act of the reconciliation of man with God.'[58]

Barth sums up the relation between Christology and reconciliation in this way: 'we have to develop the whole doctrine of reconciliation in accordance with our Christology and the three basic christological aspects. We shall do so in three sections which correspond to the three aspects. *The Christology is the key to the whole*. From each of the three aspects suggested it will be our starting point and will necessarily control all the detailed developments.'[59]

To gain a concrete understanding of the foregoing and its implications for the christological perspectives and so for the whole theology of Karl Barth it is necessary to set out what is the starting point and centre from which the whole being and work of Jesus Christ is understood and interpreted. Some[60] believe this is the incarnation in its traditional form with the atonement following. For Barth, while the incarnation is certainly central, it is not the starting point. For him it is in fact the whole Christ event as it is focused in the cross and the resurrection. The event of the cross is the fulfilled reconciliation accomplished by the condescension of the Son of God and revealed in the resurrection.[61] This is, moreover, the key to the whole of Barth's theology and has far-reaching consequences.

Berthold Klappert[62] has given a thorough exposition of this whole question, and shows its implications for the restructuring of the doctrine in relation to reconciliation. He draws several conclusions from this:

(1) The unity of Christology and reconciliation in the person of the Mediator. In Jesus Christ we meet with the reconciling God and reconciled man and with both in their unity. 'As this One he is the subject of the act of reconciliation between God and all men.'[63] It is the completed event of reconciliation on the cross that at once reveals the being and action of God and man in Jesus Christ and is the centre from which one sees and interprets the whole. Thus, it is Christology and reconciliation as they mutually interpret each other.

(2) The doctrine of the *two natures* is interpreted in the light of this unity of person and work. Jesus Christ is the Mediator, the unity of the reconciling God and reconciled man. In the event of reconciliation there is clearly implied the *nature and being* of the One who is active therein. We know him as wholly God and wholly man in their unity and totality. The old formula cannot be avoided, 'very God, very man, very God-man',[64] for as Barth himself puts it, 'there can be no question of abandoning the *vere Deus, vere homo*. If it is a matter of the reconciliation of man with God in Jesus Christ, i.e., the reconciliation of man with God and by God, then obviously we have to do truly and wholly with God and truly and wholly with man.'[65] This conclusion, however, is reached, as can be seen in the context, from the event of reconciliation itself. Klappert writes 'From the unity of Person and Work . . . and from the two dimensions of this work, viz, the reconciling God and reconciled man, Barth deduces the "being" of Jesus Christ as true God and true man.'[66] Or, as he puts it otherwise, 'the doctrine of the atonement is therefore not a deduction from the doctrine of the two natures and the person related to the incarnation. On the contrary the two nature theory is an implication of the doctrine of reconciliation as it is orientated on the cross.'[67] This is the new point of departure for Christology with Karl Barth.

The same is true of the *two states*. They do not describe 'a being in the particular form of a state, but the twofold action of Jesus Christ, the actuality of his work',[68] reconciliation. In other words, 'The double movement of the reconciling God and reconciled man implies the humiliation of the Son of God (*status exinanitionis*) and the exaltation of man (*status exaltationis*).'[69] The doctrine of the two states did not intend to have two static and timeless conditions related to the incarnation but 'two sides or directions or forms of that which took place in Jesus Christ for the reconciliation of man with God'.[70] It is the one action of God in Jesus Christ in reconciliation that implies the two movements of humiliation and exaltation in the being of Jesus Christ, true God and true man. Barth can relate these two aspects clearly in this way. 'There is a humiliation and exaltation . . . it is not something incidental to his being. It is the actuality of the being of Jesus Christ as very God and very man. We cannot, therefore, ascribe to Jesus Christ two natures and then quite independently two states. But we have to explain in mutual relationship to one another what Jesus Christ is as very God and very man and what takes place as the divine work of atonement in his humiliation and exaltation.'[71]

One could sum up Barth's position and relate the various aspects in this way. It is in reconciliation on the cross in this differentiated but necessary unity that God proves himself to be the true God and man to be true man. God is the true God, *vere Deus*, in his self-humiliation, (*status exinanitionis*) in reconciliation on the cross (the atonement), and man is true man (*vere homo*) in his exaltation (*status exaltationis*) by virtue of this condescension. It is in this way by virtue of Christ's self-humiliation on the cross that Barth sees the three aspects of traditional Christology and the atonement reinterpreted, and it is in this illuminating way that he modifies and actualizes traditional Christology.

Klappert states this as follows:

(1) 'Jesus Christ is the God who reconciles man on the cross (unity of person and work) who, as such and in fulfilment of the atonement, accepts the judgment on man (humiliation of the Son of God) and thus proves his true deity (*vere deus*).'

(2) 'Jesus Christ is man reconciled on the cross (unity of person and work) who, as such in fulfilment of the atonement, is exalted by God (exaltation of the Son of Man) and therein proves his true manhood, (*vere homo*).'

(3) 'Jesus Christ is the unity of the God who reconciles and of man reconciled on the cross (unity of person and work) who, as such is the Guarantor and Witness of God in his self-humiliation and man in his exaltation (coincidence of states). It is in this way that he proves the unity of God and man, his being as the God-man.'[72]

There are, however, two questions that Klappert's interpretation—correct as far as it goes—raises. These are

(1) Is this interpretation of Barth's a later change or modification of his earlier position which may have been expressed in a more traditional form of language, or is it basically the tenor of his exposition as a whole? Again, what is the place of the incarnation both in Barth's earlier and later theology and in their relation to each other? Klappert, by implication, raises this issue but does not expressly answer it.[73] The answer is, I believe, that Barth's basic position remains unchanged though it comes to its full fruition in the doctrine of reconciliation. It is true that in the Prolegomena[74] he does express himself in a more traditional way and at times seems to limit the incarnation to the coming of God as man, i.e. to the beginning of the life of Jesus. But this is not the spirit of his exposition as a whole. The incarnation is indeed God becoming man, but this reaches forward to and includes his life and cross. 'He . . . completed his incarnation on the cross.'[75] Or, again and quite clearly, he links Christ's life and death as follows: 'Of the incarnation of the Word of God we may truly say both that in the conception of Jesus by the Holy Spirit and his birth of the Virgin Mary it was a completed and perfect fact, yet also that it was continually worked out in his whole existence and is not therefore exhausted in any sense in the special event of Christmas with which it began.'[76] There is revealed here as elsewhere a certain tension, though no necessary contradiction between an event which is in a sense complete from the beginning yet which, since it must proceed to a goal, has at the same time a movement towards fulfilment. Here the judgment of Otto Weber may be regarded as correct when he writes: 'But, however one may regard individual sections of C.D., I/2, one must say that the uniting of the doctrines of the person and work of Christ, of Christology and reconciliation, is in full agreement with the main thrust of Barth's work which he has long since achieved.'[77]

(2) The second question Klappert's exposition leaves unanswered, though an answer is implied, is how, in the light of Barth's later doctrine of reconciliation, we relate it to the incarnation and what is now the meaning of the incarnation? Klappert rightly rejects Pannenberg's view that Barth's is an incarnational Christology in the sense that it has the traditional form of this doctrine as its prime basis and that any modifications are made in the light of the incarnation so understood. What, however, he fails to show is that Barth goes on in C.D., IV/1 and particularly in C.D., IV/2 to speak repeatedly of the incarnation and relates it to the atonement.[78] The answer may be that for Klappert, it is sufficient to say that the incarnation is now covered by what Barth says of Christology in the wider context of reconciliation, i.e., in relation to the working Person and the personal work of Jesus

Christ. If so, it would have been better to have said so. His exposition, however, almost gives the impression that the incarnation is now excluded. But this can hardly be his intention and is certainly far from Barth's own position. As it is there is a lacuna in Klappert's otherwise fine and illuminating interpretation.

Moreover, it is not entirely correct to say,[79] as Klappert does, that 'The Way of the Son into the Far Country'[80] is not the incarnation. Barth explicitly says that it is.[81] Nor does Barth ever separate John 1:14 and 2 Cor. 5:19b in the way Klappert tends to do by giving almost sole prominence to the latter.

Klappert[82] himself raises the question whether Barth, in several places, does not in fact suggest an incarnation, cross, resurrection sequence as in classical christology—a view Pannenberg assumes is Barth's also. While it is true that the three aspects of reconciliation, viz, *The Way of the Son into the Far Country, The Judge Judged in Our Place,* and *The Verdict of the Father*[83] do not, in Barth's interpretation, mean simply incarnation, cross and resurrection, nevertheless there is an approximation to these though the starting point is the cross. It is in the coming and existence of the Son that reconciliation takes place. It is the cross that manifests the whole scope and meaning of the incarnate life and it is in the resurrection that Jesus Christ is revealed as the One he is. In other words the three are closely inter-related and co-ordinated.

What then is the relationship between incarnation and atonement? Friedmann[84] puts the question in this way: 'Are the cross of Christ and the incarnation two separate but parallel events so that the death on the cross only makes clearer what has already happened in an incomparable way in the incarnation?' The first part of the question must be answered in the negative; the latter in the affirmative. Again, he asks, 'Does Jesus Christ follow a way which took its beginning in his human birth and was fulfilled in his death on the cross?'[85] This is partially true but, as we have seen, the coming of God as man is both complete from the beginning and yet awaits this fulfilment on the cross in the completed event of reconciliation.

In the whole context of Barth's theology we see the relationship between incarnation and reconciliation in these terms. Incarnation, which means God's coming as man, and reconciliation, which concerns what happens when he comes, are two sides or aspects of the one movement or action of God in Jesus Christ. The former, while in one sense relating more to the coming of the Word in the flesh, at the same time includes all that he was and did when he came and so reconciliation. Reconciliation, on the other hand, is the completed event in which as true God and true man he fulfilled the will of the Father and the purpose of his coming, in which the incarnation is fully realised and so included. In one sense it is the end or purpose of his coming; yet in another it is the whole of his being and action in his coming. The two, incarnation and atonement, enclose, embrace and interpret each other and are really one though distinguishable.

Only in this way can one do justice to Barth's concern for the unity of Jesus Christ as the one Lord and God active for our salvation. Only so can one do justice to his concern to give full place to all the diverse and inter-related elements in the one being and work of Jesus Christ as a whole. Certainly, there can be no question of the incarnation falling out or disappearing or, as in the case of Klappert, failing almost to be mentioned. Instead it must be given this wider scope and greater significance as the content of the being of Jesus Christ as true God, true man and their unity as the Mediator in the action of reconciliation in his life, death and resurrection. What Barth says in interpretation of the incarnation and of John 1:14 in particular is indicative of his position as a whole. 'God went into the far country *by becoming man* in his second person or mode of being as the Son . . . man—this one Son of Man— returned home . . . to fellowship with God . . . The atonement as it took place in Jesus Christ is the one inclusive event of this going out of the Son of God and coming in of the Son of Man.[86] Here Barth is clearly speaking about the one event and yet he refers to it as both incarnation and reconciliation. Klappert is thus right to see reconciliation (atone- ment) as the place where we start and from which we view the whole. For it is here that we learn who Jesus Christ is and so the meaning of the incarnation. That this interpretation agrees with Klappert's intention (though unexpressed) is clear from a quotation of his from H. G. Geyer.[87] What the incarnation is 'is seen nowhere else than in the history of Jesus Christ especially in his movement from the old life of death to life from the dead, i.e., in the specific *unity of Jesus Christ's death on the cross with his resurrection from the dead. This unity of Good Friday and Easter* . . . (is) the fundamental *unity of the history of Jesus Christ* and so in the language of tradition—the incarnation'.

The question may be asked at this point whether Barth is entirely fair to traditional Dogmatics. Certainly it is right to do as he does and see everything in the light of the unity and totality of Jesus Christ, while at the same time having a particular centre of interpretation and dis- tinguishable features. This must always remain a major achievement of Barth's theology and a continuing challenge and corrective. Again, let it be said that the traditional forms do have within them the danger of isolation and abstraction, as Barth shows. But in practice did they not also see the one aspect and truth in the light of the others and of the whole, and were these emphases as divisive and dangerous as Barth thinks? The answer must be probably not, but Barth's own exposition is greatly superior and points to the comprehensive unity of the one Lord Jesus Christ.

(b) *The Dynamic Actualism of Barth's Perspectives.*

In an important section[88] Barth gives both a summary of his own position and interpretation of Christology and at the same time a critique of traditional formulae not so much in content and intention as in form. In doing so he shows us why he has to use the formulae and terminology of action, movement and history in preference to those of a static or abstract nature as in earlier expositions. For Barth, form and content cannot be separated. His terminology therefore derives from the nature of the subject which conditions it and its uses. The terms are, in other words, not chosen at random but because they best correspond to and express the nature of the object of Christology. Since their content is the living Lord Jesus Christ in movement and action and in a saving history with and for man which is at the same time God's history the terms used must be actualistic and dynamic.

First, Barth states his own consistent position. 'From the very first we have understood and interpreted the doctrine of the incarnation ... in historical terms, as an actuality, as an *operatio* between God and man fulfilled in Jesus Christ as a union of God with man. We have represented the existence of Jesus Christ as his *being* in his *act*.'[89] Here the ideas of movement, action and history prevail. Over against the older Christology Barth states his position. 'In a basic attachment to the Reformed tradition, but without following it in detail, and transcending it at some points, we have given this a sense and position which it did not have in all earlier Christology. We have actualised the doctrine of the incarnation, i.e., we have used the main traditional concepts, *unio*, *communio* and *communicatio* as concentrically related terms to describe one and the same ongoing process. We have stated it all ... in the form of a denotation and description of a single event. We have taken it that the reality of Jesus Christ, which is the theme of Christology is identical with this event, and this event with the reality of Jesus Christ.'[90]

There are several implications and conclusions to be drawn from Barth's position.[91] The reality and being of Jesus Christ as the union of God and man cannot be divorced from the act and history in which God becomes and is this man. He 'exists in this way only in the act of God, and therefore the occurrence of this history. Can we see what he became in this act, "God and man", but ignore—or leave behind as a mere presupposition—the act in which he became it and therefore his becoming? Can we say *Verbum caro* but conceal or give no emphasis to the *factum est*?'[92] In other words the action in which God becomes man in Jesus Christ is the very being and nature of Christ and of this union and the two cannot be divorced. '*Esse sequitur fieri*'[93] becomes the phrase which expresses this truth. There is, therefore, a real *being* of God in Jesus Christ but understood always in terms of his *actuality* in *becoming*

man. 'Barth's actualism does not mean . . . that his theology leaves no
room for the idea of a "state" of things. It only denotes that there can
be no "state" which does not arise out of God's constant giving.'[94]
Barth himself sums up the point finely 'Presupposing that we are
speaking of the living Jesus Christ, can the *being* of Jesus Christ be
distinguished from what *actually takes place*, as the *act of God*, in his
existence as the Son of God and Son of Man?'[95]

Further, this action and history[96] of God and man in the concrete
reality of Jesus Christ while a once for all act of reconciliation is at the
same time a history that is all embracing and becomes real and actual
again and again. By this Barth does not mean that the sacrifice of Christ
is repeated or that the Church is an extension of the incarnation, though
he does call it the *totus Christus*,[97] i.e., Christ and his own. He means
rather that because it is an act of God in this man and this history, i.e.,
because this man's history is the history of God, it can always be
present and actual to us and we to it. It means also that since God has
united man with himself in the act of becoming man in his Son all men
are included in Christ's reconciliation. It has a universal inclusive
scope and significance, a history which comprehends all other history
in itself.[98]

(c) *Christology from 'Above' to 'Below'*

This approach to the incarnation (in line with though modifying the
classic statements of the past) has been characterized as that 'from
above to below'.[99] In this Christology we begin in our thoughts with
the action and movement of God to man, his assuming our humanity,
his becoming and being true man, one of us, our brother. This was the
common approach in the early church and is characteristic of the
Alexandrian Christology of Athanasius in the fourth century. It has
obvious points of departure in the New Testament itself (e.g. Phil.
2:5ff.; Romans 8:3; Gal. 4:4).[100] However, Pannenberg criticizes this
whole approach and believes that the primitive Christian traditions of
the New Testament begin with the man Jesus and in the light of the
resurrection proceed to demonstrate his unity with God. This is how
Pannenberg believes Christology should begin today with the man
Jesus and his history and its relation to the Old Testament history.
Nevertheless he speaks later of a 'relative justification' for the more
traditional way of approaching the question; 'one cannot claim that the
incarnational theology which has ruled the history of the development
of the christological doctrine was simply a mistake'.[101]

It is, however, possible to combine a genuine theology 'from below'
with the classical statements. In a sense the starting point as such is
unimportant save as it may point to a particular Christology. Emil
Brunner, following Luther, has changed his approach in his *Dogmatics*

partly in the light of his stronger emphasis on the functional aspects of the Person of Christ. He believes, in his later writing, that one must approach the doctrine of the Person of Christ through his work.[102] He quotes Luther as saying 'The Scripture beginneth very gently and leadeth us to Christ as to a man and after that to the Lord of all creation, and after that to a God. Thus I come into it gently and thus I learn to know God. . . . We must begin at the bottom, and afterwards rise to the heights.' It is, however, clear that both Luther and Brunner, while taking this as their practical point of departure for the New Testament view of Christ, are at the same time aware that the Scriptural testimony affirms the God-man and does not start simply with a man and then go on to that of his unity with God. Proof of this is seen in the fact that Brunner's exposition as a whole and his conclusions are not essentially different, save in emphasis, from those in his earlier book *The Mediator*.[103] His is indeed quite clearly, as over against Pannenberg's, an incarnational theology. One can therefore speak of a relative justification of this approach as well.

Karl Barth, in his own distinctive way, combines both approaches. He speaks (*C.D.*, IV/1, Section 59) of God the Son going into the far country of man's disobedience and alienation and sinfulness, taking these to himself and so becoming man, uniting man with himself. At the same time (*C.D.*, IV/2, Section 64) he speaks of man's exaltation to unity with God. It is a movement from man to God but one which is wholly determined by God's movement to and for man and is in fact identical with it. His method can more correctly be described as 'from above to below' and vice versa, related to the God who is self-humbled on the cross.

Berthold Klappert[104] has given a good and balanced summary of the different starting points and methods of several modern theologians. They can be grouped into five different types:

(1) The classical incarnation Christology *from above to below*.

(2) Christology *from below* represented by Friedrich Gogarten's conception of Jesus as that of pure personal being.

(3) Christology *from below to above*—Pannenberg.

(4) Christology seen in the contemporaneity of *above and below*, (*a*) in the Kerygma (Bultmann), (*b*) in the kerygmatic encounter with Christ (O. Weber, *Dogmatik*, II, pp. 36ff).

(5) Christology of the contemporaneity of *above and below* in the history of humiliation on the cross (Karl Barth).

It is this distinctive nature of Barth's Christology which has as its starting point the humbled Son of God on the cross and whose method is at once from above to below and vice versa, that is Barth's chief contribution to this aspect of the christological debate to-day.

(d) *Relation to Chalcedon and Tradition*

Barth's general attitude to the dogmatic inheritance of the Church and its doctrines, especially the more classical statements, can be summed up in this way as 'a respectful freedom and independence in relation to tradition'.[105] The position from which he judges the correctness or otherwise of these statements is Jesus Christ as he is attested in Holy Scripture. 'Obviously', he writes, 'it is not a powerful tradition . . . but only the Subject itself', i.e., Jesus Christ in his reconciling life that is determinative, 'the law controlling what we think and say about a given matter.'[106] Nowhere can this be seen more clearly than in his relation to the christological statements of the early Church.[107] We shall take Chalcedon as an example. The respect comes first. Chalcedon is 'normative' and its truths and insights must be reaffirmed and safe-guarded. Indeed in all Barth's christological statements, however new or different the form and shape, the content is always the Chalcedonian, very God, very man and very God-man. In his interpretation of Barth's earlier Christology in the Prolegomena (*C.D.*, I/2), H. Volk says, 'any real doubt that Karl Barth's Christology is not sincere in its acknow-ledgement of Chalcedon can no longer arise. The formal and material agreement is thoroughly convincing'.[108] This is equally true of the massive treatment of Christology in the doctrine of reconciliation. It is throughout—whatever criticisms may be offered—primarily a respect-ful reaffirmation of the truths stated at Chalcedon.

But, Barth's attitude is also one of a constructive, critical freedom and independence. The sole criterion is the Word of God, Jesus Christ him-self. In this light, and in view of Barth's own restatements, Chalcedon has its weaknesses while 'factually right and necessary'.[109] It represents Christ in such a way that it tends towards abstraction, a lack of contact with history and a kind of timelessness. 'We must not forget that if in the doctrinal decisions of . . . Chalcedon it was a matter of the being of Jesus Christ as such, these decisions had a polemical and critical character, their purpose being to delimit and clarify at a specific point. They are to be regarded as guiding lines for an understanding of his existence and action, not to be used, as they have been used, as stones for the construction of an abstract doctrine of his "person". In himself and as such the Christ of . . . Chalcedon naturally was and is a being which even if we could consistently and helpfully explain his unique structure conceptually could not possibly be proclaimed and believed as One who acts historically because of the timelessness and historical remoteness of the concepts (person, nature, Godhead, manhood, etc.). He could not possibly be proclaimed and believed as the One whom in actual fact the Christian Church has always and everywhere proclaimed and believed under the name of Jesus Christ.'[110]

Hence Chalcedon can only be properly seen and understood in

relation to the history and action of God in Jesus Christ as a whole and not in the isolation it tends to have in the traditional doctrine. So interpreted, it is misunderstood since there is no Jesus Christ apart from what he was and did as God and man in reconciliation.

Notes to Chapter 1 will be found on pp. 137–144.

CHAPTER TWO

The Incarnation

I. THE ETERNAL BASIS OF THE INCARNATION.[1]

In the theology of Karl Barth the basis of the incarnation is in God himself, in his eternal and gracious purpose to become man and so to reconcile sinful man to himself in his Son Jesus Christ our Lord.[2] Therefore, before beginning to expound the meaning of the incarnation, we must speak of its eternal basis in God himself. In making this emphasis Barth is in line with the traditional teaching of the Church,[3] though he gives it a much richer and fuller treatment than most previous theology.[4] In particular it is related specifically to God's election of grace in Jesus Christ and to the being of the triune God. The incarnation therefore has its beginning in God, in his being, action and choice in Jesus Christ.

(a) Election

God is the self-revealing God and as such he is the electing God. As Barth puts it 'If we hold fast the revelation of God as the revelation of his eternal will and good-pleasure, if we acknowledge God's freedom in the revelation in which he has proclaimed and enacted it, then as the beginning of all things with God we find the decree that he himself in person, in the person of his eternal Son, should give himself to the son of man, the lost son of man, indeed that he himself in the person of the eternal Son should *be* the lost Son of Man. In the beginning with God, i.e., in the resolve of God which precedes the existence, the possibility and the reality of all his creatures, the very first thing is the decree whose realisation means and is Jesus Christ ... It is a decision which is the basis of all that follows.'[5]

This comprehensive statement includes more than concerns us at the moment. Let us note, however, in this connection several points. The eternal basis of the incarnation in election is first of all a self-determination of God in which he affirms and confirms himself.[6] It is, further, the election of Jesus Christ as God's eternal will to give himself for the sake of man as created by him and fallen from him.[7] God has chosen Jesus Christ and in him man for salvation and to himself he has

Notes to Chapter 2 will be found on pp. 144–151.

ascribed perdition and death.[8] It is an exercise of his free, sovereign grace in which he chose not to be God only in his own inner life or, as Barth puts it, in his loneliness,[9] but to be God in his condescension in, with and for man by making man's cause and sin his own, removing sin and so establishing communion with a being other than himself. It is the transition from God's being in and for himself to his being as Lord of creation and so as the God of man in Jesus Christ. 'From all eternity God posits his whole majesty . . . in this particular relationship to this particular being over against himself. God pledges and commits himself to be the God of man'.[10]

(b) *Relation to the Trinity*

It is obvious that if the Son of God, the second person of the Trinity, became man there is a clear relationship between the incarnation and the Trinity. Barth's view of the Trinity is that the one God, Father, Son and Holy Spirit in the divine freedom and love lives a life complete in itself, though this is only known in and through the incarnation. This divine life has its own history and relationships. In the complete equality and unity of the divine nature the Son is nevertheless subordinate, obedient to, comes from, follows on the Father. He (the Father) rules in majesty, is the original fount of the Trinity, whereas the Son is in a relation to him, humble yet at the same time wholly and fully God.[11] It is these internal relationships of Son to Father within the Trinity that are the basis of and in a sense make possible God's self-activation and revelation *ad extra* and so creation, incarnation and reconciliation. Ultimately one must also include the person and work of the Holy Spirit. The act of love, condescension and obedience, in which the Son became man has therefore its source and possibility in the eternal relation of Father and Son, corresponds to and is continuous with this. The Scriptural basis for this Barth finds in the obedience of the Son during his earthly life which corresponds to the divine being and nature.

The Son in this obedience can go into the far country of man's disobedience, humble himself, be lowly, be other than himself in the incarnation while still remaining himself. He can do so because in the divine life there is in God himself an above and a below, a *prius* and a *posterius*, a superiority and a subordination.[12] This direction downwards in the divine action has therefore its own inherent dignity. It is not the lessening of deity but its supreme affirmation. In the incarnation God empties and humbles himself but 'he does not do it apart from its basis in his own being, in his own inner life'.[13] He determines, as it were, his own inner being to take outward form. Klappert states the relationship in this way 'This first, this *primum* is, according to Barth, *the self-determination of God for fellowship* with man which, in turn, is based on

the Being of God in his relation to himself as the One who loves in freedom
and is free in his love.'[14]

It is, however, only the Son who becomes man because only he lives
in this mode in the life of the triune God. The incarnation is thus 'the
work of the eternal Son, determined in God's eternal decree and taking
place in time, as the meaning and basis and power of the reconciliation
of the world with God. It can be his work, and it must indeed be his,
because he—the one God in the mode of being of the Son—in unity
with the Father and the Holy Ghost, in the deepest harmony of the
whole Holy Trinity of the one God—is the humble God, and therefore
exalted with the Father and the Holy Ghost.'[15] In this sense and for this
reason therefore one can speak of the Trinity as also the eternal basis
of the incarnation.

A further trinitarian perspective should also be mentioned since it
was the divine Son only who became man. We are, however, not
speaking here of a part-god but of God in his entire divinity. In
common with the traditional dogmatics[16] Barth states (*a*) negatively
that it is not the one nature of God as such but the one nature in the
mode of existence of the Son who became incarnate. In other words not
the whole deity as such Father, Son and Holy Spirit became man but
the Son in his entire divinity. 'The statement that it is the Word or the
Son of God who became man therefore asserts without reserve that in
spite of his distinction as Son from the Father and the Holy Spirit, God
in his entire divinity became man.'[17] (*b*) Positively on the other hand we
must add that because of the unity of the divine nature the whole
Trinity is involved; the *opera trinitatis ad extra sunt indivisa*. The
incarnation is thus the common work of Father, Son and Holy Spirit.
'The Father represents, as it were, the Divine *Who*, the Son the divine
What and the Holy Spirit the divine *How*.'[18] Yet in spite of the mutuality
of this triune work it was only the Son who assumed humanity. The
act of assumption is the work of the Trinity but the *terminus* is the Son
alone.[19] This can be otherwise expressed. The Son, eternally loved by
the Father and loving him eternally in return, became man because he
is sent by the Father and comes in obedience. But it is he and not the
Father who becomes man. Similarly he does not do so without the
Holy Spirit who is the eternal love between the Father and the Son.
The Son thus becomes incarnate in the omnipotence of the Father and
the mutual love of the Father and the Holy Spirit.[20] 'This One, God,
the Son, became and is also man. He became and is—according to the
will of God the Father, in the humility of his freely rendered obedience
as the Son, in the act of majesty of the Holy Spirit.'[21]

It is clear that God's eternal purpose to become man and so take the
cause of sinful man upon himself and its basis in the Trinity are closely
related, indeed, in a sense are one. Barth puts it succinctly like this

'The Son of God determined to give himself from all eternity. With the Father and the Holy Spirit he chose to unite himself with the lost Son of Man. This Son of Man was from all eternity the object of the election of the Father, Son and Holy Spirit. And the reality of this eternal being together of God and man is a concrete decree . . . This decree is Jesus Christ.'[22] Here five elements are clearly one yet distinct. The eternal decree of God to become man; yet the Son alone doing so; the unity of the divine Trinity in the action of the Son; the one object of God's election the lost Son of Man; and all this actualised and realised in Jesus Christ. This sums up the interrelationship between God's election of grace, the Trinity and the incarnation. This whole complex of truths can be otherwise stated by saying that it is the eternal will of the Father to send the Son and of the Son to come in the power of the Holy Spirit.

Or, again, it may be so stated that in the mutual love of Father, Son and Holy Spirit in which God maintains and demonstrates himself in sovereign freedom the Word became flesh. What, therefore, God does *ad extra* in Jesus Christ is in the closest possible correspondence with his trinitarian being and life.

The question arises from Barth's exposition of the eternal basis of the incarnation; Would God have become man apart from man's sin? Or has the incarnation only meaning, significance and reality in relation to man's *'felix culpa'*? Some of his statements tend to speak of a possible incarnation apart from man's sin. While God's eternal purpose is the incarnation of the Word (for us men and for our salvation) Barth seems to imply that *propter nos homines* would have applied even without *propter nostram salutem*. 'In delivering and fulfilling this first and eternal Word in spite of human sin and its consequences *as he would in fact have delivered and fulfilled it quite apart from human sin*, sin is also met, refuted and removed in time.'[23] Here Barth states that what God decreed, namely the incarnation, destroys and removes in time man's sin, but because it had its basis in God's eternal decision would have been a reality in any case. The phrase in the above quotation is almost inserted here as an aside but it is in fact fully consistent with Barth's basically supralapsarian exposition of election. Since actual man is sinful man, the question does not arise as to how we can conceive of the God-man apart from our salvation. J. C. Scott is, however, right in querying Barth at this point when he asks: 'Is it not going too far to use the word Mediator of the relationship of Christ to unfallen man? Is there any reference in Scripture which clearly and unambiguously states that the "eternal purpose" of God for the unfallen world would have been that the Word should become flesh?'[24] Barth is not completely explicit here but incarnation without sin is at any rate implied and the strictures of Scott must be accepted as correct when he again

asks 'Can we then say with dogmatic assurance that without human sin there would have been no cross, but there would certainly have been Jesus Christ the God-man?'.[25] The answer would certainly seem to be no. Rather must we say that the New Testament knows of no other God-man but the crucified Lord Jesus. It would have been better had Barth at this point, combined the absolute and the relative bases of the incarnation, as Heinrich Vogel does. By so doing he would stress that God's choosing in absolute, sovereign freedom to become man is always related to the salvation of actual sinful man. What Barth is, however, seeking to maintain here is a twofold truth, namely that God's eternal will and purpose is to be the God of man—this is the implication of election (but does this necessitate incarnation?). The other is to show that sin, while real, is but an 'incident' (Zwischenfall) in the whole context of God's dealings with man and must never be co-ordinated with grace which is the superior and triumphant will of God for man in Christ Jesus. Nevertheless, as Klappert points out, for Barth the two aspects, God's primary will and his reaction to sin, are in fact one and the same.[26]

2. THE INCARNATION—THE DIVINE SUBJECT

The incarnation as understood and interpreted by Barth is not something which is open to men to know and understand by themselves; it is, in his own words, 'the mystery of revelation'.[27] It can be described expressly as 'the great Christian mystery and sacrament beside which there is, in the strict and proper sense, no other'.[28] Two deductions can be made from this. (*a*) We have no control over God's revelation and incarnation; in it he controls and masters us. (*b*) We cannot know the *how* of God's becoming man, being both God and man but only *that* he does so. It is thus beyond man's understanding but is disclosed to him by the Holy Spirit as God makes himself known to him. Barth speaks of the task of theology as the description of this event and the merit of primitive Christology and Chalcedon that it 'did not intend to solve the mystery with its formula about the two natures of Christ . . . It began and ended with the realization that this was simply impossible'.[29]

Yet it is known to us in revelation which in its objective reality is the incarnation of the Word, the one true God present with us and for us (reconciliation) as true man. But even in revelation it is and always remains a mystery. We can only know its meaning by the Holy Spirit creating faith in us and this knowledge is at the same time acknowledgement or confession.[30] The revelation of the incarnate Word will be thus manifest to us in its truth by its own cogency and agency and not by any capacity belonging to us.

Barth defines and sums up the mystery of revelation in this way; it

'consists in the fact that the eternal Word of God chose, sanctified and assumed human nature and existence into oneness with himself, in order thus, as very God and very man, to become the Word of reconciliation spoken by God to man. The sign of this mystery revealed in the resurrection of Jesus Christ is the miracle of his birth, that he was conceived by the Holy Ghost, born of the Virgin Mary'.[31]

(a) The Word in becoming man is and remains what he is, the true and eternal God, the One who participates without restriction in the divine nature and existence; the eternal Son. The Word was God (John 1:2); 'God is free for us, in such a way that his Word by becoming man at the same time is and remains what he is, the true and eternal God, the same as he is in himself at the Father's right hand for ever and ever'.[32] His condescension signifies no loss of divine majesty but its manifestation and triumph.[33] There is of course a veiling, *kenosis* and passion,[34] an externalization compared to the divine form in a form familiar to man. One can say that in the incarnation the divinity is latent, hidden, 'veiled in flesh'. But it is only veiling not the abandonment or the lessening of it. The one who in Jesus Christ manifests himself to us for our salvation is and can be nothing less than wholly and completely God—the 'Very God' of the Creeds and Confessions. God thus became man, the Creator creature without for one moment ceasing to be God.

He becomes that which was other than, different from himself and still remains the same. God does not renounce his deity or change himself into a man or become another thing halfway between God and man. Nor does it mean that 'in him a changed God who loses his deity becomes and is a changed man who loses his humanity, but the one unchangeably true God becomes and is unchangeably true man'.[35] He cannot cease to be God even in the slightest. How could he be *God's* revelation to us and his reconciliation of us if he did?[36] He remains wholly the divine Subject, in the freedom of grace, in the divine act of humility. This is the secret of the grace of God that he does not do despite or become unfaithful to himself in becoming lowly but in the incarnation is most properly himself in the fulness of his divinity.[37]

(b) The incarnation took place in the divine *freedom* of the Word.[38] He is the Subject who acts and not the one who is acted upon. This implies that there was no human co-operation, no mutual interaction or reciprocity between God and man. Furthermore, the incarnation was not a human possibility, not a determination immanent in man,[39] nor that of a higher law superior to both God and man. Nothing in the world processes or any man compels the Son so to act; no higher evolutionary possibility could have produced the Word (contra

Schleiermacher).[40] The incarnation 'is not a realization of one of the
possibilities immanent in the created cosmos'.[41] It takes place within
world history and is related to it but cannot be deduced from it. It is an
'act of divine majesty'—'an absolutely new event'—'a new act of God',[42]
a free act of divine Lordship. Because the incarnation means God
becoming *man* it is continuous with world history, but because it is
God becoming man it is a new event; he 'here initiates a new series in
the sequence of his whole action . . . there takes place an event which is
sui generis'.[43]

(c) Further it is not a *necessity* resting upon the inner nature of Godhead or forced by man's sin. 'God did not owe it to man. He did not
owe it even to the man Jesus. He did not owe it either in his eternal
counsel or in its execution. He did not owe it even to himself, to an inner
dialectic of his Godhead. Both in eternity and in time it was the act of
his divine power and mercy as it is founded only in his freedom, in his
love to the world . . . It has no basis or possibility, and certainly no
necessity, apart from his gracious good-pleasure'.[44] What God *must* do
can only be determined by what he has done, 'by pointing to what is in
accordance with his good pleasure',[45] i.e., read off from the Christ event
itself. Indeed the incarnation was for the purpose of redemption;
revelation is reconciliation, but the Word would have been as divine
and as free without the incarnation. That he did come in the freedom of
divine grace, is, 'a miracle, an act of God's mercy'.[46]

(d) The equation God became man is *irreversible*. 'The Logos can
never become predicate or object in a sentence the subject of which is
different from God'.[47] To speak of man becoming God, the flesh
becoming Word would be impossible and blasphemous. The Word or
Son is what he is even apart from and before he became flesh but the
flesh 'could not be the flesh apart from the Word . . . would have no
being at all, far less be able to speak, act, prevail, reveal or reconcile'.[48]
The flesh which the Word assumed is mortal on its own but is alive by
this union with the Word. The flesh as such profiteth nothing, does not
reveal God but the Word becomes flesh and so quickens it. God always
remains the subject of the action of the incarnation. 'The Godhead of
God without change or commingling remains undiminished in Jesus
Christ. Even in Jesus Christ God and man cannot be exchanged. Therefore it can only be said that God has assumed humanity and not the
opposite. God can only be the Subject, in no sense can he ever become
the predicate or the object of human action. The earlier concern of
Barth to preserve and emphasise at all times the fact that God and man
are not interchangeable has not been given up.'[49] Barth rejects the
'Jesus of history' movement since it deals with a Jesus who never

existed; the only Jesus we know is One not apart from the Word but in and with the Word. For the same reason he strongly condemns the hero worship of Jesus and the teaching on the sacred heart of Jesus in Roman Catholicism. These are a deification of the creature and its worship rather than the Creator.[50]

3. THE WORD BECAME FLESH—THE HUMANITY OF THE WORD

Barth turns next to deal with the object or predicate in the sentence from John 1.14. The Word became 'flesh' means that he became true man, the object and theatre of the acts of God. 'That the Word was made "flesh" means first and generally that he became man, true and real man, participating in the same human essence and existence, the same human nature and form, the same historicity that we have. God's revelation to us takes place in such a way that everything ascribable to man, his creaturely existence as an individually unique unity of body and soul in the time between birth and death, can now be predicated of God's eternal Son as well.'[51] H. Volk writes: 'The true humanity of Jesus Christ is also called human nature. Barth is decisively against every form of docetism; equally he is against spiritualism as if man could preferably exist before God in his spirit. The body does not disqualify and the spirit does not save.'[52] It is human nature in its unity and totality that the Son of God assumes. He could have come in his invisible glory or in a being wholly foreign to us. But he came as one of us; had he come in any other way it would have been the end. But he came in this gentle fitting way choosing not to meet us in naked divinity and thus in judgment and destruction but as one of us, our brother.[53]

The Word thus became a man like ourselves with a true body, flesh and mind. He took or assumed our *humanitas*, i.e., 'human essence and existence, human kind and nature, humanity, *humanitas*, what makes a man man as opposed to God, angel or animal'.[54] As this cannot be real except in the concrete existence of one man we must say also that he became a man, assumed individual existence. But it does not mean that a man existed and that the Son became that man. To think and speak like this lands one in innumerable difficulties and is the basic mistake and danger of those who begin simply with a human Jesus. We must say rather that in the incarnation the man received concrete reality and existence because he was given such by the Son of God and our humanity as such was assumed by him. The two ideas of a man and our humanity are in Jesus coterminous. But the idea that God assumed our humanity without at the same time being one particular man is impossible.[55]

This whole discussion is therefore in fact an exposition and inter-

pretation of the *anhypostasia* and *enhypostasia* of the ancient Church.
What is meant by these terms? T. F. Torrance has given a good
definition as follows: 'By *anhypostasia* classical Christology asserted that
in the *assumpto carnis* the human nature of Christ had no independent
per se subsistence apart from the event of the incarnation, apart from
the hypostatic union. By *enhypostasia*, however, it asserted that in the
assumptio carnis the human nature of Christ was given a real and
concrete subsistence within the hypostatic union—it was *enhypostatic* in
the Word. *Anhypostasia* and *enhypostasia* are inseparable. In the incarnation the eternal Son assumed human nature into oneness with himself,
but in that assumption Jesus Christ is not only real man but a man.'[56]
This is the same as Barth's position when he states of the union of God
and man in Jesus Christ, 'from the utter uniqueness of this unity
follows the statement, that God and man are so related in Jesus Christ
that he exists as man, so far and only so far as he exists as God, i.e., in
the mode of existence of the eternal Word of God. What we thereby
express is a doctrine unanimously sponsored by early theology in its
entirety, that of the *anhypostasis* and *enhypostasis* of the human nature of
Christ. *Anhypostasis* asserts the negative. Since . . . Christ's human
nature has its existence . . . in the existence of God, meaning in the
mode of being (*hypostasis*, "person") of the Word, it does not possess it
in and for itself, *in abstracto* . . . *Enhypostasis* asserts the positive . . .
human nature acquires existence (subsistence) in the existence of God,
meaning in the mode of being (*hypostasis*, "person") of the Word.'[57]
Barth has been criticized for his doctrine of *anhypostasis* (*impersonalitas*)
on the grounds that it denies the true humanity of Jesus and is a form of
concealed Docetism.[58] He answers his critics in this way: 'It rests
simply upon a misunderstanding of the Latin term *impersonalitas* used
occasionally for *anhypostasis*.'[59] The early Church writers did not teach
that Christ's human nature lacked personality or individuality but had
this. *Personalitas* was their word for existence or being and what they
denied was that this being of Christ's flesh had an existence of its own
apart from the Word or Son.

When Barth therefore speaks of the *humanum* or *humanitas* that was
assumed he is not thinking of an abstract or impersonal substance
called human nature which was somehow there and is the object of
the *assumptio* or *unio*. Rather he is thinking in terms of a possibility
which becomes real and concrete in an individual and representative
man in union with the Word, in the assumption of the flesh in the
incarnation. The humanity of Jesus Christ is true and real because it is
given such by the Word in the hypostatic union.[60]

Jesus Christ is thus not only true God but also true man; this does
not mean that God and man exist side by side. This would be a duality
and not a union, would be akin to the Nestorian heresy. Barth means

rather that the Son of God who is true God is also at the same time true man in identity in the one Lord Jesus Christ. 'What is added to the Word in his incarnation is not a second reality alongside of him, but his own work upon himself, which actually consists in this, that he assumed human existence.'[61] Moreover, Jesus is not a demi-god or an angel or an ideal man but true man and so God himself is the Subject of a real human being and action.

Barth takes a further step in his exposition and interprets the flesh or humanity of Christ as that of man under sin.[62] In this he departs from the majority of theologians throughout the ages, but there can be little doubt that his interpretation is thoroughly biblical at this point and is to be accepted. It was 'flesh' that the Son of God assumed, i.e., man liable to the judgment and verdict of God, incurring his wrath and subject to death. The Son in assuming flesh goes on the side of the enemy—while remaining what he is becomes what we are as well. Only in this way can he save us. However, by the Holy Spirit he was sanctified and though tempted did not sin; nevertheless both inwardly and outwardly his position was the same as that of sinful man. Thus, though Jesus Christ was not and could not be a sinner, he came in our humanity under the weight of guilt and sin's curse, liable to judgment and death. 'It is our own familiar humanity out and out, namely, not only with its natural problems, but with the *guilt* lying upon it of which it has to repent, with the *judgment* of God hanging over it, with the *death* to which it is liable. The Son of God could not sin—how could God be untrue to himself? But all of this, the entire *curse* of sin, which is what Holy Scripture means when it calls men flesh, this curse the Son of God has taken upon himself and borne by becoming a man.'[63]

The Word in becoming man becomes flesh, sinful human nature and by obedience within the terms of this humanity fulfils the righteous judgment of God on man's sin, bears it away and reconciles us to God.

4. THE EVENT OF THE INCARNATION (EGENETO)—THE UNITY OF GOD AND MAN IN JESUS CHRIST

In this section we see quite clearly the dynamic nature of Barth's theology compared with the more static character of traditional statements. God's being is action, movement not only in and of himself but in and for man. Indeed while in one sense we must say that the incarnation is a completed event that has taken place in another it is continually present.

The fact that the *Word became* points to the centre and mystery of revelation, to God's gracious choice, movement and action on our behalf. The question must be asked: does he the Word of God by becoming something else thereby surrender his divinity? As we have already seen the answer must clearly be NO; but if God becomes man without in the slightest surrendering his divinity it is a miraculous act, an act of mercy on God's part. This action is known in theological language as the *assumption* (see Phil. 2:7; Heb. 2:16). God the Son or Word takes, assumes humanity into union with himself. As Barth puts it, the Word 'assumes or adopts or incorporates human being into unity with his divine being, so that this human being, as it comes into being, becomes as a human being the being of the Word of God'.[64]

The act of God in becoming man can thus be stated as the personal or hypostatic union of the Word or Son with our human nature—*the unio personalis*. In his exposition here Barth emphasizes four main points:

(a) As the union of the Word with humanity it is, therefore, primarily a personal union and only then and in consequence a union and communion of the divine natures. 'Thus by the whole of early dogmatics the unity of God and man in Jesus Christ is described primarily as a *unio personalis sive hypostatica* and only secondarily as an *unio naturarum*. And, moreover, the *unio naturarum* is decidedly always regarded from the standpoint of the *unio personalis*.'[65] H. Volk writes of Barth's exposition, 'In this way the question of the unity in Christ is clearly answered in accordance with the meaning of Chalcedon.'[66] Again Volk explains Barth's position thus: 'Jesus Christ is not first described as true God and true man but in the unity in which the two natures are one in the Person so that this man is God and God is this man and revealed in him.'[67] The reason for this emphasis in Barth is clear. We should speak primarily of the *Word* becoming flesh rather than of the union of the divine with the human nature (though naturally the latter is also true). But it was the Son who in his (the) divine nature was united with the human—hence this essential emphasis and distinctive usage. It is therefore not the Godhead or divine nature that became incarnate but the divine Son.[68] The hypostatic union is thus central and has a 'key position in the classical doctrine of the incarnation'.[69]

(b) In dealing with the hypostatic union in Jesus Christ the Greek and scholastic Lutheran tradition diverged from the classical position by laying more emphasis on the *unio naturarum* whereas the Reformed in their dogmatics were closer to the traditional Christology. Yet both agreed as to the starting point in the *unio personalis*. 'For all their pressing interest in the *communio naturarum*, the Lutherans could as little dispute its presupposition in the *unio personalis* as could the Reformed, for all their reticence in this respect, the consequences of the *unio personalis* in the *communio naturarum*. The accents were obviously put in different places, but the two schools were agreed among themselves (and with the traditional Christology of the primitive and mediaeval Church) that thinking must start at that proper and primary and central union and unity.'[70] Barth sees the different emphases in this way. The Reformed were interested in the *act* of union, the Lutherans 'in the result of the act as such'.[71] i.e., in the effect of the union.[72] While Barth gives his preference to the Reformed he sees the dangers and weaknesses in each which they were not slow to point out to each other in the dispute. The Reformed spoke of a ' *"nuda" sustentatio*' of the humanity by the Word which had in it the danger of no real union and of a separation or a duality leading in a Nestorian direction.[73] The Lutherans, on the other hand, spoke of a communication of the divine to the human nature in such a way that there was the danger of a reciprocal relation between Creator and creature as well as of Eutychianism.[74]

For all their differences Barth believes that these divergences point, not to a difference in the faith, but to two schools of thought.[75] They could moreover have met on a more common ground had the Reformed emphasized the *sustentatio* as a real union and communion and had the Lutherans been more concerned with 'the primacy of the existence of the Logos'[76] since both had a common starting point and intention.

(c) The union of God and man in Jesus Christ cannot, however, be conceived of in the same terms as God's relation with other men or with nature generally, as a union with something or someone independent though owing its existence also to God. Here there is no independence since the man Christ Jesus does not exist through God or with God; he is himself God.[77] Barth states the position he adopts (again in line with classical orthodoxy) in this way. 'Our older dogmatics was at one in the fact that the *unio hypostatica* must be distinguished even in the formal sense from all other higher or lower unifications and unions; that it is *sui generis*, and therefore to be understood only in terms of itself.'[78] This statement is, however, not absolutely correct since Schmid speaks of 'analogies which furnish us with at least an approximate conception of it'.[79] i.e., the hypostatic union. However, Barth does point out that occasionally the Fathers so spoke[80] and even Calvin 'is strangely guilty in this case',[81] i.e., in seeing in the relation of soul and body a suitable human analogy to the *unio hypostatica*. In the main, however, the orthodox divines rejected any such analogies. In the last resort, according to Barth, they simply gave 'a fresh definition of the *unio hypostatica*'. They did so because 'in Jesus Christ we have to do with an event and being which, as the direct revelation of God, not only speaks for itself, but speaks also for its own uniqueness, i.e., for the fact that it is analogous only to itself and can be understood only in terms of itself'.[82] Nothing similar or analogous exists in the natural order and only such real analogies are valid as are established and made possible by the incarnation itself.[83]

(d) *Communio naturarum*. If priority is rightly given to the *unio personalis* and so to the Reformed emphasis Barth pursues the Lutheran intention in a way different from the Lutherans but consistent with the basis in the hypostatic union. There is a genuine union and communion of natures. It is not based on a general view of God and man as two opposites that cannot ordinarily be united nor on any idea of metaphysical union as was the tendency in speculative interpretations.[84] It is based rather on the fact that there are two such natures in the one Lord Jesus Christ and that this union is an act of God the Subject in the person of the Logos. 'The unification of divine and human essence in him, the One, and therefore his being as very God and very man, rests absolutely on the unity achieved by the Son of God in the act of God.'[85] But on this basis there is a real participation by both divine and human essences—but from above to below and only so from below to above. The Son of God did not need the human but gave himself in this man to human essence. The man Jesus does not take it upon himself to be the Son of God and participant of the divine essence. Both are given to him by the free grace of God.[86]

So it is a union based on a unity, a *unitio* based on a *unio*. It is a union in which the two natures, while one, are yet distinct, *inconfusi* and *immutabiliter* (Chalcedon contra Alexandria). In this union there is no change of natures nor any self-alienation from either side. 'The mystery of the incarnation consists in the fact that Jesus Christ is in a real simultaneity of genuinely divine and human essence, and that it is on this presupposition that the mutual participation is also genuine.'[87] On the other hand it 'is a real and strict and complete and indestructible union'.[88] The two are indivisibly and totally united so that no part of either is untouched by the union. They are therefore not to be divided but are *indivise* and *inseparabiliter* (Chalcedon contra Antioch). So 'we do not have here a divine and eternal and heavenly Christ who is not wholly of human essence, nor a human and temporal and earthly Jesus who is not wholly of divine'.[89] Rather we must conclude on this side that 'the mystery of the incarnation consists in the fact that the simultaneity of divine and human essence in Jesus Christ is real, and therefore their mutual participation is also real'.[90] If one asks further how in fact Barth pursues his aim to relate the divine and human in the person of Jesus Christ the answer is that he does so in three ways.[91]

(1) The mutual impartation similar to the *communicatio idiomatum*[92] which says that statements made of either nature can be made of the one Lord Jesus Christ. There is impartation of the divine to the human

and reception of the human by the divine in this irreversible order. Yet this does not mean the acceptance of the Lutheran theory of the *communicatio* which in its form of *genus majestaticum* must be rejected.[93]

(2) The address of the divine to the human essence—*communicatio gratiarum*[94] 'It is human essence as determined wholly and utterly from the very outset and in every part, by the electing grace of God.'[95] This is, in effect, the incarnation in which human essence clearly receives 'not only its first but also its last and total and exclusive determination . . . This is the exaltation which comes to human essence in the one Jesus Christ'.[96]

(3) The common actualization of divine and human essence.[97] This corresponds to the *communicatio operationum*, the *genus apotelesmatum* of the older orthodoxy i.e., the co-ordination of each to serve a common end. The divine and the human move along the same lines towards the same goal, namely, the reconciliation of man.

Notes to Chapter 2 will be found on pp. 144–151.

CHAPTER THREE

Jesus Christ—The Revelation of God

Traditional Protestant dogmaticians of the post-Reformation era, in affirming the full deity of Christ, followed a line of argument now largely abandoned, i.e., that of direct 'proofs' from Holy Scripture.[1] Now this is not a wholly indefensible approach. Though it does take the Bible in a sense as a textual quarry, one must grant that combined with this there was a personal awareness of God in Jesus Christ. However, this way of putting the theological statement of Christ's deity as simply deduced from proof texts makes this awareness and emphasis much less prominent than it should be. It simply says that Jesus is God because the Bible says so; as such it is not fully related to revelation, faith, the Christian life and the experience of the Church and so cannot be regarded as an entirely satisfactory way of setting forth the meaning of Christ's deity.

Karl Barth does not wholly reject this approach for he too believes in the supreme authority of Holy Scripture but by his own explicit exposition he does to a large extent set it aside. That he is equally emphatic on the confession of Jesus Christ as true God with its implications for the Trinity is clear. That he is in line with the traditional belief of classical orthodoxy is also evident. He comes, however, to this same conclusion by a different path. It is based on the fact of God's self-revelation testified in the Scriptures as a whole. It deals less with isolated texts (though of course he does deal with texts and expositions of Holy Scripture in the course of his treatment) than with the total revelation—the whole content of it as God himself addressing us, speaking to us in his Word and so himself disclosing his divine nature to us in Jesus Christ.

The difference between the older and the more recent approach needs some explanation. Briefly it is this. The Bible in the more recent view is seen as being not simply an authority on the basis of whose texts we accept that Jesus Christ is divine; this would be an external proof which, in many ways, would be no proof at all or at least only a secondary one. On the contrary, the Bible is now seen as an authoritative testimony to God's action in Israel and in Jesus Christ, i.e., to revelation, to the

Word of God. This testimony is confirmed when through it and by the Holy Spirit we meet with Jesus Christ, by faith acknowledge and confess him to be true God, or as Barth can also put it, when he speaks his self-authenticating Word to us which is believed and obeyed. An external proof on the basis of the Scripture alone does not do what it claims to do, viz., 'prove' the deity of Christ. Rather it is through the testimony of Scripture working faith in us by the Holy Spirit that we are enabled to know that this man Jesus of Nazareth is at one and the same time the Son of God, divine.

Emil Brunner states this view somewhat baldly when he counters both Roman Catholic and Protestant Scholasticism and says 'According to the Biblical conception of faith we believe in Jesus as the Christ not because it is taught to us by the Church or in the Bible, but because he, Jesus, the Christ, meets us as the true Word of God in the witness of the Scriptures. We do not believe in Jesus the Son of God because the Bible teaches this, but we believe in the Bible because, and in so far as, through it we have come to know Jesus as the Christ. The Bible is not the authority, on the basis of which we believe in Christ, but the Bible is the means which shows us and gives us the Christ. We cannot believe in Jesus Christ without the Bible; but we should not believe in Jesus the Son of God *because* the Bible says so.'[2]

Barth equally and 'decisively breaks with the view of Protestant Orthodoxy at this point'[3] and rejects the idea that the Bible as such possesses a divine power apart from or unrelated to the divine action and the effect upon the hearer or reader.[4] It is not a *vis* or *potentia* but action; in other words it is as its testimony is received and believed in the power of the Holy Spirit that it becomes and so is the Word of God to man.[5] His way of putting it is this. 'The statement that the Bible is the witness of divine revelation is itself based simply on the fact that the Bible has in fact answered our question about the revelation of God, bringing before us the lordship of the triune God'[6] There is, therefore, a distinction between revelation and the Bible, the latter being a true witness to the former, i.e., to the Lordship of God, Father Son and Holy Spirit and so to the full deity of Christ. Yet, at the same time, the two are inseparable. Revelation comes to us in and through the Scripture. 'A real witness is not identical with that to which it witnesses, but it sets it before us.'[7] It is in this way that the true meaning of witness (the witness of apostles and prophets, i.e., of the whole Scripture) must be understood. G. W. Bromiley writes: 'The word "witness" is a dangerous one if used in its ordinary sense, but if we think of the Bible as a witness in the way in which the Bible itself describes the prophets and apostles as witnesses—"he that receiveth you receiveth me" it is perhaps not quite so objectionable as some critics of Barth suppose.'[8] The Bible is thus at one and the same time a human witness and God's self-authenticating

Word. In and through it God speaks; testimony is given to Jesus Christ as Lord and God.

H. R. Mackintosh summarizes Barth's view thus 'The Bible gives authoritative witness inasmuch as it lets something else be the authority, viz., God's revelation thus attested. *It must never be identified with the revelation itself.* The revealed Word of God is the Word he spoke to prophet and apostle in Jesus Christ, and speaks through their instrumentality ever anew to man.'[9] A similar view is expressed by P. T. Forsyth. The apostolic witnesses 'share in the self-certainty of God . . . on these great central matters of faith, not he (Paul) spoke but Christ spoke in him'.[10] Forsyth can say that Christ interpreted himself in his Apostles in the New Testament.[11] This does not imply infallibility or inerrancy in every statement. In other words, for Forsyth as for Barth, a witness is not only a human observer who speaks of the particular event he has seen in Christ. He is in a kind of sacramental relationship to the object of testimony. His witness is thus both a pointer to Christ and by the Holy Spirit instrumental in conveying him to men.

1. REVELATION

Testimony to the deity of Christ as true God fully, and unchangeably, God is borne by the revelation as a whole which the Scripture attests. The deity of Christ is made known to man in and with God's revelation of himself.[12] In Jesus Christ it is the one, true, eternal God who makes himself known to us, in whom we believe, whom we acknowledge and confess as *our* God.

At this point it will be necessary to set out briefly what Barth means by revelation in order to show its precise relevance to the deity of Jesus Christ in particular and to Barth's christological perspectives in general. Barth's view of revelation can be stated in three ways:

(a) It is the divine self-disclosure in all that Jesus Christ was, said and did in his life, death, resurrection and reign.[13]

(b) It is related in particular to the resurrection which as God's act is the revelation of reconciliation in Christ in its definitive form.[14]

(c) More specifically it is the function of the prophetic office of Jesus Christ. It is the light of Christ's life, the manifestation and making known of all that he did in his reconciliation.[15]

It is the first of these in particular as set forth in the *Prolegomena*[16] that we have to look at now.

What then is the Christian concept of revelation? 'Corresponding to . . . the real theme of the biblical witness Barth begins with the *event* of revelation, with "God's *action* in his revelation".'[17] This event of revelation is identical with Jesus Christ in all that he was and said and did. 'Revelation has to do with Jesus Christ who was to come, and who finally, when the time was fulfilled, did come—and so with the actual, literal word spoken now really and directly by God himself.'[18] Jesus Christ is thus not one who came simply to tell us about God but is himself the divine word and action of God for us. Hence we may say very definitely that revelation is the self-disclosure of the very being and nature of God in saving action for men. It is always and everywhere at the same time God's reconciliation.

Barth puts this truth of revelation in a variety of ways. It is *'Dei loquentis persona'*[19] The biblical witness to revelation is thus witness to God himself. 'In God's revelation, God's word is identical with God himself.'[20] If therefore we can equate, as Barth believes the biblical witness does, God's word with Jesus Christ, it is God himself with whom we have to do in him. In other words, here we look at revelation primarily as a testimony to the deity of Jesus Christ and so to God himself.[21]

Again revelation is testimony to the Lordship of God. 'That he reveals himself as the Son is what is primarily meant by saying that he reveals himself as the Lord. Actually this Sonship is God's lordship in his revelation.'[22] Since, according to Barth, only through God is God known the statement ' "God reveals himself as the Lord" means that he reveals what only he himself can reveal, *himself'*.[23] In this revelation in Jesus Christ God takes historical form, while always at the same time remaining Lord and God. In meeting this man we meet with 'Immanuel, God with us . . . could say thou to him, could pray to him',[24] could in fact call him God.

The best way to express this, according to Barth, is with the concept of form. 'It is the concept of form (Gestalthaben) which we must single out . . . as the decisive one. Whoever and whatever the self-revealing God may be otherwise, this is certain that in his revelation, according to the witness of the Bible, he takes form, and that this taking form is his self-unveiling.'[25] This can again be described as God being 'his own double in his revelation',[26] himself in the *event* of his manifestation. More particularly 'the form is here, the *humanitas Christi* . . . the incarnation of the Word'[27] Friedmann writes, 'In the first volume of the *Church Dogmatics* the accent is not yet on the incarnation but on the freedom of the Word, on its character as event, on the transcendence of God.'[28] This is indeed true though one should add that the incarnation, while not explicitly dealt with in volume I/1, is implied. What else can the *form* of revelation, the *humanitas Christi* and this express reference here to the incarnation mean except this? Certainly when one looks at Barth's doctrine of revelation as a whole the incarnation is at the very centre of it. In volume I/2 this is quite explicit: 'The incarnation of the eternal Word, Jesus Christ, is God's revelation.'[29] T. H. L. Parker has brought this out very clearly.[30] He writes 'It is in Jesus Christ that God reveals *himself*' and interprets this as follows 'The incarnate existence of the Word of God is God's self-revelation. When he encounters us, God himself encounters us. When we know him, we know God himself. In sum, when we have to do with him, we have to do with God.'[31]

So it is with God who became man in the *humanitas Christi* that we have to do in revelation. Here we come up against 'one of the hardest problems of Christology'. Barth asks 'Is the *humanitas Christi* as such the revelation? Does Jesus Christ's Sonship to God mean that God's revealing has now, so to speak, passed over to the existing of the man Jesus of Nazareth, and the latter has now become identical with the former?'[32] Barth answers that this could only mean a dissolution of the deity. 'We may at once conclude . . . that the power and the continuity in which the man Jesus of Nazareth, according to the testimony of the evangelists and apostles, was in fact the revealed word, consisted here also in the power and continuity of the divine action in this form and not in the continuity of this form as such.'[33] The *humanitas Christi* is therefore not directly the revelation of God since it conceals as well as reveals and it was only a few who saw in Jesus Christ the revelation of the Lord. Indeed revelation can never be ascribed to it as such. It is the resurrection (the Awakening) that reveals this man who was crucified to be the Lord. 'To speak in the language of the later period, the divinity is not so immanent in the humanity of Christ as not also to remain transcendent over it.'[34]

H. R. Mackintosh expresses here the queries of many who ask if we may not speak of the words and deeds of Jesus in the Gospels as themselves a revelation of the true nature of God. 'Was Jesus' behaviour to the woman that was a sinner no true revelation of the Father's mercy, but only a sign of it?'[35] Barth's answer would be that it is not the human actions of Jesus as such that are the revelation of God since to many they conceal rather than reveal. But, since the human is assumed and used by the divine it does and can become an instrument of revelation. He writes 'the form as such, the means, does not take the place of God. It is not the form that reveals, speaks, comforts, works, helps, but God in the form'.[36] That is one answer. Another would be that, since the human being of Jesus is analogous to and reflects the divine, the eye of faith will see in the words and works of Jesus a counterpart to the attitude of God to sinful man.

We can therefore say that God takes the form of a man in his revelation. As such he shows that he is not hostile to his being revealed.[37] It does no despite to his deity but is one of its possibilities. He does not remain inscrutable to and hidden from man but in the deepest condescension gives himself to be known by coming to and living as man. 'Revelation, *revelatio*, (*apokalypsis*) means the unveiling of the veiled.'[38]

Parker comments: 'Thus Barth, to fasten our minds upon the primary sense. Apart from Jesus Christ, God is hidden from us and unknown. We do not know that he is, we do not know who he is, we do not know what he is like. But in his incarnate Son he withdraws the veil and shows himself, discloses himself and makes himself known.'[39] Yet he is and remains the Subject of revelation not only in his hidden form of being as *Deus absconditus* but also as the *Deus revelatus*. He cannot be unveiled to man save as it is a *self-* unveiling. 'In this way revelation remains *God's* revelation and is protected from becoming an event in which God loses himself.'[40] The self-unveiling of God as sole Subject of the revelation points again to the Lordship and deity of the Son who reveals.

2. REVELATION AND THE TRINITY

When the Bible speaks of revelation it speaks also of the revealer and revealedness (Offenbarsein). It is with Jesus Christ that we begin and without whom we would know nothing of the other two. More correctly, though the centre is Jesus Christ we cannot know the one mode of God's being without the other so that both historically and theologically it is with revelation that we take our starting point and this revelation is that of the Son—the deity of Jesus Christ. 'The other two questions here too have achieved expression primarily as a necessary counterpart to the question about the Son, namely, that about the Father and that about the Spirit of the Father and the Son.'[41] This does not mean that they are less important or that we can understand God or the deity of the Son apart from them but rather that they are to be approached and understood only in their relationship to the Son. Revelation, then takes three forms and we can only know the one in and with the other.[42] Another way of putting this is that the Lordship of God is in his revelation as triune, but this is made known to us uniquely in the Son. Revelation, however, is not as such a direct statement about the Trinity but implies and involves it.[43] Barth speaks of revelation as the *root of the doctrine of the Trinity* since it points to the three forms or modes in which the being of God is manifest and exists. 'And it is as the answer to the question about the God who reveals himself in revelation that the doctrine of the Trinity interests us.'[44] On the other hand because it is the being of *God* who is revealed, the doctrine of the Trinity 'is a part, in fact the decisive part, of the doctrine of God'.[45] So 'it is the doctrine of the Trinity which fundamentally distinguishes the Christian doctrine of God as Christian—it is it, therefore, also, which marks off the Christian concept of revelation as Christian, in face of all other possible doctrines of God and concepts of revelation'.[46]

Barth states the threefold truth of revelation in this way: 'God reveals himself. He reveals himself through himself. He reveals himself.'[47] Of this John McIntyre says: 'He is making three emphases in this order. In the act of revelation, it is God who takes the initiative, and the whole event has its roots in divine grace. He executes the revelation not through any medium less than himself but through his *alter ego*. Finally, as a result of this process he genuinely reveals himself to man.'[48] So we are here pointed in the revelation of Jesus Christ to God himself and to his nature as triune.

Barth discusses the question whether there are, as traditional theology of almost all Churches has stated, *vestigia trinitatis*[49] in the structures of created reality and so 'a second root of the doctrine of the Trinity'.[50] He is convinced that this is false and dangerous teaching and leads automatically to the *analogia entis*.[51] It is solely God's revelation in Jesus Christ that gives us knowledge of God and leads to the doctrine of the Trinity. Hence the true *vestigia trinitatis* are in revelation itself. There God is manifest as the revealer, revelation and revealedness. 'Our assertion then is that we designate the doctrine of the Trinity as the interpretation of revelation, or revelation as the ground of the doctrine of Trinity; we find revelation itself so attested in Holy Scripture that our understanding of revelation . . . i.e., of the self-revealing God, must be this very doctrine of the Trinity.'[52]

Parker puts this truth in this way: 'The one who reveals himself is none other than God himself; God the Father of his eternal Son, and in him our Father; God the Son, who in his flesh suffers, dies and rises again for our salvation; God the Holy Spirit, the bond of unity within the Godhead and of our union with him in Jesus Christ. It is not as if in Jesus Christ anything different from God were revealed, or anything less than God, or merely one part or aspect of God. He whom Christ reveals is God himself in his wholeness. If that which is revealed were different from God or less than God or even just an aspect of God, we should no longer be able to speak of Christ being the revelation of God. In that case, if we wished to know God, we should have to turn elsewhere for our knowledge.'[53] In this Parker quite clearly and strongly affirms the truth of Barth's position that it is God himself and God in the fulness of his being who is revealed to us in Jesus Christ. Revelation is identical with God himself making himself known to us and is a clear testimony both to the deity of Christ and to the triune nature of God.

If this is so then there is no higher authority to which we can appeal; 'revelation is the self-interpretation of this God. If we have to do with his revelation we have to do with himself, and not, as modalists of all periods have thought, with an entity distinct from himself'.[54] Those who discovered and taught the *vestigia trinitatis* were wrong in so far as they forgot this and tried to find traces of the Trinity within the created cosmos rather than in God's revelation alone. For only God himself is competent to interpret himself and to be his own witness. However, those who did so pointed to a truth, namely, that 'theology and the Church, and before them the Bible itself, speak in fact no other language than that of this world'.[55] This ability is, however, not something native to the language itself but is accorded it as revelation lays hold upon it and presses it into its service.[56]

(a) *The Revealer.* Beginning therefore with the revelation of God in Jesus Christ Barth discusses the three aspects of this one event. It points first of all to a revealer who in his hiddenness would not be known apart from revelation. Since God has taken form in Jesus Christ and so is manifest there is in him the ability 'to distinguish himself from himself', to be 'a being of God in a mode of existence, not subordinate as compared with his first hidden mode of being as God, but just different, one in which he can also be existent for us'.[57] This revealed form of God's mode of being points to a hidden form to be distinguished from it yet at the same time one with it, in other words, to God the Father Almighty. 'God reveals himself as the Father, that is to say the Father of the Son in whom he assumes form for our benefit.'[58]

The revelation of Jesus Christ reveals a God who cannot be known by man. This sentence is only apparently contradictory. It means that there is nothing in the created world or in man which could discover the God manifest in revelation.[59] Jesus Christ is the revelation of the otherwise hidden God but the true revelation of God. There is no difference between God revealed and God concealed; he is one and the same in both. 'That God is for us, that he is not only hidden as he is in himself, but precisely as the God who is hidden is revealed to us, that must have its source in the very being of God.'[60] 'Since it is the God who according to his nature cannot be unveiled to man, who unveils himself there, self-unveiling means that God does what man himself cannot do in any sense or in any way; he makes himself present, known and significant to them as God.'[61]

(b) *Revelation.* However, it should be made clear that in the form of the Son it is one and the same God who is revealed. God is one yet distinguishable in three modes of his being because he has thus distinguished himself. Moreover, the revelation of God in Jesus Christ does not mean that God is now manifest to all. He remains veiled even in his revelation. It is only the eye of faith that 'sees' in Jesus Christ the second mode of being of the one true God. He does not give himself manifestly or obviously to be known by all but remains a mystery thereby demonstrating his Lordship and the freedom of his sovereign grace. So 'even in the form which he assumes by revealing himself, God is free to reveal himself or not to reveal himself'.[62] 'God's self-unveiling remains the act of sovereign divine freedom.'[63]

(c) *Revealedness*. Revelation has, however, a third aspect, that of being revealed and as such reaches man in his historical situation. 'Revelation . . . means the self-unveiling *imparted to man*.'[64] Again this shows that its power, reality and possibility are not in man but solely in the God who reveals. 'God's revelation has its reality and truth wholly and in every respect—i.e., ontically and noetically—within itself.'[65] But it really has a goal and fulfills its purpose for 'the Bible always regards what it calls revelation as a concrete relation to concrete men'.[66] It is self-authenticating and 'it reaches man . . . It belongs to the concept of biblically attested revelation, to be an historical event',[67] not in the sense of historical positivism but as 'a definite event, distinct from all others, and therefore incomparable and unrepeatable'.[68] Barth can therefore speak of revelation as 'God's being imparted, of a revealedness in God'.[69] Therefore, God's revealedness makes it 'a relationship between God and man, the effective meeting between God and man'.[70] God can and does become the God of man. Jüngel writes of this third aspect: 'We are thus concerned here too with the *being* of God, with a mode which is peculiar to him. This aspect of revelation is grounded in the being of God himself. And the basis of revelation in the God who reveals himself is made known by revelation itself.'[71] The whole event is a self-enclosed circle but one which at the same time reaches out and embraces man. So there is only one God who reveals himself. Here he is known as the Spirit. 'God reveals himself as the Spirit . . . the Spirit of the Father and of the Son.'[72]

Parker speaks of this as God's freedom to make man free for himself and the apprehension of revelation. 'It is effectual revelation from both sides—because it is the powerful work of God, overcoming all obstacles in its path, and because in its form it is apprehensible by man. Revelation would not be genuine if it occurred in a sphere which man could not enter and if it were totally alien to man. But God revealed himself in man's own sphere, in the humanity of Jesus Christ. Not in some foreign form, an angel, maybe, or some different creature, but in this other man God reveals himself to and is known by man.[73] H. R. Mackintosh correctly presents Barth's view in this way: 'Revelation explicitly includes the bestowing on man of the gift to recognise and believe it. The imparting of the Spirit, creating faith within, is an essential element in revelation itself. The event called revelation in the New Testament is both things—a happening *to us* and *in us* . . . In other words, the revelation *is* revelation only when by the Spirit it "gets through" to man.'[74]

But says Mackintosh 'We are led to ask how the "once-for-allness" of the event of revelation in Jesus Christ is to be harmonised with the contention that revelation, as complete, includes man's believing acknowledgement of its reality.'[75] There seems, however, to be a misunderstanding here in the use of the word 'complete'. For Barth, the revelation of God is Jesus Christ in all he was, said and did. As such it is the one, full, complete revelation of God to man. Yet this revelation at once puts us in touch with the Father, the Revealer (true God) from whom are all things and with the Holy Spirit (true God) whose work it is to open up men's lives to receive Jesus Christ as grace and truth. There is no real contradiction here since it is all God's work and the Holy Spirit does not add a new completeness to an already finished work but only 'completes' revelation by making the completed work known to us and real in us. This is stated by Barth adequately when he points to Jesus Christ as the objective reality of revelation[76] and the Holy Spirit as the subjective reality.[77] Since revelation is all of God and since it is the triune God who is made known, one must so speak of revelation in its objective and subjective aspects. Nor should it be thought that this in any way takes away from man's choice or his faith or freedom. It is, in fact, the possibility and the power of all three.

It is to this point that revelation as it is attested in Holy Scripture has led us from its centre in the Christ event where God is manifest as triune, the one living and true God.

3. THE DEITY OF CHRIST—FALSE VIEWS

If, as Barth asserts, the deity in its fulness, without restriction, is to be applied to Jesus Christ since he reveals God and is attested as Son and Lord in the New Testament, it is also important to state clearly how we are not to understand it. This has to be done because certain false and misleading ways of stating it have appeared in the history of the Church. Barth is thinking particularly of two very ancient heresies which appeared in the early Church and continually re-emerge in Church history, namely, Ebionitism and Docetism. Ebionitism affirms the true humanity of Jesus but fails to do justice to his full deity[78] while Docetism states that Jesus Christ is true God but had only the appearance of a man; his deity was real but not his humanity

Barth has his own characteristic way of describing these two heresies.

(a) Ebionitism. This believed that the New Testament started with the historical figure of Jesus who in the course of the early Church was transformed by faith into the heavenly Son of God.[79] Jesus was a man exalted to divinity; beginning as a great man he had more and more qualities attributed to him so that he could literally be called Son of God and lived on by the 'Spirit'. He could be said to be adopted as Son at his birth, baptism or resurrection. The error here is that no man can become God or God's Son; no human being can become divine. We cannot reverse the *logos sarx egeneto*, the Word became flesh. In Jesus we do not meet with One who has been adopted as God's Son but with God the Son himself in the identity of his being with the man of Nazareth.

(b) The other way the New Testament statement of the divinity of Christ has been misunderstood is as 'the personification of an idea otherwise very familiar, of a general truth'.[80] The idea takes concrete form in Jesus of Nazareth—it may be the idea of redemption, of 'die and be reborn' etc., but it could take root and does so elsewhere. Consequently, the human Jesus is only important as an embodiment of a divine idea. It is the idea or conception that matters, not the form. This has also to be completely rejected since in the New Testament it is God himself who came in Jesus and no mere idea, and he came clothed in full humanity and not in any mere appearance of it. Barth's way of stating a docetic view of Christ is unusual but nevertheless is true as one aspect of it. Basically the two ideas of Jesus are closely allied and both are wholly rejected by Barth as they have been repeatedly by the Church. 'The New Testament statement of the divinity of Christ can, in fact, only be understood on the assumption that it has nothing to do either with the apotheosis of a man or with the personification of an idea of God or of a divine idea. It bars these alternatives . . . (it) means anything only as witnessing to God's revelation.'[81]

However, although Barth rejects the two heresies mentioned, he now takes up the theme of revelation from the two points of view they were trying to express but failed adequately to do so, viz., that *God* was in Christ and that in *Jesus* we meet with God. He seeks to state it in a more acceptable way by showing that Jesus Christ is a man in whom one meets with *God* and in *Jesus* God is made known to man. In dealing with these twin aspects of the One Lord Jesus Christ we are not involved with a dialectic at a two dimensional level but with a third dimension, the revelation of God himself in this man of Nazareth. Had the New Testament witnesses been guilty of such 'idealising of a man or mythologising of an idea'[82] they would have been expelled from the New Testament community as guilty of blasphemy and idolatary. To Palestinian Jews the statement about the divinity of Jesus (i.e., Jesus is Lord) must have been an 'axiomatic assumption . . . a pure beginning of their thought, previously supplied to their thought'[83] as much as Yahweh was to the Old Testament people.[84]

Barth states the two-fold aspect of revelation in this way: 'The Word or Son of God became a man and was called Jesus of Nazareth; therefore, this man Jesus of Nazareth was God's Word or God's Son.'[85]

The New Testament witness rarely says this in so many words either as a two-fold statement or in its constituent parts. It often prefers other ways of speaking and usually in each comes to this or similar formulations only at certain solemn climaxes. We do not find the deity of Christ stated in the New Testament with the exactitude we might like as we do in dogma. The christological dogma is like that of the Trinity not the text but the commentary on it. Moreover, it does not always appear where one would expect it; the confession that Jesus Christ is Son of God does not come lightly to their lips.[86] It is to be read between the lines and inferred, waiting, as it were, the hearer's own confession. Emil Brunner says much the same thing when he speaks of how seemingly reluctantly the affirmation that Jesus Christ is the eternal Son of God was made in the New Testament. Yet if we do not make this affirmation we are left only with the possibility of Adoptionism.[87] 'If Jesus be the Revealer, in a different sense from that of the prophets, that is, not merely in his Word, but in his being, in his Person, then he must be God. If Jesus be really Reconciler and Lord then he is God.'[88]

The New Testament has this reserve because it is witness and proclamation but it is a reserve which, as both Barth and Brunner state, presses on insistently both in faith and theology to the two-fold statement that Jesus Christ is God's Son, God's Son is Jesus of Nazareth. What these witnesses say in very inadequate words is 'We have met God, we have heard his *Word*—that is the original and ultimate fact.'[89]

4. THE ETERNAL SON

Jesus Christ is thus known and confessed as the One 'who reveals the Father and reconciles us with the Father, is the Son of God'.[90] We must go on now to speak of Jesus Christ as the *eternal* Son of God.[91] Sonship neither comes into existence in time nor is it conferred on Jesus but is his eternal nature and being. There is no other reality of deity behind his Sonship, no other God behind or above God the Son. 'No, revelation has eternal content and eternal validity. Throughout all the depths of deity, not as the penultimate but as the ultimate thing to be said about God, God is God the Son, just as he is God the Father. Jesus Christ, the Son of God, is God himself, as God his Father is God himself.'[92] The divinity of the Revealer and Reconciler is the very last word. The New Testament assumption confirmed and stated in the Church's dogma rests on the simple yet momentous belief that 'Jesus Christ is Son of God because he is so (not because he makes this impression upon us,[93] not because he fulfils what we fancy we should expect from a god, but because he is so).'[94]

The dogma of the eternal Sonship of Jesus is thus a fundamental statement but it is not to be found as such in the biblical texts though it is their correct interpretation. 'Therefore', says Barth, 'we throw in our lot with it in declaring that the divinity of Christ is true, eternal divinity. We recognise that divinity in his action in revelation and reconciliation. But it is not revelation and reconciliation that creates his divinity but his divinity that creates revelation and reconciliation.'[95] Jesus Christ, therefore, reveals God himself, is God the Son himself, reconciling. What he is in his revelation and reconciliation he is in himself from eternity to eternity. 'He is the Son or the Word of God for us because he was so *previously in himself*.'[96] In other words what God does 'for us' in Jesus Christ he is in himself. What Jesus Christ does for us is identical and continuous with and corresponds to his eternal life within the divine Trinity. What he is for us he is previously in himself yet not God the Father, but God the son.[97]

Modern Protestantism of the later nineteenth century tried erroneously to interpret the Reformers as being against the dogma of the eternal Sonship of Christ on the grounds that it involved an untheological metaphysical speculation. It is true that the Reformers' primary emphasis was on the appropriation of salvation, the so-called *beneficia Christi*,[98] but they did not thereby deny the reality and truth of the Son's eternal nature. Barth sees Melanchthon's seeming antitrinitarian bias as a passing mood and not basic and Calvin as never denying the Trinity. Rather both were against Scholasticism. Luther warned against thinking and speaking speculatively about God in heaven apart from Christ. He affirmed the deity of Christ which was known only in revelation in the *beneficia* and *humanitas Christi*. In Christ we do see what God is in himself. The facts are clear: 'The Reformers never dreamed of letting Christology resolve or dissolve into a doctrine of the *beneficia Christi*.'[99] Modern theologians wrongly distinguish between what God does for us and what he is in himself, between his forgiveness and the means of it. But the two are one; it is the true God who forgives, the eternal Son whose *beneficia* are known in Jesus Christ. There is a difference between the Son 'in himself' and 'for us' but it is that between his nature as such and the grace which, in his divine freedom, is made available for us men and for our salvation.

Notes to Chapter 3 will be found on pp. 151–157.

CHAPTER FOUR

Jesus Christ—the Reconciler

In the doctrine of reconciliation we come to the heart of the theology of Karl Barth. Here in an original and stimulating way the Person of Christ is specifically related to and treated in the context of reconciliation or the atonement.[1] Here is the centre of the *Church Dogmatics* whose circumference is the doctrines of creation, the last things, redemption and consummation. 'The covenant fulfilled in the atonement is its centre.'[2]

Before, however, dealing with reconciliation Barth relates it to the covenant[3] between God and man which it fulfills. The covenant is the presupposition of reconciliation. It is universal in its scope and significance, first in the Noachic one made with the race and then in the Abrahamic made with Israel but with a view to all men. For Israel has a mission to all nations. Finally, there is also the promise of a new covenant, that 'of the free but effective grace of God'.[4]

Jesus Christ is the fulfilment of the covenant, the atonement for Israel and the whole race. He accomplishes God's will in face of man's sin and its consequences. It is an act of God's faithfulness to himself in fulfilment of his will to bind himself to man by creation. He atones because he cannot tolerate that his communion with man should be broken.

Moreover it is a covenant of grace, free and undeserved, beneficent and redemptive, engaging man's gratitude as God's partner. While it is true that the atonement is the reaction of God to our sins, it is basically, primarily the fulfilment of his original covenant with man, his purpose to be our God. 'The atonement in Jesus Christ takes place as a wrestling with and an overcoming of human sin. But at the same time and primarily it is the great act of God's faithfulness to himself and therefore to us.'[5] As we saw in the first chapter, for Barth Person and Work are one in Jesus Christ. He both reveals God to us and is the Reconciler with God. Reconciliation in Christ is therefore testimony to the true deity of Christ since it is God alone who can do this work for us.

Notes to Chapter 4 will be found on pp. 157–165.

The Lord as Servant

Barth gives this title to the whole subject of reconciliation in relation to the deity, thereby indicating that it is not to be understood apart from the action of the Son in becoming not only man but the suffering servant who atones on the cross. Humiliation is not simply (as in the older dogmatics) identified with the man Christ Jesus; it is now associated with the deity of Christ. It is in and through it that we know and most clearly affirm the Godhead of the Son.[6]

The framework in which Barth sets this whole exposition is that of the Parable of the Prodigal Son.[7] This does not become obvious until the second part-volume of the *Church Dogmatics*[8] but is clearly outlined and intended here as well. This is seen in the general title of the Christological section of 'The Lord as Servant', which is 'The Way of the Son of God into the Far Country'.[9]

Barth clearly admits the right of exegetes to affirm that the Son of God is neither mentioned nor directly intended in the parable and that therefore no direct christological exegesis is in order. However, if such a strained exegesis is to be avoided it is equally wrong 'to miss what is not expressly stated but implied'.[10] What should be stated, according to Barth, is that 'we do not do justice to the story if we do not see that in the going out and coming in of the lost son in his relationship with the father we have a most illuminating parallel to the way trodden by Jesus Christ in the work of atonement, to his humiliation and exaltation'.[11] This is a christological exegesis which, as Barth indicates, is, if not direct and explicit, nonetheless indirect and implicit.

The main thesis of Barth is that it is precisely in this going into the far country of our disobedience and rebellion that the true deity of Jesus Christ is manifest. His divine majesty is seen in his obedience, in his offering of himself to be our brother and so taking our place, being judged by judging himself and dying on our behalf.[12] The centre where the deity is affirmed is the cross.

The exposition of Barth's treatment of 'The Way of the Son of God into the Far Country' will be carried out in three parts:

(1) The atonement wrought in Christ shows us God in an act of condescension and grace coming into our situation, making our lost cause his own, and in the midst of man's contradiction, rebellion and sin affirming his deity and showing forth his glory.

(2) The atonement wrought in Christ shows us the Lord as servant, as suffering, the self-humiliation of God—the divine work *ad extra*. This means no limitation of the deity as in *Kenosis* and its allied theories, but the true expression of it in its opposite and supremely on the cross. The attributes or perfections of deity are to be ascribed to Jesus Christ in his humiliation, lowliness and weakness.

(3) The atonement wrought in Christ has its source in the divine nature *ad intra*—in the obedience of the Son. Humiliation is its expression not its contradiction. It affirms the equality and unity of the deity and implies no limitation or subordinationism.

I. THE CONDESCENSION OF THE SON

We notice first that God concerns himself with man in Jesus Christ who is the atonement, the special history of God with man. This condescension of God in his grace is his binding himself to us in all our humiliation, weakness and perversion. Nay, more, it is God making all these his own without ceasing to be God. He does not hold aloof but 'in being gracious to man in Jesus Christ, he also goes into the far country, into the evil society of this being which is not God and against God. . . . In being neighbour to man, in order to deal with him and act towards him as such, he does not need to fear for his Godhead. On the contrary. We will mention at once the thought that will be decisive and basic in this section, that God shows himself to be the great and true God in the fact that he can and will let his grace bear this cost, that he is capable and willing and ready for this condescension, this act of extravagance, this far journey.'[13] He writes: 'God is not proud. In his high majesty he is humble. It is in this high humility that he speaks and acts as the God who reconciles the world to himself.'[14] Here we see clearly that at each point in this exposition we are dealing with the action and work of the Lord God. We are also dealing with his deity not as opposed or contrary to but precisely in, with and under the humiliation in the man Christ Jesus and his cross.

Berkouwer has stated Barth's position admirably here: 'Through the man Jesus Christ, God himself is revealed as the divine subject in the work of Christ. This conception brings us to the heart of Barth's doctrine of reconciliation. . . . For Barth, the truth of the whole of dogmatics rests on this *God himself*.'[15] It is the decisive presupposition not only of reconciliation but of *all* that follows.[16]

That God himself is revealed in Jesus Christ can be seen in various ways:

(a) *Christological Titles*. In the man Jesus Christ attested in the Scriptures and especially in the Synoptic Gospels we meet with 'One who is qualitatively different from all other men.'[17] He is, therefore, 'not simply a better man, a more gifted, a more wise or noble or pious, in short a greater man'.[18] He stands not only on this side but on the other side of reality and confronts men with the lordship of God. This qualitative difference or deity is seen in Christ's power (authority), in his being Lord, Law-giver and Judge, in the fact that his word to and about man is final and unique and that he is the only Saviour. Klappert points out[19] that this juridical terminology, Lord, Law-giver and Judge, points forward to the dominance of similar language in the work aspect of reconciliation,[20] 'the Judge judged in our place', but also backwards to the Old Testament covenant as the presupposition of the atonement. 'When God becomes his partner, as the *Lord* of the covenant who determines its meaning, content and fulfilment, he necessarily becomes the *Judge* of man, the *Law* of his existence.'[21] Klappert continues: 'This juridical trilogy, taken from the Old Testament terminology . . . is, according to Barth, the real, material content of the New Testament christological titles.'[22] As Barth himself points out: 'In attestation of this understanding of the man Jesus the New Testament tradition calls him the Messiah of Israel, the Son of David and the Son of Man, the *Kyrios*, the second Adam come down from heaven, and, in a final approximation to what is meant by all this, the Son or the Word of God. It lifts him right out of the list of other men, and as against this list (including Moses and the prophets, not to mention all the rest) it places him at the side of God.'[23]

(b) *The Earliest Strata of Tradition* point in the same direction. In doing so these New Testament witnesses were not divinizing a man but simply according him his true place, confessing the reality of *God* in Christ. This majesty of Jesus Christ as true God is not something added later,[24] no apotheosis, no according him something he wasn't nor simply a 'religious valuation' (Loofs) but a true estimate of his Person. At every level of the New Testament witness he is given this place— that due to God alone. 'There is no discernible stratum of the New Testament in which—always presupposing his genuine humanity— Jesus is in practice seen in any other way or—whatever terms may be used—judged in any other way than as the One who is qualitatively different and stands in an indissoluble antithesis to his disciples and all other men, indeed to the whole cosmos. There is no discernible stratum which does not in some way witness that it was felt that there should be given to this man, not merely a human confidence, but that trust, that respect, that obedience, that faith, which can properly be offered only to God. Allowing for every difference in viewpoint and concept, the heavenly Father, his Kingdom which has come on earth and the person of Jesus of Nazareth are not quantities which can be placed side by side, or which cut across each other, or which can be opposed to each other, but they are practically and in effect identical.'[25] The titles which embodied this were not 'conferred' on him who didn't deserve them. They affirm the reality and truth of his person. And 'this would still be true even if it could be proved and not merely suspected that Jesus himself did not expressly speak of his majesty, his messiahship, his divine Sonship'[26] in the days of his flesh.

(c) *His Lordship* (deity) is thus a fact prior to the apostolic witness and apart from our acceptance or rejection of this witness. 'Prior to any attitudes of others to him or statements of others about him, the man Jesus did in fact occupy this place and function, ... prior to any knowledge of his being or temporally conditioned confession of it, he actually was and is and will be what he is represented in the reflection of this witness, the Son of the Heavenly Father, the King of his Kingdom, and therefore "by nature God".'[27] What the apostolic records seek to do can therefore be summarised in this way: 'They aim to be his witnesses. They answer his question. They give an account of his existence. He has placed them in this attitude. He has put these titles of majesty on their lips. They do not try to crown him in this way, but they recognise him as the One who is already crowned, to whom these titles belong.'[28] So when they speak of him as Christ, *Kyrios*, Son of Man, Son of God, the Exalted One they appeal to himself; he himself continually attests himself as such. It is 'his self-attestation of his majesty, of his unity with God'.[29]

We can sum up Barth's position on the deity of Christ by saying—we know that this man is also divine (*a*) because of 'the practical attitude to Jesus' mirrored in the tradition and (*b*) by 'the titles of majesty conferred upon him'[30] and (*c*) by his own self-testimony by the Holy Spirit through the apostolic witness. All of these reflect the truth that he is, was and will be divine. It was this truth which 'the dogma of the fourth and fifth centuries tried to formulate' and at this point the spirits divide. 'And to this day there is hardly a point of Christian knowledge and confession which is not positively or negatively, directly or indirectly, related to this one point.'[31]

(d) *The Nature of the Deity* in the Cross and Humiliation. It is necessary not only to confess and affirm Christ's deity but equally the extraordinary way in which it is known.

The mystery of Christ's existence consists in this—the identity of the majesty of God with the man Jesus—not an outward and obvious splendour but its opposite. When the New Testament speaks of Lordship it speaks at the same time of obedience which shows itself in the condescension, lowliness and suffering of this man Jesus, identified with sinners, crucified, dead and buried. This is the decisive testimony to the deity of Christ—Jesus in ignominy and suffering and so under the wrath and judgment of God—Jesus Christ the Crucified.[32]

Two things follow from Barth's position: (1) the centre for the interpretation of the deity of Christ is the suffering and death, the cross of Jesus Christ—this has been brought out particularly clearly by Klappert[33] and by Jüngel;[34] (2) the true *nature* of God is here manifest in the cross of Jesus Christ in contrast to all false ideas of God which we might imagine and conceive.[35]

(1) Klappert points out the indirectness of Barth's method in affirming the deity of Christ.[36] 'In the development of his christological starting point it is a question of the indirect knowledge of the Godhead of Jesus in the mirror of his humanity.'[37] This is seen in two ways, in his obedience and his suffering unto death,[38] an obedience reflecting that of the Son in relation to the Father, and a suffering occasioned by his willingly undertaking the divine work of reconciliation.

Obedience and suffering are not therefore an optional way but the one and only way for the Son of God. 'He is a suffering servant who wills this profoundly unsatisfactory being, who cannot will anything other in the obedience in which he shows himself the Son of God.'[39] The New Testament witness 'reveals the character of the whole story of the man Jesus as a story of suffering.'[40] From this Klappert concludes: 'Barth reaches his basic thesis: the character of the whole history of Jesus Christ as the history of humiliation on the cross is the centre from which he interprets the early Christian confession of the deity of Jesus'.[41] He goes on to show that this can be seen when Barth (following M. Kähler) sees the words and works of Jesus as an introduction to the passion, and the Gospels as 'the history of the passion with an extensive introduction'.[42] This is brought out particularly clearly in the following quotation, 'In the whole of the New Testament he is the *Crucified*, enclosing in himself the whole of his being within this limit.'[43] This is a quite typical, indeed a classical remark, already anticipated in the previous volume when Barth writes, 'What the New Testament witnesses obviously saw and understood, the proper being of the one true God in Jesus Christ the Crucified.'[44] Klappert sums up: 'Here on the cross the Son of God reveals himself, necessarily and essentially and not accidentally or by way of confirmation or completion, as the One he is.'[45] From this he concludes that Barth does not approach the question of the deity of Christ from the point of view of the incarnation as traditionally understood but derives it primarily from the cross.[46]

(2) If it is true that it is the cross of shame that reveals the true nature of the deity, this runs counter to our natural conceptions of who God is. His own position Barth states thus: '*Who* the one true God is, and *what* he is, i.e., what is his being as God and therefore his deity, his "divine nature", which is also the divine nature of Jesus Christ if he is very God—all this we have to discover from the fact that as such he is very man and a partaker of human nature, from his becoming man, from his incarnation and from what he has done and suffered in the flesh (i.e., the cross). For—to put it more pointedly—the mirror in which it can be known (and is known) that he is God and of the divine nature, is his becoming flesh and his existence in the flesh.'[47] It is thus in the greatest humiliation as Jesus Christ bears our sins and God's judgment

and suffers on the cross that we see the heights and depths of Godhead
—not only that he is divine but the character and the miraculous nature
of the divine.

In contrast any god we could conceive, imagine or fashion would be
proud and unbending, the result of our human pride and so other-
worldly, supernatural, 'Wholly Other'.[48] The true God shows his
majesty in humility and thus contradicts what we generally know of
God, all our general concepts. No human cognition could grasp, know
and conceive the real nature of the deity. The glory of the true God
consists in the fact that 'the Almighty exists and acts and speaks here in
the form of One who is weak and impotent, the eternal as One who is
temporal and perishing, the Most High in the deepest humility. The
Holy One stands in the place and under the accusation of a sinner with
other sinners. The glorious One is covered with shame. The One who
lives for ever has fallen a prey to death. The Creator is subjected to and
overcome by the onslaught of that which is not. In short, the Lord is a
servant, a slave.'[49]

It is in this way and only in this way that he is 'the Almighty, the
Eternal, the Most High, the Holy One, the Living One, the Creator,
the Lord'.[50] This revelation comes to us in the weakness and judgment
of the cross of Jesus Christ. 'In *him* we are able to discern the true
features of this God and discover that he does not terrify us by his
distant and infinite majesty and pure absoluteness but that he is near to
us in the "powerlessness" of humiliation and cross.'[51] Barth himself
expresses this in the following way: 'He is God in the fact that he can
give himself up and does give himself up not merely to the creaturely
limitation but to the suffering of the human creature, becoming one of
these men, himself bearing the judgment under which they stand, willing to die and, in fact, dying the death which they have deserved.'[52]
It is therefore in the light of his reconciling cross that we know the true
God and that our false ideas are corrected. 'It is in the light of the fact
of his humiliation that . . . all the predicates of his Godhead, which is
the true Godhead, must be filled out and interpreted.'[53]

(e) *The Relation to the Old Testament. The Old Testament as Background
and Framework of the Humiliation of Christ on the Cross.* By relating the
history of Jesus Christ to the Old Testament background Barth seeks
to show why and how his deity must be interpreted in terms of suffering
and death. He states that it is only in relation to Israel, to the Jewish
'flesh', that Jesus assumed that his history has real meaning and that
the incarnation and atonement have a more than accidental or incidental significance. He was this particular man 'not a man in general, a
neutral man, but . . . the One who fulfills the covenant made by God
with this people'.[54] So we do not have in Jesus 'a kind of ideal picture

of human existence . . . who was and is the Son of God',[55] quite apart
from Israel. It is his connexion with Israel that gives to his history
'its contour and colour, its definiteness and necessity'.[56] And as the One
who is the conclusion of Israel's history 'he is the obedient Son and
servant of God and therefore the One who essentially and necessarily
suffers'.[57] His coming therefore is 'not a historical *novum*, not the
arbitrary action of a *Deus ex machina*, but . . . the fulfilment—the
superabundant fulfilment—of the will revealed in the Old Testament
of the God who even there was the One who manifested himself in this
one man Jesus of Nazareth—the gracious God who as such is able and
willing and ready to condescend to the lowly and to undertake their
case at his own cost'.[58] In this we are reminded that 'the nerve of the
history between God and man . . . the history of redemption, is essentially the history of the passion . . . a history of victory only with this
orientation'.[59] From this it can be concluded that the *essential* background to understanding the revelation of the deity of Christ on the
cross and the nature of that deity is the Old Testament history and the
coming of Jesus into it as Jewish 'flesh'. In this sense, Jesus's coming
was a divine necessity prescribed by God in and through Israel. Barth
points out that there are three things in particular that derive from the
history of Israel and are the prophecy of and fulfilled in Jesus Christ.

(1) There is the election of Israel itself. The fulfilment in Jesus Christ
means that 'he is the same high God who in supreme humility elected
himself the God of this one small people'.[60] In other words, already in
the Old Testament the high God acts in the lowliness of our humanity
and for our humanity. God limited himself in this way from the very
beginning.

(2) The chosen people prove to be a faithless and rebellious people
who reject God and turn against him. But Jesus identifies himself with
and comes in this 'flesh'. 'This involves an obvious sharpening of the
idea and concept of the humiliation of the Son of God, of the alien life
in which he identifies himself with the man Jesus'.[61]

(3) The Old Testament goes one step further and shows man negated
by God, under his wrath and curse and so under his sentence and judgment. Since Jesus Christ the Son of God is also man he takes man's place,
accepts his suffering and 'gives himself to this most dreadful of all
foreign spheres'.[62] The Son is truly in the far country.

Klappert sums up the meaning of these three points as follows: 'This
threefold reference to God, who in the Old Testament covenant history
already previously goes into the far country, has this meaning. . . . The
Son of God humbled on the cross is the God who chooses the particularity of the man Jesus, exists in solidarity with the sinful and disobedi-

ent people of Israel, comes under the sentence and judgment of God and so of necessity suffers.'[63]

We see that, for Barth, as the cross and resurrection are the centre from which one interprets the deity of Christ this is the fulfilment of the Old Testament covenant history which was a foretaste and prophecy of that which was to come.

2. THE SELF-HUMILIATION OF GOD

The Possibility of the Self-Humiliation of the Son of God on the Cross

The question that Barth raises here is the important one of how then God can remain God and yet become man, suffering and dying for us and so reconciling. *Quo iure Deus homo*? 'It is the question concerning its *possibility* from the standpoint of God.'[64]

It is a free, divine act in the truest affirmation of the deity of God and it is an act in which he is and remains wholly and completely God despite all appearances to the contrary and all seeming contradictions or threats to his deity. It is in this way and only in this way that he is our Reconciler. This is 'the mystery of his deity in his work *ad extra*, in his presence in the world'.[65] The possibility of his becoming man does not lie in his being less than God or in being in contradiction to himself but in the very nature of God himself. i.e., the freedom of his election and action. We can, therefore, describe the incarnation as God's *self-humiliation*; in it he acts as free, sovereign Lord whose will and power alone it is to become man.

(a) *Kenosis*

The main teaching, however, which Barth is concerned to counter at this point is the famous *kenosis* theory[66] of Christ's person prominent in the late nineteenth and early twentieth centuries but actually having its origin earlier in seventeenth century Lutheranism. But before entering into a brief exposition and exposé[67] of this teaching Barth sets out his own.

The basis of the *kenosis* theory is Phil. 2:7, *ekenosen eauton*—he emptied himself. For Barth this does not mean giving up anything of the deity; on the contrary, it means that God was not bound, deity was not his sole or exclusive possibility. He was not committed to being in the form of God only (*forma Dei*) but could at the same time, take upon himself the form of a servant (*forma servi*). True, in this form he came concealing his majesty but nonetheless bringing it in its wholeness, undiminished and unlimited. Moreover, Barth maintains that nowhere else but here in his own act of self-humiliation is God to be found. Here alone is the one true and living God.

(b) *The Question of Paradox*

The Kenotic theories, while incorrect, did point to an ambiguity which Barth now takes up and discusses. Indeed he sees in it a further stage, a more refined and more dangerous form of the *kenosis* theory. It is to the effect that the existence of God in the *forma servi* indicates a logical paradox (Seinsparadox), a cleft or rift between 'his being and essence in himself and his activity and work as the Reconciler of the world created by him'.[68] In himself he remained fully God, immutable and omnipresent, almighty, eternal, etc. For us he became limited, lowly, impotent, etc.—in other words he became a being in antithesis to, in contradiction with himself, a 'God against God'.[69] 'On this view God in his incarnation would not merely give himself, but give himself away, give up being God.'[70] Is this the possibility of the self-humiliation of the Son of God on the cross? The incarnation certainly does mean God giving himself up to our contradiction against him and so the above view is plausible. What is Barth's answer to the question of a Seinsparadox? He rejects it completely for two reasons: it would contradict the unity of God and make reconciliation impossible. Furthermore, it is contrary to the nature of God whom we know in self-humiliation on the cross. There he is the reconciler and as such is the one true God.

In his interpretation of this paradox Klappert refers to three views.[71]

(1) The inner-divine Paradox of Being (Seinsparadox) just referred to which had a very small basis in traditional Christology and which divides God's being in himself from the *Deus pro nobis*. Barth rightly rejects this. Indeed it is one of the characteristic features of his theology that he shows the *Deus pro nobis* to be God as he is in himself in full unity and at peace with himself, even (indeed supremely) *in* his submission to the contradiction of sinners. The God who is God is such for us and it is in the *pro nobis* that he reveals his true nature to us as a reconciling and so a gracious God.

(2) The existential paradox (Existentialparadox). This is associated with H. Vogel[72] who asks the question: 'Does the self-revelation of God stand under the sign of a contradiction or is it only the existence of the sinner in relation to this truth that does so? At the decisive point is it a matter of a paradox of existence (Existentialparadox), i.e., of a contradiction . . . in the existence of man in the presence of God?'[73] He answers that the self-revelation of God 'means God giving himself up to the contradiction of man against himself. There is no contradiction based on or dividing up the being of God himself. . . . Rather the contradiction runs through our existence.'[74] This is also Barth's meaning when he says: God 'makes his own the being of man in contradiction against him, but he does not make common cause with it'.[75] In other

words God does not contradict himself when he enters the area of man's contradiction against him.

(3) The Paradox of Judgment (Gerichtsparadox). For Vogel[76] this contradiction in our existence means the divine wrath which God in Christ also undergoes. Jesus Christ, according to Vogel, undergoes the judgment of God on this contradiction. In the same way Barth speaks of Christ 'placing himself under the judgment under which man has fallen in this contradiction, under the curse of death which rests upon him',[77] which results from the reality of sin in his existence.

Klappert states that for Barth these two paradoxes do not reach into the being of God but are a moment in the act of reconciliation. Similarly to Vogel[78] ('He reveals himself as Lord of the contradiction'). Barth says: 'He acts as Lord over this contradiction even as he subjects himself to it . . . he overcomes the flesh in becoming flesh. He reconciles the world with himself as he is in Christ.'[79] Barth speaks of these as only 'apparent paradoxes' since in Jesus Christ 'the unity of God and man . . . cannot be *judgment* more profoundly and strongly than it is now really *grace* . . . that is, reconciliation of man to God. If God himself in Jesus Christ bears the *curse* that must fall upon the transgressors of his law, then it really *is* borne.'[80] Again he writes: 'He does not cease to be God. He does not come into conflict with himself. He does not sin when in unity with the man Jesus he mingles with sinners and takes their place. And when he dies in his unity with this man, death does not gain any power over him. He exists as God in the righteousness and the life, the obedience and the resurrection of this man.'[81] There we see God acting in full unity with himself. There he has accepted and overcome our contradiction and shown himself to be a God of peace in whom is 'no paradox, no antimony, no division, no inconsistency'.[82] If it were otherwise he could not reconcile the world with himself. The deity would have no value to us if in becoming man he left it behind. Self-contradiction in the deity would be an even greater blow to reconciliation than the earlier Kenotic views and would leave us in greater contradiction to God than ever. Such a God would 'only be the image of our own unreconciled humanity projected into deity'.[83] But we know him as the Reconciler so that 'if he has revealed himself in Jesus Christ as the *God* who *does* this, it is not for us to be wiser than he and to say that it is in contradiction with the divine essence'.[84]

The possibility of the self-humiliation on the cross lies, therefore, not in *Kenosis* nor in a Seinsparadox but in the divine nature itself which is a 'love in which he is divinely free'.[85] The question of the possibility Barth answers by the reality.[86] It has happened and in this light is possible. Klappert sums up in this way what Barth has done in this section: he has linked the divine self-humiliation on the cross as divine revelation with the divine potentiality and possibility of revelation. In this way, beginning *a posteriori* with the fact of reconciliation and so showing its possibility in God from his action, Barth 'has avoided the *a priori* method of Anselm and the dangers of a paradox theology. . . . The *scandalon* of the cross is drawn into the idea of God'[87] and becomes its point of reference and its interpretation.

3. THE OBEDIENCE OF THE SON

The Necessity of the Self-Humiliation of the Son of God on the Cross

In this section Barth goes on to speak of what he calls the divine Word and Being *ad intra* and takes up a theme of some importance and complexity, viz., the eternal obedience of the Son. It might be thought that obedience could only be attributed to the man Jesus in relation to God, but Barth speaks of an obedience of the Son as an essential and basic aspect of Christ's deity. 'The way of the Son of God into the far country is the way of obedience . . . the first and inner moment of the mystery of the deity of Christ.'[88]

The question Barth raises and seeks to answer here is, *Cur Deus homo?* what 'is the character of the self-humiliation of God in Jesus Christ as the presupposition of reconciliation'.[89] His answer is that its essence is obedience—the obedience of the Son of God. This has three aspects: (*a*) It is not simply the human obedience of the man Jesus, but, since it is the self-humiliation of God in Jesus Christ, it is an obedience grounded in the being of God himself and is in fact the supreme characteristic of the divine being. (*b*) The way of humiliation is a *necessary* way for Jesus Christ the Son of God because it is in accordance with the very essence of God in his own inner life. That it is and was possible for God to humble himself on the cross has this sure basis. The Son does it in obedience to the Father's will and is accompanied on it by the Father. 'The possibility of the condescension of God on the cross has in this way the full weight of the divine necessity.'[90] (*c*) In the act of self-humiliation the Son of God is thus not following a capricious or disorderly way nor an arbitrary choice of lowliness. Rather he is following the divine order, a way chosen by God in the freedom of his will but in agreement with his own divine nature. It is in this way that 'the being of Jesus Christ in humility, his suffering and dying, and therefore the act of atonement made in him, are marked off by their characterization as an act of obedience from the accidental events of nature or destiny. Jesus cannot go any other way than this way into the depths, into the far country.'[91] So while Barth can speak of all this taking place in the freedom of God, it does so 'in the inner necessity of the freedom of God and not in the play of a sovereign *liberum arbitrium*'.[92] In the divine condescension of the Son on the cross 'we have to do with a divine commission and its divine execution, with a divine order and a divine obedience'.[93]

Barth expresses the relation between the man Jesus and God's action and being in this way: 'He is in our lowliness what he is in his majesty . . . he is as man, as the man who is obedient in humility, Jesus of Nazareth, what he is as God.'[94] So Jesus Christ was obedient unto death, obedient as man but also as Son and so both a human and a divine obedience. In this way his obedience reflects and is the very being of God himself. Humiliation, lowliness and obedience are three inter-related moments in God's self-revelation in reconciliation. Obedience is primary because the necessary basis of the other two. They are the forms in which it is expressed in human terms and correspond to the inner 'history in which he is God'.[95] It is in fact 'the real key to an understanding of it',[96] 'the dominating moment in our conception of God'.[97] But since the proper being of the one true God is in Jesus Christ the Crucified for Barth it is from the cross as the starting point that one learns of this the true and supreme expression of the nature and deity of God, viz., obedience. Klappert remarks, 'These closing observations of Karl Barth give a more precise connotation to the early Christian confession of the deity of Jesus Christ. Here for the first time it finds it real climax and necessary conclusion.'[98]

When we speak of an obedience within the Godhead, then a question arises. Does not obedience in God compromise the unity and the equality of the divine being? Does it not imply two divine beings, a greater One who is properly divine and a lesser One who is improperly so? If, however, we so argue we end up with a being who is less than God, who is a creature and so 'not qualified to be the subject of the reconciliation of the world with God'.[99] We end with the heresy of Subordinationism which dissolves the deity of Christ. The other false way is to say that in his proper being as God he can only be unworldly whereas in his lowly, humiliated, obedient existence he is but a form or appearance of deity. But this also equally compromises the full deity of Christ since it is now only an improper form of God and not the true God himself. This is the heresy of Modalism associated with Sabellius.

Both these views clearly deny the true deity of Christ and make a real reconciliation impossible. But the deity is manifest in the greatest possible humility. The key to the divine nature is to be found precisely where it is thought to be impossible—Christ's obedience unto death, the atonement. 'It is from this point, and this point alone, that the concept is legitimately possible'.[100] Both Subordinationism and Modalism evade this the true meaning of the cross. 'Their common presupposition is their denial that the obedience of Jesus Christ can be taken up into the conception of his Godhead.'[101]

It is this stark yet absolutely necessary combination of seeming opposites that is the most distinctive feature in Barth's teaching on the deity of Christ. God in Christ not only does the seemingly impossible and enters the sphere of his counterpart, our humanity. He enters the area of our God-forsakenness, condemnation and death and atones and thereby affirms in the most emphatic way his real nature, his true deity and its supreme characteristic—obedience.[102]

Notes to Chapter 4 will be found on pp. 157–165.

CHAPTER FIVE

Jesus Christ—The Atonement

Deity and Humanity in the Cross

'Barth deals with the doctrine of the "true *deity*" of Jesus Christ under
two headings—"*The Way of the Son into the Far Country*", and "*The
Judge judged in our place*".[1] Having looked at the former aspect of it we
now deal with the latter. While it is true that the former deals primarily
with the Person of Christ as Subject of the Incarnation, i.e., the true
deity of Jesus Christ, and the latter with his work as the subject who
became object of the action of atonement, nonetheless in the context of
Barth's theology the two cannot be divided. They are distinguishable
but inseparable. The result is that in the former while the Subject and
Person aspect predominates it is always related to the work he, the
divine Son, does. In the latter, however, where the work and object
aspect, the atonement, is in the forefront, the question of the Subject of
this work is always there as well. The doctrine of the true deity of Jesus
Christ never disappears but accompanies and informs the exposition
throughout. Klappert rightly comments: 'If, in the former, Barth was
concerned with the christological aspect of "the working *Person*" in the
latter he is concerned with the christological aspect of "the personal
Work".[2] Although the deity of Jesus Christ is not the main purport of
Barth's exposition, it is sufficiently significant and prominent to merit
separate treatment here. In looking at it from this angle we shall also
inevitably indicate something of his humanity as well as some of the
aspects of Barth's teaching on the atoning work of Jesus Christ. It is
these three inter-related and interdependent christological perspectives
that we are dealing with here.

The position of Barth is clearly stated at the beginning—and this is a
consistent and central theme with him. The Incarnation involves and
includes reconciliation and redemption.

But in what Christ does for us in salvation we meet with the true God
acting for us, *Deus pro nobis*.[3] However, in this aspect of reconciliation
we meet him primarily as the Judge.[4] This is the testimony of the evangelists, particularly in the early part of the records. But he is (1) the

Notes to Chapter 5 will be found on pp. 165–171.

Judge, (2) who undergoes the judgment we merited; he was judged in
our place; (3) whose judgment was in the death on the cross and (4)
who in this is the One who does right, establishes and reveals the
righteousness of God.[5]

There is then a fourfold *pro nobis* of reconciliation on the cross.[6]
These four aspects of the atonement will now be examined to show in
what way they testify to and express the deity and humanity of Jesus
Christ. Barth summarizes his position in a passage that can be taken as an
introduction to all that follows. 'We should have to suppress or obviously misinterpret the first great section of the Gospel story—Jesus in
Galilee—if we tried to ignore the fact that as he judges for us it is
decided *who* it is that lets himself be judged for us in order to pronounce
that divine word of power by which we are pardoned: the one who is
justified and who overcomes for us. He is the subject and not the object
of what happens—the subject even when he is object. He is the Lord
as he fulfills the work which he has undertaken for us, the work of his
own deepest humiliation. He has the omnipotence in the power of this
work to bear our sins, to bear them away from us, to suffer the consequences of our sins, to be the just One for us sinners, to forgive us our
sins. He has this because primarily he himself is the Judge who over-
looks and eliminates our liability to be judged. . . . This is all a sovereign
action. It is completed and its meaning is revealed in the *passion* of Christ,
on the cross. Even on the cross it is a *divine act*.'[7]

Barth here clearly states that it is because of his work as Judge that
Jesus Christ makes atonement and can forgive, that this is a divine
work[8] and that hence the testimony to Jesus as Judge is a testimony to
his deity. It is in his being for us as Judge that he is *Deus pro nobis*. The
centre and focus of this is the reconciliation on the cross.

1. JESUS CHRIST THE JUDGE

The first *pro nobis* of reconciliation on the cross is 'Jesus Christ was
and is "for us" in that he took our place as our Judge'.[9] That he is the
Judge who has removed us from the judgment seat and is in this way
pro nobis is, according to Barth, the first main theme (though not the
only one) of the first part of the Gospel narratives.[10] In Barth's examination of this work of Jesus Christ there are three aspects.

(a) *The Judge*
Jesus Christ as Judge manifests the divine judgment, the divine
being of the Subject who judges. He speaks and acts with ultimate
authority. 'With his existence, there will fall upon them in all its con-
creteness the decision, the divine and ultimate decision.'[11] As such
there can be no appeal beyond it because Jesus Christ 'exercises and
executes . . . the judgment of God'.[12]

He does so not by teaching or pointing to the fact that God is Judge but by being, as the Son of God, the divine judgment in person. According to the Gospel presentation of Jesus Christ 'there has passed through the midst of all these men One who is absolutely superior to them, exalted above them, and fearfully alone . . . the Lord has been among them. And in the course, and as a result, of his being among them, in fulfilment of his proclamation and work, and as its consequence, the Lord has shown himself their Judge.'[13] Jesus Christ is Judge because he is and brings the holy kingdom of God which opposes and exposes all human unrighteousness.

The function of Judge belongs to God alone but is clearly claimed and exercised by Jesus Christ. 'This function is that of God himself. It is this function of God as Judge which has been re-established once and for all in Jesus Christ.'[14] This is seen in the unique place he occupies, doing what no one else can do. 'He is the only One who has come and acts among us as the Judge.'[15]

(b) *As Judge he removes from us our position as judge*

For Barth the sin of man consists in 'the arrogance in which man wants to be his own and his neighbour's judge'.[16] In this way he tries to take the place of God—*eritis sicut deus*—pronouncing himself right and others guilty. This is original sin 'when man thinks that his eyes are opened, and therefore that he knows what is good and evil, when man sets himself on the seat of judgment (Weltrichters)'.[17] But because we set ourselves up in this place reserved for God alone and usurp his sole right we have to be abased, jeopardised, and displaced and God must come to us as our Judge. For he alone can and does exercise real and true judgment. 'It is for this reason that God himself encounters man in the flesh and therefore face to face in the person of his Son, in order that he may pass on the one who feels and accepts himself as his own judge the real judgment which he has merited.'[18] But, because man thinks he can be his own judge, the coming of the Son in humility as the one true Judge can only mean 'the divine accusation against every man and the divine condemnation of every man'.[19]

The action of disclosing the falsity and wrong of our judging and of displacing it is a divine work and the person who performs it is the Lord himself. Hence, man has been not only radically accused and condemned but displaced from his position as judge. 'He is no longer judge. Jesus Christ is Judge. He is not only over us—a final court which we must finally remember and respect. He is radically and totally for us, in our place.'[20] By this is meant that, since he is Judge, we cannot be such but are threatened and removed. However much we transgress we are no longer 'what we wanted to be because he is for us, he—the man who knows and judges and decides for us'.[21] This is the negation his judgment brings. 'It is a matter of the *very man* Jesus of Nazareth in whom *God* has crossed our path and by whom we find ourselves deposed. . . . If this man is my *divine judge* I myself cannot be judge any longer.'[22] Jesus Christ thus shows men up to be bad judges and himself alone to be the one true judge of all. Klappert sums up these first two points in this way: 'Jesus Christ is the true Judge who has come on the scene, who judges in our place, displaces us as judges, removes us from the judgment seat, acts in our place and is in this way for us.'[23]

(c) *Judgment as salvation and liberation*

The traditional concept of Jesus Christ as Judge was that of One who pronounced for or against man in ultimate decision. Barth does not do away with this picture entirely or in any way lessen the true nature of the wrath and curse of God due to us for sin. He does, however, give to the conception of Jesus as Judge a new and more biblical interpretation, by relating it to God's saving acts.[24] 'The judgment of the judged in our place is in the service of salvation.'[25]

Barth defines the role of the judge as follows: 'Basically and decisively . . . he is the one whose concern is for order and peace, who must uphold the right and prevent the wrong, so that his existence and coming and work is not in itself and as such a matter for fear, but something which indicates a favour, the existence of one who brings salvation.'[26] Therefore in Jesus Christ as Judge we meet primarily with a divine Saviour who acts to prevent and overcome wrong, establish righteousness, and so bring man his salvation. 'He comes, therefore, as a helper, as a redeemer, as the one who brings another and proper order . . . he comes as the kingdom of God in person.'[27]

For us this means liberation and hope since all judging and anxiety are taken out of our hands, the intolerable burden of being a judge is removed. For his judging is but an aspect of his great, divine work of reconciliation and peace. In this way God acts 'in the exercise of his kingly freedom to show his grace in the execution of his judgment'.[28] Again this saving judgment is the work of God alone and so testifies to the deity of the Judge in the man Jesus.

2. THE JUDGE JUDGED IN OUR PLACE

The second *pro nobis* of the atonement on the cross is as follows: 'Jesus Christ was and is for us in that he took the place of us sinners'.[29] He is thus not only the One who 'judges for us' but the One who 'lets himself be judged for us'.[30] He does this as One for all in his unique and so quite lonely task. 'As such he is quite alone amongst us, the only One who is judged and condemned and rejected, just as he is the only One who has come and acts among us as the Judge.'[31]

(a) *The Gospel Testimony*

In the second half of the Synoptic Gospels and particularly in the passion narratives we meet with what Barth calls 'the inconceivable severity of this matter'.[32] The story takes a quite unexpected turn. The judge, instead of judging and condemning the wrong-doers, lets himself be judged by taking their place. This is the harsh but true reality of the passion—the subject becomes object but at the same time always remains subject, the Judge the One judged but always Judge. God takes the place in this man Jesus of sinful man but always remains God. Indeed in this way, as we have seen, he proves and demonstrates his deity in the highest degree. 'The One who is prosecuted according to this story, the One whose passion is enacted in all its stages, is the only innocent One, the One who has indeed divine authority to accuse in the midst of sinful Israel, the "King of the Jews". There is, in fact, a complete reversal, an exchange of roles.'[33] Barth believes that Jesus Christ 'becomes the object of this judgment from the time of the episode in Gethsemane onwards'.[34] He was, therefore, the Judge 'who allowed himself to be judged in execution of his judgment'.[35] In other words it is precisely in this strange exchange that the true nature of the Judge in his authority, power and deity is manifest.

Barth points out[36] that there is practically no commentary on this section in the Gospels, nor any actions of Jesus but simply his silence and passion. He thereby indicates that it is what he does and the whole manner of his doing it that is silent but eloquent and sufficient commentary on the meaning of it. It says quite clearly that he took our place, that of the guilty, lost and helpless, of God's enemies and, as our representative and substitute, was our Saviour. 'The Gospel story says this factually. It does not offer any theological explanation. . . . But in telling us what it has to tell, and in the way it does, it testifies that we are dealing with the event which at bottom cannot bear any other theological explanation than that which we have here tried to give it in actual agreement with every Church which is worthy of the name of Christian.'[37] In other words he became our substitute, bore our sins, God's judgment and just condemnation, did for us what we could not do for ourselves and so reconciled us to God.

(b) *His action as the One judged*

Since Jesus Christ took the place of us sinners he made the evil case of man's his own without himself committing sin. 'He as One can represent all and make himself responsible for the sins of all because he is very man in our midst, one of us, but as one of us he is also very God and therefore he exercises and reveals amongst us the almighty righteousness of God.'[38]

In acting in this way, God not only establishes and reveals his righteousness but shows the mystery of the divine mercy. Mercy and righeousness meet and are as one. It was the mercy of God that prompted him, as it were, to act in this hard but righteous way and so from within man's sinful situation convert the world to himself. On the one hand, while it is true that he is judged as man and so takes our place, it is nevertheless God himself with whom we have to do in this action. One cannot, in any sense, lessen the emphasis on this point here. 'If anything is in bitter earnest it is the fact that God himself in his eternal purity and holiness has in the sinless man Jesus Christ, taken up our evil case in such a way that he willed to make it, and has in fact made it, his own.'[39] As a result we are totally displaced and now exist in him and his righteousness. God sees us and accepts us in Jesus Christ. The really scandalous thing is that *God* takes the place of the godless in accordance with the divine purpose, accepted by the Son, in the eternal election of grace.

(c) *The Totality of Christ's identification*

Barth takes a further step in showing how Jesus Christ is 'for us'.[40] The *totality* of the salvation of Jesus Christ points to the *totality* of man's corruption, i.e., to man's sin in the whole of his being. 'The fact that Jesus Christ died totally for the reconciliation of every man as such . . . means decisively that this corruption is both radical and total.'[41] Consequently the change required and effected in man 'does not consist in a partial alteration' but 'in his total conversion'.[42] 'Man himself in his totality is unreservedly converted to God.'[43]

Furthermore, the result of the totality of the atonement is that it is impossible 'to separate between us and our sins, between what we are and what we do'.[44] We exist as sinners in what we do and commit, i.e., sin. 'Man is what he does'[45] Hence 'there is no place for any distinction between himself as the neutral doer of sin, and sin as his evil deed'.[46]

Since Jesus Christ is *Deus pro nobis* he identifies himself completely with us, 'by confessing himself one with sinners, by making their situation his own, by declaring and creating his own solidarity with them'.[47] This is the highest expression of his true humanity, his substitutionary atonement for the whole man and all humanity. It is, therefore, 'the situation of sinful man in its totality which Jesus Christ has made his own. . . . It is for the whole man, man in his unity of being and activity, for whom he has died.'[48]

This means (*a*) that one is here dealing not with a neutral object, sin, but with an active and wholly rebellious subject—man the sinner; (*b*) that sin is one's own responsibility since it is one's own personal failure. 'Sin is my *own* fault, if it is understood as the failure of a person.'[49] It must therefore be borne as my own personal responsibility, (*c*) that in order to do away with sin, God must do away with the sinner. All this happens in Jesus Christ and in and through him to us.

Primarily it is Jesus Christ himself who is the new man who displaces the old and we who by his death and substitution are in him.[50] As Weber shows this is the place for the inclusive character of the work of Christ on the cross. And this is also obviously Barth's meaning too.[51]

3. THE JUDGE PUT TO DEATH IN OUR PLACE—THE PASSION OF GOD IN THE DEATH OF CHRIST

Here Barth deals with the third *Deus pro nobis*. 'Jesus Christ was and is for us in that he suffered, and was crucified and died.'[52] The passion of God in the death of Jesus Christ is the theme of this section. It is as the Judge judged in our place, suffered and died that what has been set forth in the first two sections was fulfilled. On the other hand, the first two aspects are quite indispensable for our understanding of this third. Here we are dealing with the fulfilment of the judgment in the specific sphere of time and history. 'The judge Judging and judged in our place is identical with Jesus of Nazareth, crucified and put to death on the cross.'[53] The extraordinary exchange and substitution takes place in the passion of Jesus Christ.

We look at this from three standpoints:

(a) *Passion* as *action* in the death of Jesus. If, in the first part of the Synoptic history we meet with the 'sovereign action' of the Judge, in the second we see the One who is judged and suffers, the passion and death of Jesus. So we have this inter-relation between action and passion. The first part of the story is thus a commentary on the second and *vice versa*. 'His passion and the cross are therefore to be understood as his action. It is as the One who carries his cross to Golgotha that he comes to judge the quick and the dead.'[54] It is as the Judge lets himself be judged and so suffers that the action and work of God are manifest and done. 'He conquers by suffering. Without ceasing to be action, as action in the strongest sense of the word, as the work of God on earth attaining its goal, his action becomes passion.'[55]

This again is related to the subject who acts here. 'In it as a passion we have to do with an action. That in it the subject of the Gospel story became an object does not alter this fact. For this took place in the freedom of this subject.'[56] So it is a divine action, the work of God in the passion and death of Jesus Christ. Klappert writes: 'Because Jesus Christ is this subject, this sovereign Judge, this qualitatively Other, who belongs on the divine side, therefore this passion is decisively action. The decision in the question of the subject is at the same time the prior decision in the question of the passion.'[57] This means that it

is the nature of the subject who is here active that determines the
meaning of the passion and makes it quite different from any other.

W. Pannenberg[58] practically eliminates the *action* aspect of the cross
and sees it almost exclusively as Jesus's passion. In this his death differs
from his preaching and earlier life. 'His *passion* and death remain something that happened to him and are not to be understood as his own
action in the same sense as his activity with its message of the nearness
of the kingdom of God.'[59] Hence Jesus did not foresee or foretell his
cross and passion; they were a fate that happened to him. While this
clearly contradicts the predictions of the passion, 'critical scholarship,
since Wrede, has judged these predictions to be *vaticinia ex eventu*'.[60]
According to Klappert, Bultmann,[61] Käsemann[62] and Marxsen[63] all see
the passion of Christ as something that happened to him, however
differently they interpret it. But if it is merely such this means 'the
practical elimination of the cross as a salvation event (Heilsereignis)'.[64]
The divine action of the Son as subject of this event is excluded and he
becomes a mere object who is acted upon.

The crucial question arises: is this how the passion predictions are to
be understood, so eliminating the active knowing and willing of Jesus
in the pre-passion period, or, are they substantially correct and in
context? Pannenberg quotes Marxsen[65] with approval when he sees
the passion predictions as the work of the later community and in no
sense the words and action of Jesus himself. Joachim Jeremias,
however, gives a more balanced and correct assessment[66] (as does
Klappert[67]). Jeremias argues that the predictions of the passion belong
to an early stratum of the tradition and so go back in essence to Jesus
himself. He gives the following reasons for this conclusion: (*a*) The
course of Jesus's ministry forced him to reckon with suffering and
death. (*b*) The nature of the predictions themselves. Their form is late
but their nucleus, a *māšāl*, is early. (*c*) They form only part of other
comprehensive material which confirms their content and character and
these others are mostly early tradition. Jeremias concludes: 'This is not
to argue that each of the many passion sayings is pre-Easter. . . .
Nevertheless we must note the total result that there can be no doubt
that Jesus expected and announced his suffering and death. . . . Certainly the three so-called passion predictions are, in their present form,
constructed *ex eventu*, but they go back to an early Aramaic *māšāl*.'[68]
Jeremias deduces from this: 'If he reckoned with the possibility of a
violent death, then he must have been concerned with the question of
the meaning and the atoning power of his death.'[69] He must, in other
words, have been the active subject as well as the passive object,
giving his life for many as well as being the suffering servant on the
cross. In the same way Barth states: 'According to the common consent
of the Gospels, Jesus Christ not only knew but willed that this should

happen . . . it is with a free self-offering of this kind and therefore with an act and not a fate that we have to do in this passion.'[70]

(b) The *passion* of Jesus Christ in its *spatio-temporal* character. This emphasises the particularity of the atonement, the so-called 'scandal of particularity'. It also underlines the true, historical humanity of Jesus Christ. The Judge who judges but lets himself be judged 'fulfills this strange judgment as the man who suffered under Pontius Pilate, was crucified, dead and buried'.[71] Thus 'we are dealing with an act which took place on earth, in time and space, and which is indissolubly linked with the name of a certain man'.[72] Here we have no 'myth which is cyclic and timeless and therefore of all times . . . (but) a unique occurrence for which there is no precedent and which cannot be repeated'.[73] The Judge took the place of man 'not merely as God but as man'.[74] It is in this way also and specifically that he is *pro nobis* in this action and place at 'a very definite point in world history which cannot be exchanged for any other'.[75]

(c) *The passion of God*. In Barth's exposition the passion of Jesus Christ is to be distinguished from all other suffering of men in the world.[76] It is a unique event, but 'it was not the intention of the New Testament . . . that the fundamentally unique occurrence should be found in the human passion as such'.[77] The mystery and uniqueness of the passion of Jesus are 'to be found in the person . . . of the One who suffered there . . . it is the eternal God himself who has given himself in his Son to be man, and as man to take upon himself this human passion'.[78] He gives himself as object to suffering, submits to this humiliation and dishonour. And this, rather than endangering his deity or meaning its renunciation or capitulation, is the way in which he gives it its highest expression. 'In this humiliation, God is supremely God . . . in this death he is supremely alive,' so 'that he has maintained and revealed his deity in the passion of this man as his eternal Son'.[79]

Moreover, it is the suffering of God in this man Jesus, threatened with destruction, the Nihil (das Nichtige), eternal death, but in which he actively overcomes. Put precisely, it is the suffering of God himself to accomplish reconciliation. Man cannot do it, only God can. 'It needed nothing less than God himself to remedy the corruption of our being and ourselves. . . . That God has intervened in person is the good news of Good Friday.'[80] In the passion and death of Jesus 'God himself is for us'.[81] 'So, in this sense, according to Barth, the uniqueness of the passion of Jesus Christ is based on the uniqueness of his person',[82] i.e., on God himself suffering and reconciling in him.

That Barth emphasises so strongly the passion of God in the death of Jesus Christ means that he is critical of the teaching of the early

Church when it stated its doctrine of the divine *apatheia* that God could not suffer. According to Jüngel it is 'no paradox when we speak of the nature of God as One whose existence in suffering is his action. This sentence would be a paradox if God were in his nature incapable of suffering, as the early Church in part asserted when it followed the metaphysical idea of God of Greek philosophy.'[83] The passion of God is clearly asserted by Barth when he states that in the incarnation God takes the misery and degradation of man to himself, and so in that sense suffers. This is a necessary implication of incarnation and reconciliation. 'It is not at all the case that God has no part in the suffering of Jesus Christ, even in his mode of being as the Father. No, there is a *particula veri* in the teaching of the early Patripassians. This is that primarily it is God the Father who suffers in the offering and sending of his Son, in his abasement. The suffering is not his own, but the alien suffering of the creature, of man, which he takes to himself in him. . . . This fatherly fellow-suffering of God is the mystery, the basis, of the humiliation of his Son; the truth of that which takes place historically in his crucifixion.'[84] Jüngel sums it up thus: 'The Father participates in the passion with the Son so that the divine unity of God's modes of being are demonstrated in the suffering of Jesus Christ. The Being of God *is* a being in the act of suffering. But also in suffering God's being *remains* a being in *action*, a being in the act of *becoming* (ein Sein im *Werden*).'[85] Again we see clearly that the God who is active in the person of Jesus Christ is no static, immobile being in and for himself, but the God who moves towards man, acts in the history of this man Jesus and feels and suffers for and with man in his Son. This is what is meant when Jüngel speaks of Gottes Sein im Werden; it is a movement in which God does not become different from what he is, but in which he demonstrates most truly who he is, what is his real nature, in the action in which he participates and suffers with and for man in Jesus Christ.

(d) *The passion, human sin and death.* A further and final aspect of God's action for us in the passion of Jesus Christ relates to sin and death. *Sin* is the obstacle to be destroyed in God's act of reconciliation; its wages is *death* (Romans 6:23), not simply ordinary death, but eternal death, subjection to destruction, to the Nihil which, in consequence of sin, threatens all human existence. Klappert sums up in this way: 'Death, so understood is nothingness, the overwhelming, threatening power of destruction, separation from God towards which man as sinner is impelled.'[86] The reality of the atonement is that it both overcomes the obstacle, sin and bars the way to the threat, death.

In this death the Son of God 'has saved us from destruction and rescued us from eternal death'.[87] It is thus a divine action which destroys the primary evil in the world and closes the path to perdition. It is the victory of God in Jesus Christ. 'God has done this in the passion of Jesus Christ. For this reason the divine judgment in which the Judge was judged, and therefore the passion of Jesus Christ, is as such the divine action of atonement which has taken place for us.'[88] Throughout its whole course and in every aspect of it, it is not only the action of a man but in and through Jesus Christ, it is the divine action, judgment and atonement that are executed.

In his exposition Barth is critical of the theory of Anselm and his successors which sees the atonement 'either in the sense that by his (Christ's) suffering our punishment we are spared from suffering it ourselves, or that in so doing he "satisfied" or offered satisfaction to the wrath of God'. Of these he says: 'The latter thought is quite foreign to the New Testament. And of the possible idea that we are spared punishment by what Jesus Christ has done for us . . . the main drift of the New Testament . . . is not at all or only indirectly in this direction.'[89]

However, Barth does take up the conception of satisfaction put forward by Anselm and uses it in his own way. It is not the wrath of God which is 'satisfied'; we must put it rather in this way that God's love, because of its radical nature, must, when it meets sin, work itself out as wrath and so destroy the old Adam. In this way God is satisfied, does what is sufficient (*satis fecit*). 'Here is the place for the doubtful concept, that in the passion of Jesus Christ, in the giving up of his Son to death, God has done that which is "satisfactory" or sufficient in the victorious fighting of sin to make this victory radical and total. He has done that which is sufficient to take away sin.'[90] It is divine action in the passion of Jesus Christ with this victorious conclusion.

4. THE JUDGE WHO DOES RIGHT IN OUR PLACE

'Jesus Christ was and is for us in that he has done this before God and has therefore done right.'[91] This is the fourth aspect of the *Deus pro nobis* in the cross and its reconciliation.

(a) *The righteousness of God*
The first three aspects of the *pro nobis* of the reconciliation of the cross *seemed* to be mainly negative, particularly in their second and third forms. But 'this action which is negative in form is the great positive act of God within and against the world which is hostile to him'.[92] It is an act done to and by a man but the man Christ Jesus who is one with the eternal God himself in his being as action. In all three seemingly negative aspects Jesus Christ is acting positively, is the 'righteousness of God . . . the omnipotence of God creating order . . . this righteousness cannot come from the world, from us . . . it is the righteousness of

God'.[93] Klappert shows that 'in this last aspect Barth is concerned to prove the great positive act of God as the real *telos* of the radical negation of man, as it took place in the death of Jesus Christ'.[94] Moreover, in doing so Barth modifies the traditional conception of *justitia* as a righteous condition (Stand) which must be satisfied. Jesus Christ is present as the One who acts savingly not only to judge and negate but in doing so to restore right relations, to bring salvation. So, in this last section, Barth 'draws out the soteriological-anthropological consequences'[95] of this conception. Jesus Christ is the just man who acted as Judge, was judged and put to death in order, in accepting God's righteous judgment on sinful man, to create order, peace and salvation, to show and to bring the love and grace of God. That judgment was 'only the negative form of the fulness of a positive divine righteousness, which itself and as such is identical with the free love of God effectively interposing between our enmity and himself, the work and word of his grace'.[96] That was the absolutely necessary No of God to rebellious man but a No subordinate to and in the service of his Yes. And it is 'because Jesus Christ is the Yes of God spoken in world-history . . . that God is in Jesus Christ *pro nobis*'.[97] The two sides of the total action of God in Christ can be summed up in Luther's famous words that it is the *opus alienum* in the service of God's *opus proprium*. So the divine being of Jesus Christ is manifested even in the negative form but with the positive purpose and result of creating and establishing righteousness—the salvation of God.

(b) *The Righteous man*[98]

To the omnipotence of God creating order, establishing righteousness, bringing salvation there corresponds the one righteous man who is identical with this order. He fulfils this righteousness in obedience and freedom, corresponding to and expressing in human terms the obedience of the Son to the Father. He is in fact that obedience and freedom, reflected in this one man, and in this one man fully. 'As this man he has revealed and made operative the righteousness of God on earth.'[99] This is expressed in his sinlessness—no mere negative or abstract virtue. Rather it means that in our place he did what we refused and refused what we did. In other words he acted rightly and refused to act wrongly. He gave God his right. By occupying our place and being sinless there he put God in the right against man, i.e., against himself. He has confirmed the righteous judgment of God, become the one righteous man thereby and established righteousness, salvation—a new man. Klappert writes: 'The *iustitia hominis* which corresponds to the *iustitia dei* as the omnipotence which creates order means *deum justificare* (Luther) to put God in the right against himself . . . Jesus Christ is the "righteous man" who puts God in the right against him, who affirms

God's judgment and so corresponds to the righteousness of God.'[100]

Barth sums up what he has to say of Jesus Christ, our representative and substitute, in all four aspects as follows: 'Everything depends upon the fact that the Lord who became a servant, the Son of God who went into the far country, and came to us, was and did all this for us; that he fulfilled, and fulfilled in this way, the divine judgment laid upon him.'[101]

Two other points require to be made in concluding this survey of Barth's doctrine of the atonement.

(a) Barth is aware that he has expounded the atonement in exclusively juridical or forensic terms, yet believes that he has covered the whole of the ground in doing so. However the New Testament also speaks in financial terms (paying a 'ransom'), in military terms (victory over the devil) and also in cultic or sacrificial terms which are of special importance. The older Dogmatics used the latter terms freely but combined them with the forensic 'in a way that was more or less foreign to the Bible itself',[102] To show that the sacrificial or cultic imagery is patient of an interpretation along the lines of the above four selected concepts Barth proceeds[103] to give a short exposition of the atonement in these terms. In doing so he says nothing new but the same thing in other words.

(b) The other thing to be noted is that in his doctrine of atonement Barth gives maximum space to biblical exposition and direct commentary and minimum to a critique of the dogmatic tradition of the Church on this doctrine. This is in marked contrast to other parts of the *Church Dogmatics*, notably those dealing with the person aspects of reconciliation where expositions and critiques of earlier writings are offered in abundance. No particular reason is given for this procedure. It may be that since disputes about the Person of Christ dominated the early Church and the work aspects are taken up later Barth feels these need less mention (only Anselm is briefly touched on here). Or, it may be (and this is more likely) that since he is carrying on a sustained though quiet and indirect debate with Bultmann[104] in *C.D.* IV/1 he adopts the same method with regard to the history of the doctrine of the atonement. Klappert's remarks showing that Barth modifies the traditional statements at several points would indicate the latter conclusion.

Notes to Chapter 5 will be found on pp. 165–171.

CHAPTER SIX

Jesus Christ—True and Exalted Man

In the theology of Karl Barth the humanity of Jesus Christ has a quite central and indispensable place. Jesus is completely, truly and fully human else the incarnation and atonement lose their meaning.

In his teaching on this subject Barth has clearly in mind and keeps to the fore the *Enhypostasis* of classical Christology. His discussion is given in the first instance in the context of his teaching on man as creature and then in relation to reconciliation. The man Jesus has his being and nature from the Word (*Enhypostasia*) and as such reveals to us not only the being and nature of God but real and true man. We are therefore not to judge the human nature of Jesus by other standards or from other sources but from the man Jesus himself. He is his own criterion and standard. 'We must form and maintain the conviction that the presupposition given us in and with the human nature of Jesus is exhaustive and superior to all other presuppositions, and that all other presuppositions can become possible and useful only in connexion with it.'[1] In making these statements and taking this course Barth is conscious of a decisive break with the treatment of man and the man Jesus in classical Christology. He leaves the traditional path 'which was to try first to establish generally what human nature is, and on this basis to interpret the human nature of Jesus Christ in particular'.[2] Barth's approach is a complete reversal of this ancient tradition and is 'revolutionary in content'.[3] We can only understand true human nature from the nature of this one particular man Jesus Christ as the Word and revelation of God, and not from ourselves since sin in man destroys true humanity. 'Thus the incarnate Word of God, Jesus Christ, is really the true Word about man as well as God, and about the nature of man.'[4] This is Barth's text here and the rest is but commentary on it.

Nevertheless Jesus Christ is a *real* man. We can say of him 'that he was hungry and thirsty, that he ate and drank, that he was tired and rested and slept, that he loved and sorrowed, was angry and even wept'.[5] It is true again that 'he is born of a human mother; he lives and works as a man; he sees and hears as a man; he speaks in human language; he suffers and dies as a man'.[6] Indeed he lives and will come

Notes to Chapter 6 will be found on pp. 171–174.

again as man. Barth insists that these human qualities of his existence
as a whole man with body and soul[7] living in time and space only
indicate his possibilities as man and are not what make him true man.
They do point away from Docetism but do not show us what he truly
is. Barth thus makes a distinction between the *reality* of his humanity
which is like ours in all these characteristics and *true* humanity which
is his being in full and right relationship with God[8]—a relationship
which ours lacks. Thus Jesus is both real and true man in time as his is
the human nature of the Son of God and this is seen in what he does in
and through it. For this reason Barth is against the older view of seeing
these human qualities in isolation. 'Hence the private life of Jesus can
never be an autonomous theme in the New Testament.'[9]

So while the ordinary human life and history of Jesus are always
affirmed they play a minor, dependent role, are subordinate to the true
being of man as the organ and instrument of the Son of God in his
revelation and atonement.[10] Yet if the work of God is done in and
through the real humanity it must not be underestimated either as
Barth tends to do. Even if one only regards it as the real form of the
true content of the humanity its place is vital and essential. Barth,
however, is right in underlining the dangers and in seeing the humanity
in relation to who Jesus Christ is and what he does. Nevertheless the
impression remains that these real aspects of Christ's humanity are, in
his theology, underestimated and underplayed.

I. JESUS, MAN FOR OTHER MEN[11]

'The Man for Others' is a phrase which is well known today in
radical theological circles and has been popularised largely by J. A. T.
Robinson.[12] However, in Robinson it is used to emphasise almost
exclusively the humanity of Christ and leads to a great extent to the
emptying of his true divinity of any real content and meaning. This,
however, cannot be said of Barth from whom this phrase very probably
originally derives. Jesus the man for other men is such only as his real,
true deity is fully affirmed and expressed.

If the central idea linking the whole of Barth's treatment of the
humanity of Jesus in *enhypostasia* the specific thread running through
this particular section is that of *analogy*.

To understand the meaning of this analogy one cannot resort to a
general anthropology but only to one based firmly and surely on
Christology—here specifically on the man Jesus. But who is he? Barth
speaks of him as existing for other men. As the one who is for God,[13]
does the divine work, he is also human, there in the same totality for
other men. His existence as man refers to them exclusively, originally,
totally. His is fellow—or co-humanity, an existence completely for

others. He does not exist first for himself or for a cause or ideals but for other men. 'From the very first, in the fact that he is a man, Jesus is not without his fellow-men, but to them and with them and for them'[14]—their Deliverer. Everything else that can be said about this humanity can be summed up in this and this is seen in his incarnation, in his sympathy, help, deliverance, mercy, and 'active solidarity with the state and fate of man'.[15]

This conception of the humanity of Jesus as radically, wholly co-humanity, being for other men in atonement, has certain implications.[16]

(a) *Jesus is from his fellow-men*

'Jesus has to let his being, himself, be prescribed and dictated and determined by an alien human being'[17]—his fellow-men in their sin and abandonment—in their need and peril. He does not live in the glory of his original humanity but in the lowliness and misery of ours. He identifies himself with the first Adam to be the second Adam. He represents in his person Israel in her unfaithfulness and the Apostles, his community who forsook him. He is 'the One who is supremely compromised by all these, the Representative and Bearer of all the alien guilt and punishment transferred from them to him'.[18]

(b) *Jesus is for and with his fellow-men*

But at one and the same time his life, its 'I', is also wholly *for* this other life, the 'Thou'. He could have done otherwise but instead he is for them—to maintain their cause in death and its conquest, to give them life and happiness in the giving of his life in atonement as God's grace active on their behalf.

These two aspects can now be seen together. Jesus the true man is both *from* his fellows as their Representative assuming their sinful human nature and *to* (or *for*) his fellows as their Deliverer. In this he is most truly himself. 'What emerges . . . is a supreme I wholly determined by and to the Thou. With this twofold definition Jesus is human.'[19]

(c) *Jesus as man is not separate, opposed or neutral viz-à-viz his divinity*

His humanity is clearly not his divinity but neither does it stand in an indefinite relation to it. His being from and to sinful man mirrors, corresponds to and is the image of his divinity. And the divinity has this correspondence on its side. Each is to be recognised in the other; there is this harmony and similarity between them. 'As he is for God, so he is for man; and as he is for man, so he is for God. There is here a *tertium comparationis* which includes his being for God as well as his being for man, since the will of God is the basis and man the object of the work in which this man is engaged.'[20] Jesus Christ the divine Son

is both from God and to God. As man Jesus in his being from and to
his fellows shows a correspondence (analogy) to the twofold aspect of
his divinity.[21]

(d) *Jesus' work for others is a task given by God with an eternal basis in God's will and choice*

It has, therefore, nothing arbitrary, capricious or alien about it but
comes from the eternal and unchangeable God himself, corresponds to,
reflects and exhibits his nature. In this way Jesus the man for others
exists and this is his true nature as man. 'He exists and lives in his
saving work . . . He cannot be at all, and therefore for God, without
being for men.'[22] In this way he reveals the glory, will and eternal
choice of God to be for man as his Covenant partner. 'God first and
not the man Jesus is for men',[23] but the man Jesus is the One in whom
this is fulfilled in the cosmos, the counterpart of the eternal, divine
action. Here again Barth shows us the analogy between the being of
man for God (in Barth's language here the divinity) and the humanity
of Jesus, the man for others. In this case it has two sides 'an inner
material connexion' i.e., a basis in the divine will, being and action for
man and 'a formal parrallelism', i.e., a correspondence between what
God is and does as God for man and what the man Jesus does for his
fellow men.

(e) *Finally, it rests on the freedom and love of God in which he is true to and affirms himself*

In himself he is Father, Son and Holy Spirit. In him there is an inner
relationship of 'co-existence, co-inherence and reciprocity'.[24] God's
work *ad extra* in the man Jesus creates another relationship not alien to
the Creator but appropriate and natural to him. Therefore since it is one
and the same God in each relationship 'God repeats in this relationship
ad extra a relationship proper to himself in his inner divine essence'.[25]
There is thus no identity between the two but correspondence and
analogy. The relation between God and man in the incarnation corresponds, is analogous to the relationship within the Trinity, particularly that of the Son to the Father. And 'it is this relationship in the
inner divine being which is repeated and reflected in God's eternal
covenant with man as revealed and operative in time in the humanity of
Jesus'.[26]

This is the true and original analogy. So 'the humanity of Jesus is not
merely the repetition and reflection of his divinity, or of God's controlling will; it is the repetition and reflection of God himself, no more
and no less. It is the image of God, the *imago Dei*.'[27] What this means is
that the humanity of Jesus does not simply reflect the divinity of God
the Son (though of course it also does that) but rather the life of God

in his being as Father, Son and Holy Spirit and their relationship to one another. This receives even greater precision in Barth's treatment of the obedience of Christ in relation to the obedience of the Son to the Father and should be taken as the inner core and essence of that relationship.[28] This is indeed the centre of Barth's teaching on analogy in theology. It has an eternal and therefore trinitarian basis, and is seen in the incarnation which is as such the key to the whole being of God, man and creation and their true relationships to one another. The *imago Dei*, is not man as such nor a remainder in man left over from the Fall, nor is it man as God's good creation. It is the man Jesus as we see him in the New Testament witness—the One who is assumed into unity with the divine Being and as such reflects his triune, loving nature and so his will to be our God.

However, we must make clear what exactly this means and what it does not mean. As image the humanity of Jesus 'is only indirectly and not directly identical with God'.[29] It belongs as creature 'to the outer sphere of the work of God' and not 'to the inner sphere of the essence . . . of God'.[30] Between God and God, Father and Son, Son and Father there is a unity of essence self-grounded, self-originated and self-renewed. This cannot be the case between God and man nor can it be directly expressed in the humanity of Jesus. Here one must speak in a twofold way of both correspondence and disparity—correspondence between the inner being of God and his external work in the man Jesus, yet disparity since we are dealing with God and sovereign grace on the one side and human dependence and need on the other. God alone is our deliverer. 'He does not enter into alliance with a second God in his eternal covenant with man . . . nor does man become a second God.'[31] There is no identity but similarity and correspondence. 'It is in the humanity, the saving work of Christ that the connexion between God and man is brought before us.'[32]

There are really several relationships which are in analogy not identity—and this leads Barth to speak of an *analogia relationis*. These relationships are those between the persons of the Trinity, between God and man and between the man Jesus and other men. Barth denies any *analogia entis* which he believes is emphasised by some Roman Catholic theologians and is roundly attacked in the *Church Dogmatics*. He states it thus: 'This is not a correspondence and similiarity of being, an *analogia entis*. The being of God cannot be compared with that of man.'[33] That there is a correspondence of relationships is clear. These relationships may be summarized as follows:

(*a*) The Father and the Son—the divine 'I' and 'Thou'—are in a relationship; the Son is from and to the Father.

(*b*) The divine and human are in relationship in Jesus Christ—the divine 'I' and human 'Thou'—the man Jesus being from and to the Son.

(*c*) The man Jesus is in relation to his fellows—a human 'I' to a human 'Thou'—both from and to his fellows.

This complex of relationships and analogies Jüngel[34] has summarized as follows:

(*a*) The relationship between God and the man Jesus is analagous to the relationship within the divine being, i.e., Jesus is subordinate to God as the Son is to the Father.

(*b*) The relationship between the man Jesus and man in general is analagous to that between the man Jesus and God.

(*c*) The relationship between men generally is analagous to that between the man Jesus and man in general.

(*d*) The relationship between men in general is analagous to the relationships within the inner divine being and essence.

(*e*) The relationship between God and man is analagous to the relationships within the divine being.

(*f*) Various relationships of order are analagous to that relationship of orders arising from the structure of the human being as soul and body.

These relationships are based on God's being and action in creation and reconciliation which create a correspondence in the creaturely realm to God himself and in no way, as some assert,[35] presuppose an *analogia entis*. Since all God's actions are in Christ Barth's concept of analogy is wholly christological. It is therefore at the very centre of his christological perspectives. 'I would hazard the thesis that the analogy among the relations of Father and Son, God and man, man and man, is the ground motif of the entire *Dogmatics*. This does not contradict Barth's own thesis that "in actuality Dogmatics must fundamentally be Christology and only Christology" (*C.D.*, I/2, p. 872) but rather is identical with it.'[36] With this judgment one can completely agree.

2. JESUS CHRIST—EXALTED MAN

Jesus Christ is not only true God in the self-humiliation of the Son, but, at the same time and in consequence, he is true and exalted man. God's condescension is the basis of and makes possible man's exaltation which is a second moment of the one divine act. Jesus Christ is both the humbled God and exalted man in the whole of his being and work which form a unity. This unity, however, is not an undifferentiated but a diverse one whose integrating factor[37] is Christ's death seen in the light of the resurrection.

(a) *The homecoming of the Son of Man*

In a previous chapter[38] we saw that Barth used the story of the Prodigal Son as indirectly illustrative of the nature of the deity of Christ. As the Son went into an alien land and life, so the way into our 'flesh' is the way of the Son into the far country.[39] Likewise, though there is no direct equation between the Prodigal's return and the man Jesus, there is an indirect relationship and parallel. The way of the man Jesus is the homecoming of the Son of Man, 'the way to that home of man which is not lost but remains, not closed but open; the way to his fellowship with God; the way on which he precedes all men as a King who draws them after him to share his destiny'[40]—the way to their home which is also his—which indeed he is. The parable of the Prodigal in this homecoming reflects the exaltation of the Son of Man into fellowship with God as it took place in Jesus Christ. It is an exaltation to the right hand of the Father in which he participates 'as man in his power and glory, in the exercise of his grace and mercy'.[41] It is not in any sense to be thought of as his divinization.

It is in this that Jesus Christ is true and real man—as man exalted and brought home in reconciliation. He is thus both like and unlike us. His unlikeness to us in his human nature consists in the fact that it is the same nature differently—to be precise, it is human nature exalted in the incarnation of the Son. 'He enters also as the Son of Man, upon this office and work of a Lord, the King, who is ours as he is completely like us and yet so completely unlike us in this likeness.'[42] This does not mean that his humanity is destroyed or altered or emptied of its contents but raised to a higher level in union with the Son of God. In this unlikeness he is unique since no one else is so exalted to the side of God. He is the servant exalted to be Lord and this has no parallel in our humanity but is his secret alone. Again this is based on the fact of the humbled God.

So far Barth has been considering the *form* of Christ's true and exalted humanity; now he turns to the *content* and asks what is this exaltation? He answers that it is human nature 'set in motion from its very centre by the act of the Subject who exists here—in a motion in which no man finds himself, or will or can find himself, in any other way'.[43]

Again, true exalted man is man in the person of Jesus of Nazareth whose history takes place 'in its totality, in its free, spontaneous, inward agreement with the will and decree and action of God, and therefore as a service of God, which includes also a service of man'.[44] His life is gratitude answering, corresponding to and accompanying grace. In his human nature there is a grateful affirmation of grace which is addressed to man and the whole cosmos; as man he keeps the covenant and does what we fail to do. The opposition to be sure is still there but his whole life from the beginning is a 'conquest of this opposition and tension. . . . He is the man who is faithful both to God and therefore also to himself, the man who is reconciled with God, the true man.'[45] Barth does not here mean that Jesus had to be reconciled to God but that as man he represents mankind which had. He on the contrary 'is well pleasing to God . . . is the total recipient of the grace of God',[46] sharing his peace and power. He is the servant who is here attested and proclaimed by God to be Lord. Jesus Christ is therefore both the Word of God in humility and 'in the glory of God he is himself the answer to the otherwise insoluble question of human existence'.[47] Negatively, 'the meaning of the incarnation is that now in the flesh that is not done which all flesh does'.[48] Positively, 'it is the exaltation of our essence with all its possibilities and limits into the completely different sphere of that totality, freedom, corespondence and service'. [49]This is the homecoming of the Son of Man, the exaltation and so the manifestation of true human nature in Jesus Christ.[50] In this way Jesus is true and royal man.[51]

(b) *The Cross*

This exaltation is manifest supremely on the cross. The cross is the crown, goal and completion of Christ's life and work. Jesus is thus the royal man in his life, crowned as King on the cross, manifest and made known as such in the resurrection and ascension. Barth expresses this unity, diversity and differentiated relationship in this way: 'We have not seen the Jesus of the Gospels and the whole of the New Testament properly if we do not finally take account of the fact that the light in which we have tried to see him is the light of his *death* as it shines forth in his *resurrection*, and that it is in this way that it is the light of his *life*.'[52] Nevertheless, the central and focal point of the exaltation of this man Christ Jesus as true man is *the cross* as the fulfilment of his life, 'the perfect act of redemption once for all accomplished in his previous existence and history'.[53]

The exaltation of Jesus does not therefore begin with the resurrection as in earlier theology. 'The *datum* of . . . the exaltation of Jesus Christ is the whole of his human life including his death. But his resurrection is the event and not merely the *datum* of the revelation of the One who is exalted in his lowliness.'[54] Berthold Klappert has rightly summed up the meaning of this aspect of the humanity of Jesus in a section entitled 'The resurrection as the revelation of the royal man exalted on the cross' and further specifies it as 'the Lordship aspect'[55] of his being.

The cross as the fulfilment of the whole life and work of Jesus is the coronation of the King. It is 'his supreme exaltation, the triumphant coronation of Jesus Christ the Son of Man'.[56] He is the '*homo exaltatus et regnans in cruce*'.[57] The cross is not defeat but victory, a triumph already won. Jesus Christ is Lord on the cross. The Gospels portrayed him as such. 'It was here above all, in the fact that he finally suffered, and was crucified, dead and buried, that (in the light of his resurrection) they attested him as the Lord. It was here that they found the corona-tion of the King. . . . The definitive form of the elevation and exaltation of this man . . . was that in which he gave human proof of his humility and obedience to the Father, of his humiliation, in his human suffering and dying as a rejected and outcast criminal on the wood of curse and shame.'[58] He was foreordained for this by God and this is his supreme glory and victory. He 'acted as the divinely instituted King and Lord of all men by going to his death'.[59] His cross is therefore 'the dominating characteristic of his royal office'.[60] Here the servant is decisively exalted as Lord, the royal man reigns from the tree. This is the *Christus Victor*[61] aspect of the cross. The victory of Jesus and his lordship are not therefore still to be achieved. He reigns already fully and completely from the cross over all things and over all men. He is exalted with the Son in the unity of the Trinity to reign with the Father. It is not simply in the resurrection that Jesus becomes and is Lord but on the cross.[62]

The exaltation and coronation of Jesus Christ are effectuated in his completed work of reconciliation. 'The humiliation of God and the exaltation of man as they took place in him are the completed fulfilment of the covenant, the completed reconciliation of the world with God.'[63] The fact that it was concealed *sub contrario* in the judgment of God, the ignominy and shame of the cross in no way lessens its meaning and glory. 'Everything took place in this crucifixion—the whole reconcilia-tion, the whole restoration of peace, between man and God.'[64] Only as such is it the exaltation of the Son of Man and the fulfilment of the incarnation of the Word.

All that has been said so far about the man Jesus would dissolve into meaninglessness or simply be a verbal dialectic were it not as Christ's exaltation in humiliation the will and power and act of almighty God. As death it is simply an abasement and not an exaltation and no power or thought or action of man can make it different. Humanly speaking, death relativises and compromises all man's previous achievements, be they ever so exalted. The life of Jesus is, however, totally different. 'It moves towards death to take its full form in death',[65] which is its goal and purpose. 'He has exercised and confirmed and maintained his Kingdom and Lordship in his death.'[66] It is the Lordship of God which has power and claims over all men, power to judge but supremely to save, 'the power of an incomparable lordship and supreme royalty'.[67] In the whole life and action, being and death of Jesus Christ 'we have also to do with God himself and his act. God himself is the eternally living One who intervenes and is at work in and as this man. For defeated, rejected, condemned and crucified, this man is the One who is alive from the dead, the Victor.'[68]

All the previous statements about the man Jesus are true only in the light of this supreme truth that here, in this life and death, God was at work reconciling and so exalting man. Otherwise, the whole is entirely contradictory, inexplicable.

(c) *Humiliation and Exaltation—Critique and Evaluation*

Several critical questions arise at this point in relation to Barth's exposition. These have been put clearly and forcibly by Friedmann:[69]

(1) If the humanity of Jesus is regarded as already exalted and if humiliation and exaltation are seen as two moments of the one divine action, how can this contemporaneous action be reconciled with succession, continuity and completion in the life and history of the man Jesus?

(2) If we regard the humanity of Jesus as exalted to a higher sphere by union with the divine, can it really be our humanity, like ours, and again can it have a real human growth and history?

By way of an attempted answer to these criticisms we will refer to some of Barth's own words, to Friedmann's own exposition, to the succinct statements of Walter Kreck[70] and to Klappert.[71]

(1) One must first of all be clear what exactly Barth means by exaltation. It is not intended that it should in any sense deny the reality of Christ's humanity or be confined to one moment of the life of Jesus, e.g. his resurrection, but should be regarded as the character of his life as a whole. Nevertheless, while this is true, Barth can speak of it as consummated on the cross which is Christ's definitive exaltation and which we know as such as it is illumined by the resurrection. It is in this way that Barth regards the relationship between the different aspects of Christ's life and work. In discussing the relationship between simultaneity and succession Walter Kreck seeks to reflect the various elements in the New Testament testimony. His exposition can be taken as a fairly clear reflection of that of Barth. He writes: 'The New Testament confession of Christ rests on the history which is told as successive events, yet which is to be understood as also simultaneous.'[72] The New Testament witnesses see Jesus correctly and only in the light of the resurrection. 'It is first of all the Risen Lord who makes clear who this earthly Jesus is, who above all the Crucified One is.'[73] Moreover, the resurrection reveals God's identification with the Crucified One as a reality which is true also of the previous life of Jesus. 'The humiliation of Jesus and his exaltation at Easter, his death and awakening can only be told as successive events—else were it no real humiliation and death. But

they point also to an identity of the humiliated with the risen and
exalted One. Humiliation is not equal to exaltation but the Humiliated
is the Exalted One, the condemned One is already God's dear Son, this
One who dies is the Victor over death.'[74]

Kreck remarks that while Barth emphasises strongly the identity of
God and man in Jesus Christ and so the humiliation and exaltation as
aspects of the one action of God in Jesus Christ, he also pays attention
to New Testament passages that speak of the successive elements in his
life. This is particularly true of John's Gospel which also most strongly
emphasises the two as simultaneous. There is 'a specific Easter-story in
this Gospel too, and prior to Easter the sending of the Holy Spirit is still
a future event. There is no abolishing of the distinction between before
and after'.[75] Perhaps the successive nature of the witness takes a lesser
place in Barth's theology than it should but, as Kreck remarks, 'it is not
completely missing'.[76] Kreck adds further 'both forms of proclamation,
the "story" told in successive form and the simultaneous confession
that Jesus is the Christ, that the humiliated is the exalted one, have their
necessary function and are to be understood in context. The story form
expresses the unalterable distinction between God and man . . . the
simultaneous confession expresses the unalterable unity or simultaneity.'[77] In this way he (Barth) shows an awareness of the danger
of exchanging humiliation and exaltation.

'Thus on the one hand Barth understands the history of Jesus Christ
as a "story to be told" in successive events and on the other hand brings
out clearly that humiliation and exaltation are simultaneous. He shows
that he keeps the problem that arises here clearly before his eyes—the
problem which every dogmatic outline can only approximately express
in conceptual form'.[78] Without necessarily fully succeeding Barth has at
least attempted to state the two sides of the New Testament witness.

(2) Barth says three things about the humanity of Jesus in relation to
us which it is important to distinguish. It is in its creaturely constitution
the same as ours. This is something which is constant, changed neither
by the Fall nor by reconciliation and it is this common humanity that is,
humanly speaking, the possibility of reconciliation. Secondly, the
humanity Jesus Christ the Son of God assumed is 'flesh', humanity
fallen and corrupted, subject to the wrath and curse of God and as such
it is also ours. Thirdly, it is our corrupt humanity sanctified by union
with the divine and so freed from sin and its power and in this way
exalted to be the norm and standard of true humanity. Sinful human
nature is not true humanity. Ours is in fact not genuine humanity but
untrue because of the Fall. Barth means nothing more and nothing less
than this that exalted man is true man in genuine righteousness before
God or, as he often puts it, reconciled man.

It is difficult to see what the real problem is for Friedmann here. On the one hand he states that this makes Christ's humanity so different from ours that it ceases to be truly human. But this begs the question what is true human nature. He seems to fail to see that true human nature is that expressed by Christ. Jesus is not man exalted to be more than man but man exalted to his true nature in the will and purpose of God. On the other hand no one has more clearly expressed the relationship of the three aspects mentioned above than Friedmann, despite his own criticisms. 'Jesus is true man in so far as he is like us because of his unalterable being as human, as creaturely being which makes man man. He is also man like us because of the nature of Adam's flesh, the factual determination of his being by sin. But because he assumed the being of man in this two-fold sense, and in complete openness and readiness for God overcomes its sinful nature, he shows himself at one and the same time as Son who is of the same nature as the Father and as true and new man who lives completely for God and from God and in the same nature as ourselves.'[79]

When Barth speaks of exaltation to a higher sphere, to fellowship with God, etc., he does not mean that the man Jesus becomes a different order of being and so is not really man. Here rather is the definition of true humanity. In assumption, union and identity with the divine Son, it has its true being and life and in this way is completely different from ours which is corrupted and destroyed by sin. 'In respect of all other men human essence can only be called an essence which in its creatureliness is sharply distinct from that of God, and in its perversion, alien and opposed and hostile. But this is not the case in respect of this One. In him it is certainly distinct from God as concerns its creatureliness. But it is also bound to him. And its godlessness and opposition and hostility are not only denied but removed and replaced by his perfect fellowship with God.'[80] The humanity of Jesus has thus, as Friedmann points out,[81] a double relationship to God. It is creaturely since it is also God's good creation made by and for God. And it is relational since it is the human nature of the Son of God. In this way Barth 'can think of the exaltation of human essence in Jesus Christ as the fulfilment of the determination of each man to be from and for God. In this way he can make clear the similarity and difference between Jesus's humanity and ours, without any prejudice to the genuine humanity of Jesus.'[82]

Yet despite this favourable interpretation Friedmann can still say, 'because there is constant talk of the exaltation of the man Jesus there arises the general impression that in the long run one is not dealing with a real man. And this impression is strengthened when moreover one speaks of a movement of the human being of Jesus "to heaven which is the most proper sphere of God" (*C.D.*, IV/2, p. 29) of another state etc.'.[83] However, as shown, this simply means exalted to its reality and truth and not to something which is beyond human. Moreover, Friedmann never clearly defines what he means by true humanity but seems to assume that it is generally known. And if one does this one is making an anthropological pre-understanding to some degree the presupposition of one's knowledge of the true humanity and obedience. It is this charge which Friedmann never really answers in his criticism of Barth's own position.

Notes to Chapter 6 will be found on pp. 171–174.

CHAPTER SEVEN

Jesus Christ—The Risen Lord

We have now discussed the deity and humanity of Jesus Christ in his life and death, the way of the Son into the far country and the way of man home to God. We have also seen these manifest in the divine Judge as man assuming our judgment, accomplishing thereby our reconciliation and so revealing decisively his true nature. None of this, however, would be known by us but would be hidden from us, were it not for the fact that God raised Jesus from the dead and that he was manifest to his disciples as the risen Lord. In Barth's view, it is the awakening and the resurrection that make known and declare what has previously been hidden in the life and act of Jesus. This is the transition from his life to ours in the power of the Holy Spirit.[1]

Barth distinguishes between 'awakening' (Auferweckung) and 'resurrection' (Auferstehung), though they naturally cannot be separated or divided. They are two aspects of the one, supreme, comprehensive and decisive event without which all the rest of the Gospels would be hidden and obscure. The awakening is the act of God the Father in raising his Son Jesus from the dead, whereas the resurrection is his appearing alive to his disciples on the basis of his awakening.[2] Barth writes: 'It is one thing that he "rises again" and shows himself . . . to his disciples (resurrection) as the One raised again from the dead (John 21:14). Quite another thing is the act of this awakening.'[3] Or again, he writes: 'The facts themselves tell us decisively that the event of Easter has to be understood primarily as the raising which happens to Jesus Christ, and only secondarily and (actively) on that basis as his resurrection.'[4] In other words the act of awakening of the Son by the Father is the basis and possibility of the resurrection.[5]

The basis for this is the testimony of Holy Scripture where it is primarily an act of God. In the first Jesus is the object and recipient whereas in the second he is the subject and active. This goes back to and links on to Barth's interpretation of the obedience of the Son of God, an obedience not only in the human but in the divine essence. Hence there is a subordination of the divine Son to the Father, while at

Notes to Chapter 7 will be found on pp. 174–179.

the same time the equality of the persons is maintained. Therefore, in the awakening 'not simply as man, but even as the Son of God Jesus Christ is here simply the One who takes and receives, the recipient of a gift, just as in his death on the cross it is not only as man but as the Son of God that he is wholly and only the obedient servant'.[6]

The significance of this is that it is the awakening from the dead that gives us the knowledge of the true and distinctive character of revelation and so of the deity of Jesus Christ. The Son of God who humbled himself on the cross and thus reconciled is now revealed as Lord in the awakening. It is in the resurrection that the same man Jesus appears to his own and is seen and known as such. The crucified Lord Jesus is now seen in the resurrection as exalted man. It is in this way that he is present both as Lord and God, the Reconciler and reconciled man, i.e., in the fulness of his deity and humanity.

However, while this is obviously Barth's meaning and has considerable significance for his doctrine of reconciliation,[7] the distinction is not always made particularly in his earlier volumes.[8] This may mean that Barth has later modified his earlier views and that the latter is the more significant for our interpretation. On the other hand, it is quite possible that on occasion Barth uses the term 'resurrection' and 'Easter event' for the whole divine activity in raising Jesus from the dead and in his appearances. Indeed a complete separation would be impossible since it is as God and man that he was raised and was manifest. Any distinction made, however correct, is only relative. Nonetheless a real distinction is made in Barth's later volumes.

We shall now try to show the relation of this both to the deity and to the humanity of Jesus Christ.

I. THE DEITY OF JESUS CHRIST IN THE AWAKENING FROM THE DEAD

The awakening is the revelation of the Subject who reconciles on the cross.

Barth develops what must be regarded as his definitive interpretation of the deity of Christ in relation to the awakening of Jesus Christ from the dead. He discusses the awakening and resurrection under four main headings[9]—only the first of these concerns us here. The four are: (*a*) The Awakening as the revelation of the Subject who reconciles on the cross (person); (*b*) The Awakening as the confirmation of the act of reconciliation on the cross (work); (*c*) The resurrection as the revelation of the royal man exalted on the cross, i.e., the Lordship of the crucified Reconciler (Lordship) and (*d*) The resurrection of the crucified as a real event in history (Space and Time).

In the context of (*a*) the revelation of the divine subject the awakening has three inter-related aspects.

(1) It is an exclusive act of God.
(2) It is the exemplary form of revelation.
(3) It is the free act of the divine grace to and upon the Son.[10]

'The statement about the awakening as the exemplary form of the revelation of God is the central one; that it is an exclusive act of God leads up to this and that it is a free divine act of grace to the Son derives from it.'[11]

(1) *A new, exclusive act of God.* To understand Barth's meaning here we have to see the awakening in relation to the cross. It is, like the cross, an act of God—not primarily the work and will of men. It 'is in the New Testament comprehended and understood as an act of God with the same seriousness as the preceding event of the cross'.[12] However, it is to be distinguished from the cross. The cross was at one and the same time God's act of judgment and salvation and man's evil doing. In one sense 'as the judgment of God, the event of Golgotha is exclusively the work of God'.[13] At the same time 'it has a component of human action —both obedient and good . . . and disobedient and evil'.[14] To that extent it was 'historical', though a merely historical understanding of it would lead to misunderstanding. The awakening, while also an act of God, 'is unequivocally marked off from the first happening by the fact that it does not have in the very least this component of human willing and activity. Not merely in purpose and ordination, but in its fulfilment, too, it is exclusively the act of God. It takes place quite outside the pragmatic context of human decisions and actions.'[15]

It is thus a sovereign act of God. This could, of course, be understood as God raising the man Jesus from the dead—and it certainly means that. But, as the whole context of Barth's exposition shows, the act of God has only meaning if it at the same time reveals the identity of God with the man Jesus, the revelation of God in him. In this sense God raised his Son to glory and gave him life. It is an act which, at the same time, has definitive revelatory character which is the criterion of all that calls itself revelation.

(2) *It is the exemplary form of revelation.* The awakening of Jesus Christ from the dead was '*the* revelation of God . . . the true, original, typical form of the revelation of God in him'.[16] This is so for the resurrection as a whole because 'the event of Easter Day and the resurrection appearances during the forty days were the mediation, the infallible mediation . . . that God was in Christ (2 Cor. 5:19), that is, that in the man Jesus, God himself was at work . . . going to his death, and that he acted as and proved himself, the one high and true God . . . on this very way into the far country . . . in this his most profound humili-

ation'.[17] To understand the awakening as the exemplary form of revelation it is, therefore, necessary to recall Barth's argument for the deity of Jesus Christ. It is seen in the journey of the Son of God into the far country, in the humiliation on the cross, in the real being of the true God in Jesus Christ the Crucified. It is there that God asserts and proves his deity. But this truth was veiled in its opposite on the cross. Now by the awakening from the dead it is manifest and revealed. Here we see God truly and fully manifest as he really is. Hence we can conclude: it is because the awakening shows that *God* was in Christ in reconciliation on the cross that we can speak of the divine nature of Jesus. It is for this reason that we can also speak of it as the exemplary form of revelation.

Klappert sums up: 'The awakening is the exemplary form of the revelation of God only because it makes unequivocally clear the "God was in Christ", the self-hood of the Son of God on the cross. *The awakening is the revelation of the Subject of the atonement on the cross, the exemplary form of revelation and in this way an exclusive act of God.*'[18]

As the exemplary revelation of God it is more than 'something merely formal and noetic'[19] i.e., it does not simply show us the meaning of the cross, its reverse side. It has a material and ontic side as well, is based upon objective truth and reality, is an exclusive new act of God and so is definitive and final. However, it is not unrelated to but closely follows upon the life and death of Jesus and reveals their true meaning and significance. It is therefore only the fact that it reveals what was true and hidden on the cross, viz., the divine act of reconciliation, that makes the awakening the exemplary form of revelation. It is not such merely as the raising of a man from the dead or as an event free from all human action and components. 'The divine action in the passion—hidden *sub contrario*—reveals itself in the pure divine act of the awakening.'[20]

(3) *A free act of divine grace of the Father to the Son.* According to Klappert this is Barth's 'final qualification of his basic thesis that the awakening is pure revelation of the Subject of reconciliation on the cross'.[21] Again this goes back to the fact that Barth distinguishes between the awakening and the resurrection. According to him two views are to be avoided here. (*a*) That Jesus Christ is himself, or together with the Father, the Subject of his own awakening. 'We must also be careful how we handle the thought (which is correct not merely in the sense of later trinitarian theology) that Jesus Christ as the Son of God was associated with the Father as the Subject of his own resurrection. The New Testament does not put it in this way.'[22] Barth has here modified his earlier views which tended to speak of Jesus Christ as such a Subject. 'In the very exaltation of Jesus Christ ... as in his

humiliation, Jesus Christ himself acted, that is *God* in Christ.'[23] Or again, 'It was only because he himself was God that the resurrection could and had to follow this death.'[24] (*b*) That the resurrection and the awakening are 'simply equivalents ... he himself being the acting Subject in the one case and God (the Father) in the other'.[25] This is how H. Vogel[26] views the matter, but says Barth, this has docetic tendencies since it speaks 'of a mere "impotence" of the One dead and buried from which he recovered on his own initiative and in his own strength'.[27] Klappert, while granting that Barth is essentially correct, nevertheless to some extent agrees with Vogel that in the New Testament raising and resurrection are sometimes equivalent or interchangeable terms.[28]

On the contrary and in contrast Barth believes that Jesus Christ is essentially the passive object of the divine action of God the Father who raised him from the dead.[29]

Moreover, it is Jesus Christ not simply as man but as the Son of God since 'the one whole Jesus Christ, very man and very God, was dead and buried'.[30] Hence it was an act of 'free and pure grace which as such can only be received',[31] in which the Son is 'a pure object and recipient of the grace of God'.[32] This, as we have seen, corresponds to the fact that there is 'a pure obedience, subordination and subjection',[33] of the Son to the Father. As a result we can hazard the difficult thought that 'in the resurrection of Jesus Christ we have to do with a movement and action which took place not merely in human history but first and foremost in God himself'.[34] So Barth can sum up: 'no, not simply as man, but even as the Son of God. Jesus Christ is here simply the One who takes and receives, the recipient of a gift'.[35]

This should not lead to the idea that the resurrection took place in a heavenly sphere of which the earthly is only the reflection without genuine reality as Barth has sometimes been accused of putting things. Rather it means that since we know in the resurrection that God raised his Son from the dead he does something in real history which corresponds to his true being in himself. The event of the awakening from the dead is analogous to what he is in himself in the relation of the Son to the Father. It is therefore in this free act of divine grace of the Father to the Son that the real nature of Jesus Christ as Subject of the history of humiliation on the cross is revealed.

Klappert[36] gives the following interpretation of this section in relating the different aspects to each other:

(a) 'The awakening is the exemplary form of revelation in that it reveals the exclusive action of the Father to and upon the Son who was obedient to him.'

(b) 'The awakening, as the act of God to and upon the Son, is the conferring of the name of *Kyrios* (Phil. 2:9) by the Father, is the divine confirmation and revelation of the humiliated as the Son of the Father.'

(c) 'The awakening as a pure act of the divine grace of the Father to and upon the Son reveals the act of obedience of the Son on the cross.'

The relation of the three main aspects he sees as follows: 'If the awakening as the free act of grace of the Father to and upon the Son is the revelation by the Father of the Son concealed on the cross, then it is an exclusive act of God, the unequivocal revelation of the Subject of reconciliation on the cross.'[37]

(4) *Relation to his Preceding Life.* The resurrection revealed that 'he had always been present among them in his deity, though hitherto this deity had been veiled'.[38] This means that there was no time when he was not truly, wholly and fully God, but that his deity (centred in his cross as reconciliation and revealed in the resurrection) is the truth of his life as a whole. Yet his previous life does not as such reveal but rather conceals and that under its opposite. *'Exinanitus in cruce* is basically the *tectus sub contrario*. From this it follows that the Son of God humbles himself on the cross and there reveals the glory of God *which God alone can make known.* In this sense the awakening is, for Barth, basically the exemplary form of the revelation of God, the indubitable mediation of the knowledge that God was in Christ crucified (2 Cor. 5:19a),[39] that God is "the high God in his *humility*"[40] specifically on the cross.'[41]

This means that Barth is opposed to those who, like Pannenberg, give to the awakening a retroactive significance rather than, as in Barth's own case, a retrospective significance.[42] It does not simply confirm Jesus claims but reveals a divinity already real and operative. As an exclusive, new act of God it manifests the full meaning, content and significance of his previous life and death. It reveals him as God acting in reconciliation. Previously the disciples had seen but had not understood or only very partially[43] so that he was present as God in a paradoxical way in his humanity, *sub contrario in cruce.* Now, however, he was manifest in the glory that was always his. 'He had been veiled, but he was now wholly and unequivocally and irrevocably manifest.'[44]

2. THE HUMANITY OF JESUS IN THE RESURRECTION

(1) *The Self-Revelation of Jesus Christ as Man Exalted on the Cross*

What has been said about the nature of the deity of Christ is true also of his humanity. The cross, including the previous life of Jesus, can best be described as a concealing, a veiling, or as the secret of the real character of his being as exalted man.[45] Barth sums up simply thus:

'the being of Jesus Christ as Lord, as King, as Son of Man, as true man, is a hidden being'.[46] Nor have we any capacity of our own to penetrate this secret or unveil the mystery of his being and passion.

If then knowledge of the crucified is that he is exalted, how do we come to this knowledge? Barth's answer is the resurrection. In a rich variety of images he speaks of the resurrection and ascension as the revelation of Jesus as the royal man exalted on the cross. They are his self-revelation, 'simply a lifting of the veil',[47] a stepping out of his hiddenness to make himself known as he really is. It is with this there commences his revelation 'as the One he had been and is'[48]—the man who had been exalted. The 'life' is now 'light' (*C.D.*, IV/3). It is Jesus's self-declaration, proclamation, communication or self-witness,[49] the manifesting of his glory as the One whose life was fulfilled and crowned on the cross. While it is true to say that, in one sense, the whole being and act of Christ in its totality, has the character of revelation, nevertheless the centre of gravity and point of departure for this understanding are the resurrection and ascension. They are 'the definitive and comprehensive and absolutely unequivocal exponents of the character of his being as revelation'.[50]

(2) *The resurrection is at the same time the revelation of and the counterpart to the completed reconciliation of the cross*

The resurrection and ascension are the revelation of 'the perfect being of Jesus Christ, and his accomplished reconciliation of the world with God'.[51] Furthermore, it is a *perfect* revelation which 'corresponds to *this* completion of his work, manifesting it as such, declaring its meaning and basis'.[52] In other words, he is fully revealed and known 'in correspondence to the revealed fulness of his being and work'.[53]

It is thus clear that this revelation does not add to the already completed event of Christ's reconciliation, his exaltation on the cross—it simply makes it known. 'The being of Jesus Christ was and is perfect and complete in itself in his history as . . . true Son of Man. It does not need to be transcended or augmented by new qualities or further developments . . . the exaltation of man (is) . . . the completed fulfilment of the covenant, the completed reconciliation of the world with God. His being as such . . . was and is the end of the old and the beginning of the new form of this world even *without* his resurrection and ascension. He did not and does not lack anything in himself.'[54] Again, Barth writes, 'His being and work, his history and existence, are *completed* in his death on the cross, and . . . there is made in it once for all a satisfactory offering before God for the men of all times and places—an offering which need not and cannot therefore be continued, augmented or superseded'.[55] Klappert sums this up as follows: 'In contrast to every conception of the resurrection as a completion of the being and work of Christ it is the revelation of the royal man exalted on the cross.'[56]

(3) *The resurrection confirms the Lordship of the Crucified*

Jesus is not first Lord in the resurrection but in his life as it is consummated on the cross. The resurrection confirms this, reveals him as the Lord and King he is on the cross. Klappert points out several things that this means,[57] viz., the commencement of his rule as Lord of time, his Lordship as the Crucified over all men who are included in his being and action, his prophetic work as the Victor. This means that 'the resurrection as the revelation of the completed reconciliation on the cross implies Lordship—and this relationship is irreversible'.[58]

This Lordship is confirmed in the ascension which shows the glory of the cross. 'His exaltation on the cross was also his exaltation to the Father.'[59] Klappert interprets this to mean that 'the ascension as his last appearance was on the one hand, the final revelation of the exaltation completed on the cross and, on the other, the beginning of the Lordship so revealed, Jesus's entry into full participation in the sovereignty of God'.[60] As such it is a new act of sovereignty as well as the revelation of the exaltation and majesty of Jesus.

(4) *The appearances of Jesus*

The resurrection shows Jesus alive after his passion. He appears as such to his disciples. 'He was known as the One who had been among them before and was then crucified, dead and buried.'[61] Barth lays strong emphasis on the identity of Jesus in his life and death with the risen One and criticises putting too much stress on the resurrection body of Jesus as a new and glorified body. 'It is a fault of the otherwise very fine and competent study of K. H. Rengstorff (*Die Auferstehung Jesu*, 1952) that it lays rather too much emphasis on the importance of the new and glorified corporeality in which Jesus appeared to his disciples.'[62] But this is not the main thrust of the Easter stories. 'What the evangelists really know and say is simply that the disciples saw and heard Jesus again after his death, and that as they saw and heard him they recognised him, and that they recognised him on the basis of his identity with the One whom they had known before.'[63]

There is therefore unity and continuity with what went before but also radical discontinuity since the man Jesus returns from death after death and does so in the power of God. The significance and meaning of this is that here 'we have to do with the concrete, visible, audible, tangible new presence of the man Jesus who was crucified, dead and buried'.[64] He exists in our space and time yet for a limited time in a way 'comparable with the presence and appearance of a man who has not yet died'.[65] Barth expresses this truth even more forcefully thus: 'It was his new appearance in the psycho-physical totality of his temporal existence familiar from his first coming.'[66]

What Barth is concerned to emphasise here is that it is the man Jesus in his unity and totality, as soul of his body—and therefore corporally—who is present. He is not a mere spiritual presence nor is his body so transformed that it ceases to be truly human. Two facts testify to this: (a) The appearances of Jesus to his disciples and (b) the empty tomb.[67] He was 'visibly, audibly, tangibly alive . . . Christ is risen, he is risen indeed! To be exegetically accurate we must understand by this "indeed" *corporeally* risen'.[68]

He is in our life in history yet not of it 'being present spiritually, of course, but also corporally as the same man he had been before, preceding, speaking, eating and drinking with them as with his fellows and as he had done before'.[69] In putting such strong emphasis on the corporal and real nature of Christ's manhood present again with his own, Barth sees himself as being both true to the New Testament testimony and also as affirming the necessary truth of the real identity of the post- and pre-resurrection Jesus. Otherwise the whole basis of our faith falls to the ground and our reconciliation is imperilled.

Moreover, Barth is also concerned to emphasise the genuine 'historical' nature of the resurrection. While history cannot verify, validate or prove the meaning of the resurrection, nonetheless it has this historical nexus since the man Jesus who died was present again in our space, time and history. There is thus in him a unique union of the 'historical' (human) and the 'supra-historical' (divine).[70] While the reality and meaning of the resurrection as a whole is not 'historical' in our modern sense we 'may still speak of a happening which, though it cannot be grasped historically, is still actual and objective in time and space'.[71]

Otto Weber[72] points out that the Easter stories in the New Testament all have 'external, outward characteristics' (*Ausserlichkeit*). Among these he names the appearances themselves, their limited duration, their specific 'time' and the empty tomb, and that 'the Resurrected bore the marks of corporeality which are essentially intended to underline the identity of the risen Lord with the Crucified (so, in particular, St. John) and to exclude a mere spiritual appearance (so, in particular, Luke) but nonetheless did not necessarily identify the "body of the Resurrected" with the earthly body'.[73] This latter qualification comes from Paul's interpretation of the bodily form of the resurrection which must be analogous to that of Christ.

Barth himself points in this direction when to the stark realism of his exposition (corresponding to the resurrection narratives) is added the thought from 1 Cor. 15 that the resurrection cannot mean the continuation of man in his corruption but his being clothed in incorruption.

The return of a man, a creature, from death can, 'in no circumstances, . . . be simply its autonomous continuation in life'.[74] He continues: 'Its corruptible and mortal, therefore, must as such, as that which it was between birth and death, put on the incorruptibility and immortality which are proper only to God. (1 Cor. 15:53). Its present form is not, then, dissolved or done away or destroyed, which would mean death, or a future without God. It is taken up into a new form which is not proper to it in its creatureliness but is given to it as that of God its Creator.'[75] Barth must, therefore, speak of an identity with a difference, a real difference between the life of this age and that which is to come, between our corruptible form and that of God's incorruption. How far this differs from Rengstorff's views of a glorified body, which Barth questions, is doubtful.

While Jesus Christ in his resurrection is true man, yet in it God has broken 'into the this-worldliness of his creation'.[76] But since Christ has death already behind him this means that his only future is that of God, of eternal life. And this shows further that the determination of man's life is to participate 'in the sovereign life of God . . . in the immortality and transcendance of God',[77] so revealing the divine glory.

Jesus came again into our life as a man but as a man who had death already behind him and only the life of God before him. It was the same Jesus who had lived and died but was now present with them as the One whose life had been freed from death's power and was exalted to share in the divine life and love. 'He came again in the manifestation or revelation of his prior human life as it had fallen victim to death as such, but had been delivered from death, invested with divine glory, and caused to shine in this glory, in virtue of its participation in the life of God.'[78]

One could say of Barth's exposition that Jesus was the same yet different. He was different in that in him God revealed himself definitively to men and gave to human nature a share in his eternal life but he was not different in that he was present with them in their world as the man he had been before. 'He was different in respect of his *revelation* as the true Son of God and Son of Man existing in the world. But he was not different in respect of the fact that, no less in his revelation of these days than previously in his concealment . . . he existed among them and therefore concretely in time and space in the world. He was not different in respect of the fact that even and especially in this revelation he spoke and acted among them and therefore in the world, coming again not in semblance only but in reality.'[79] Barth here emphasises that the identity of the Risen Lord with the Jesus of the flesh consists in his real presence in space and time among men whose life is moving towards death and yet who himself had gone beyond death and now comes to them from that beyond. So Jesus came again from the dead and was in this temporal life of ours in 'the light of his eternal life. His temporal and spatial life shone as his eternal life.'[80]

Finally, there are several ways in which we do not regard the appearances of Jesus in his risen life. These can be stated as follows:

1. Barth's view of the real presence of Jesus with the disciples after the awakening is against the theory that this was 'just a mental appearance in the experience or intellect of the disciples as illumined by a vision or suchlike'.[81] This is obviously primarily spoken against the ideas of Rudolf Bultmann.[82]

2. Barth believes that any view which does not speak of the man Jesus present fully as man in the resurrection life endangers the full humanity of Jesus and so tends towards Docetism.[83]

3. The appearance of the man Jesus 'who obviously died on the cross was not a prolongation of his existence terminated by death'.[84] Others came back from death to die again. This man lived and lives for ever in 'participation in the sovereign life of God'.[85]

Notes to Chapter 7 will be found on pp. 174–179.

CHAPTER EIGHT

The Humanity of God

In his earlier theology Barth strongly emphasized the *Godness* of God, his being as 'Wholly Other' than man. This was in marked contrast to the prevailing subjectivism and historicism of the times. In his later development he did not abandon his original insight but related it more fully to the humanity of God (as he called it) i.e., to God in his relationship to man in the man Jesus of Nazareth.[1] God is not God *in abstracto* but we must learn to think of and know him *in concreto* in Jesus Christ. For 'it is precisely God's *deity* which, rightly understood, includes his *humanity*'.[2]

This teaching that God is known in and through the humanity of Jesus has two bases in Barth's theology, namely, the divine election and the doctrine of Time.

(a) *The divine Election*

In his gracious election God has chosen man to be his covenant partner and in so doing has disclosed his own true nature as triune, the One who, in his eternal Son determines himself as the God of man. In 'Jesus Christ is the decision of God in favour of this attitude or relation'.[3] This is seen in three ways. Jesus Christ is the electing God himself who in Christ has chosen man for himself. Secondly, the content of this election is none other than 'the Son of God in his determination as the Son of Man, the pre-existing God-man Jesus Christ, who is as such the eternal basis of the whole divine election'.[4] Thirdly, all this has its truth and reality in the man Jesus who is himself the humanity of God. Hence, since man coexists with God in the divine will and election from all eternity one cannot speak of the Word or Son of God as a *Logos asarkos* but always and only as *Logos ensarkos*.

(b) *Time*

Barth speaks of the man Jesus as the Lord of Time. This is made known and revealed in the resurrection. Since the man Jesus in his time is one with the eternal Son of God he shares with him his divine life without in any sense himself being or becoming divine. One cannot,

Notes to Chapter 8 will be found on pp. 179–181.

therefore, speak of any time when he was not with God as the content of the divine will for man. He is in our present as the One he was in the days of the flesh, in the Old Testament time and right back to the eternity of God. Here the doctrines of election and time coincide and are one.

Barth is not saying that there was a man Jesus who pre-existed as such or was eternal as God is but that, in the light and by the power of election and incarnation, we cannot think of God without or apart from this man through whom alone he is known as God. Let us now consider the significance of this teaching of Barth on the humanity of God.[5]

I. GOD AND MAN IN PERMANENT RELATIONSHIP AND UNITY IN JESUS CHRIST

This is the foundation of Barth's whole position. In the Christian faith we are not dealing with God or man in general, in abstraction or isolation, but in their relationship and unity in Jesus Christ—a relationship and unity eternally willed and decreed, determined by God alone in the mystery of his electing love in which he became and always is the God of man, God with and for man. This is the significance of the doctrine of the *Logos ensarkos*. There is no depth of deity in which he was other than the God of man, in which man was not with and before God. The two belong indissolubly together, not by man's choice but by God's, not because it is in the nature of God or man to be so determined but because of God's action and will. It is a relation which 'once God has willed to enter into it, and has in fact entered into it, he could not be God without it'.[6]

This relationship and unity and its nature is thus described: 'In *Jesus Christ*, as he is attested in Holy Scripture, we are not dealing with man in the abstract; not with the man who is able with his modicum of religion and religious morality to be sufficient unto himself without God and thus himself to be God. But neither are we dealing with *God* in the abstract; not with one who in his deity exists only separated from man, distant and strange and thus a non-human if not indeed an inhuman God. In Jesus Christ there is no isolation of man from God or of God from man. Rather, in him we encounter the history, the dialogue, in which God and man meet together and are together.'[7] One can speak of it otherwise as the identity of God and man in Jesus Christ, 'an identity which must be thought of as a continuing *event*'.[8]

'Thus in this oneness Jesus Christ is the Mediator, the Reconciler, between God and man. Thus he comes forward to *man* on behalf of *God* calling for and awakening faith, love, and hope, and to *God* on behalf of *man*, representing man, making satisfaction and interceding.

Thus he attests and guarantees to man God's free *grace* and at the same
time attests and guarantees to God man's free *gratitude*. Thus he
establishes in his Person the justice of God *vis-à-vis* man and also the
justice of man before God. Thus he is in his Person the covenant in its
fullness, the Kingdom of heaven which is at hand, in which God speaks
and man hears, God gives and man receives, God commands and man
obeys, God's glory shines in the heights and thence into the depths,
and peace on earth comes to pass among men in whom he is well
pleased. Moreover, exactly in this way Jesus Christ, as this Mediator
and Reconciler between God and man, is also the *Revealer* of them both.
We do not need to engage in a free-ranging investigation to seek out
and construct who and what God truly is, and who and what man truly
is, but only to read the truth about both where it resides, namely, in the
fullness of their togetherness, their covenant which proclaims itself in
Jesus Christ.'[9]

Further, this relationship and unity do not exclude but properly
describe the true difference between God and man. It is precisely in the
incarnation where the relation between God and man is at its greatest
that the real distinction is seen. 'It could be formulated in this way (and
this is Barth's meaning) . . . God became man in order that God and
man can be definitively distinguished from one another.'[10] This
distinction requires some elucidation in terms of Barth's theology. It is
a further underlining of two aspects of Chalcedon (without confusion
and without change). God proves himself to be the true God, the God
of man in his humanity, particularly on the cross and in the resurrection. Here the paradox of his dealings with man is revealed since, on the
one hand, he is known only in and with his humanity, but, on the other
hand, he is not to be confused with it or changed into it. 'The God who
is definitively distinguished from man is the One who is in union with
the man Jesus; it is in this distinction from man that he proves himself
to be the God of man.'[11] The resurrection of Jesus Christ reveals the
true God who in the atoning death on the cross alone does for man
what he cannot do for himself and so is made known both as 'other'
than man and yet as the God of man. In the most real union and
identity of God and man, in the *unio personalis*, God is revealed in his
majesty and otherness. Anyone or anything else that claims to be God
is only a false conception of God.

On the other hand, man as he truly is, i.e., man in real relationship
and fellowship with God, is also fully revealed here. Man is not an
emanation or aspect of God any more than God is man raised to the
highest degree. Man is the creature of God and, moreover, a fallen
creature whose true nature (both as creature and as fallen) Jesus Christ
reveals on the cross and in the resurrection. He is 'other' than God in
this closest unity and in this has his true life, genuine freedom and real

exaltation. True, reconciled, exalted man is revealed on the cross and in the resurrection of Jesus. Any other view of man is not a genuinely human one. 'A humanity which is not definitively distinguished from God is no genuine humanity but the false degeneration of faith in the God of man into a self-representation of man who in deifying himself is in fact inhuman.'[12]

The true deity is revealed in Jesus Christ alone as is the true humanity. In this unity and distinction Jesus Christ is true God and true man.

2. THE REVELATION AND DEFINITION OF THE TRUE GOD

'Who and what *God* is—this is what in particular we have to learn better and with more precision in the new change of direction in the thinking and speaking of evangelical theology. . . . But the question must be, who and what is God *in Jesus Christ*.'[13] Two things must be clearly stated here (as Jüngel shows)[14] and they belong together, viz., God known and thought of on the basis of the revelation in Jesus Christ and so defined fully but solely in relation to him. 'Thus we have here no universal deity capable of being reached conceptually, but this concrete deity—real and recognisable in . . . the existence of Jesus Christ.'[15]

In other words the one true God is known and defined in this relationship to man and once he has entered into it, we cannot know him otherwise or apart from this. 'The divine attitude is not a matter of chance. It is not revocable or transitory. God lays upon us the obligation of this attitude because first of all he lays it upon himself. In dealing with this attitude, we have to do with his free but definitive decision. We cannot abstract from it without falling into arbitrary speculation. But we cannot ignore it. Once made, it belongs definitively to God himself, not in his being in and for himself, but in his being within this relationship. It belongs to the reality of God which is a reality not apart from but in this decision. It is so adjoined to this reality that we must not allow any objectivity of logic to prevent us from introducing the adjunct as an element in our knowledge of God. We cannot speak correctly of God in his being in and for himself without considering him always in this attitude, . . . the actual relationship in which God has placed himself; a relationship outside of which God no longer wills to be and no longer is God, and within which alone he can be truly honoured and worshipped as God.'[16]

There are several points here which are of paramount importance:

(a) God is the true God only in this relationship to man in Jesus Christ. There is no other God, no other place we can find him or speak of him, know or define him. But he is fully and truly made known here as he, the Subject, in sovereign freedom, gives himself to be known.

(b) Only from within this relationship can we legitimately speak of God as he truly is. 'The Subject God, still cannot, as it were, be envisaged, established and described only in and for itself.'[17] One must, therefore, always be clear that God as he is in this permanent relationship is God as he is in himself. It is in and through the former that the latter is known but known truly as he really is. There are no hidden depths in God which we may know apart from Jesus Christ. 'Particularly in the later volumes of the Dogmatics in contrast to the *Extra Calvinisticum* (which owes more to St. Thomas than Calvin) Barth insists that God has defined (revealed) himself *fully* in Jesus Christ.'[18]

(c) It does not mean that man is part of the reality of God. 'It is not as though the object of this relationship, the other, constitutes a part of the reality of God outside of God.'[19] God is complete in himself, does not need man nor is he compelled or constrained by man but is sovereign and free.

(d) It is a definition and revelation in which God is the absolutely superior partner who rules in grace and demands gratitude and obedience—an obedience that is not servitude, but corresponds to and reflects the very nature of the triune God himself, who, in his Son is obedient. In this respect God is not One who acts in an authoritarian way (as Jüngel rightly points out) but as many have accused Barth of teaching. Obedience is the nature of the Son who loves in freedom and who elicits an obedience in a like, loving freedom.

That Barth so speaks of God as a whole and in the various aspects of his Being is his highly relevant and invaluable contribution to the current debate about God. That he never argues about the existence but always speaks of his Being in action in Jesus Christ is also significant and suggestive, since only in this revelation, but really and completely here, is the true God known, perceived and worshipped.

3. KEINE MENSCHENLOSIGKEIT GOTTES[20] (NO NON-HUMAN GOD)—GOD IN HIS GODHEAD, HUMAN

The basis of this is, as we have seen, God's free election of grace and not simply the nature or Being of God himself. Barth repeatedly emphasises that God is not One who decides in, with and for himself, but with and for man. It is not 'made in the absence of the one who must be present as the second partner at the institution of the covenant . . . man. . . . This is what we can call a decree, an *opus Dei internum ad extra*, and therefore a pact; God's free election of grace in which . . . the Son of the Father is no longer just the eternal Logos but as such, as very God from all eternity, he is also the very God and very man he will become in time.'[21] Barth very clearly expresses the fact of the humanity of God in this passage: 'Already in the eternal will and decree of God he was not to be, nor did he will to be, God only, but Emmanuel, God with man, and in fulfilment of this "with", according to the free choice of his grace, this man, Jesus of Nazareth. And in the act of God in time which corresponds to this eternal decree, when the Son of God became this man, he ceased to all eternity to be God only, receiving and having and maintaining to all eternity human essence as well. Thus the human essence of Jesus Christ, without becoming divine, in its very creatureliness, is placed at the side of the Creator, *pros ton theon* (John 1:1). It is a clothing which he does not put off. It is his temple which he does not leave. It is the form which he does not lose. It is an organ the use of which he does not renounce . . . For he is not God to us, nor can he be known or glorified or loved or worshipped by us as God, except in and with the human flesh assumed by his Son as the Mediator of the covenant.'[22] Nothing could be clearer or more explicit than this. God is no non-human God, because he has, from all eternity, in his free election of grace, determined himself for man and man for himself. To use one of Barth's metaphors, God is God clothed with our humanity because he has revealed himself to be God precisely in his union with man in the incarnation and atonement.

In this way there is no non-human God since the Son of Man by the divine election shares in the triune life of God, 'is fully and completely participant not only in the good-pleasure of God the Father but also in the presence and effective working of the Holy Spirit . . . the Son of Man is not deified by the fact that he is also and primarily the Son of God. He does not become a fourth in the Holy Trinity. But necessarily he acquires and takes as man the same full share in its being and work in creation as he has in its inward life as God.'[23]

'It is when we look at Jesus Christ that we know decisively that God's deity does not exclude, but includes, his *humanity*.'[24] In fact it is as in love he bends down to man, commits himself to him, sacrifices himself in this deepest humility, overcomes as man man's rebellion and contradiction against himself that he is most clearly and supremely God. His deity does not exclude but includes communion with man—a communion, moreover, which God as man created in face of man's total opposition, pride, sloth and disobedience. He is one with this man of the flesh. This again is but a further definition of the true God who, in being God, takes man up, exalts and includes him in his own divine action—in fact, is not known as the divine without man but only with him. 'No, God requires no exclusion of humanity, no non-humanity, not to speak of inhumanity, in order to be truly God. But we may and must, however, look further and recognise the fact that actually his deity *encloses humanity in itself*.'[25]

This should not be seen as God standing in any need of man, since in his eternal life he is sufficient unto himself.[26] Rather, it is the expression of the freedom of the divine Love in which 'he wants in his freedom actually not to be without man but *with* him and in the same freedom not against him but *for* him, and that apart from or even counter to what man deserves. He wants in fact to be man's partner, his almighty and compassionate Saviour. . . . He determines to love him, to be his God, his Lord, his compassionate Preserver and Saviour to eternal life, and to desire his praise and service. In this divinely free volition and election, in this sovereign decision . . . God is *human*. His free affirmation of man, his free concern for him, his free substitution for him—this is God's humanity'.[27]

Put in a nutshell, the centre of the humanity of God is the death of Jesus as atonement, at one and the same time the deepest depths of God and the highest heights of man, the humbled God and the royal man, God in lowliness and man exalted. For here, Jesus Christ, God and man, takes upon himself our need and depravity, redeems us and sets us in the heavenly places. 'He perceives that the superior will of God, to which he wholly subordinates himself, requires that he sacrifice himself for the human race, and seeks his honour in doing this. In the mirror of this humanity of Jesus Christ the humanity of God enclosed in his deity reveals itself. Thus God is as he is. Thus he affirms man. Thus he is concerned about him. Thus he stands up for him.'[28] Thus, one might say, he is human, in atoning sacrifice. The death of this man Jesus is the supreme revelation of God manifest in his resurrection. Jüngel sums this up by saying: 'God in his deity determined himself for humanity. According to Barth, the deity of God is an event specifically in the death of the man Jesus',[29] i.e., in his atoning sacrifice.

4. MAN, IN HIS HUMANITY, HUMAN—NO ABSOLUTE GODLESSNESS OF MAN[30]

This is a further and most important consequence of the humanity of God. Barth is not thereby saying that there are no godless men in the generally accepted sense of the term. There can be and there is an actual godlessness of man as man rebels against his Creator and covenant God.[31] If this is so, is it not then the case that man is without God, rejected and condemned, and so separated from him, outside of fellowship with him? In one sense all this is true. Because man, by disobedience, rebellion and sin, contradicts his election of grace in Jesus Christ and does not believe, he can be characterized as a 'godless' man. He chose not what God had willed and chosen for him but its opposite—a non-reality. But the reality of man's being is God's choice of him for salvation. Because sin does not correspond to the reality of his being as elect and reconciled it is a godlessness which, though actual and powerful, has ultimately but a negative force. Man's reality, however, is that he is God's covenant partner; in the humanity of God, God has chosen man from all eternity and is faithful to him. In the incarnation God has assumed our humanity so that in and through Jesus Christ all stand in a real relationship to him which even man's sin cannot destroy or undermine. This means that man is in a real (ontological) relationship with God. Even in God's rejection and judgment, man is not godless, not apart from God but with him, since he cannot escape him. So, in the ultimate sense, because God has united man with himself, one cannot speak of an absolute godlessness of man but can only give it relative significance. Barth sums this up simply by saying, 'He may let go of God, but God does not let go of him.'[32]

This is one deduction from Barth's doctrine of election. Man must at least know God's judgment which is the reverse side of his goodness and grace. Moreover, it is this godless man who is predestinate, chosen to be God's. 'It is this very man, godless in his negative act, wantonly representing the rejected man, who is the predestinate.'[33] Barth thus distinguishes between the *being* of the elect and *his life* as such, i.e., between what he is as God's covenant partner, *realiter*, and what he is *actualiter*. His *actual* godlessness conflicts with his real godliness but cannot annul it, because of what God has done in Jesus Christ. Godlessness is not a part of man's true being, his reality, since it has been taken by Jesus Christ upon himself, borne and borne away in his life, death, resurrection and reign.

It can be expressed in this way. Man is on the edge of a gulf but has not fallen right in, for, underneath and round about is the everlasting mercy—the man Christ Jesus, God in the flesh, the humanity of God. 'In the absurd way . . . man is able to be the edge of this gulf, and therefore relatively, although not absolutely and ontologically, godless. But he cannot really escape God. His godlessness may be very strong but it cannot make God a "manless" (non-human, menschenloser) God. . . . We should be abandoning our starting point . . . if we were to try to ascribe to man an absolute and ontological godlessness. Man has not fallen lower than the depth to which God humbled himself for him in Jesus Christ. But God in Jesus Christ did not become a devil or nothingness.'[34] He became flesh but remained man. So from the point of view of man's election and reconciliation which took place for all there is no longer any absolutely godless man; God himself has gone into the depth and has borne the uttermost of man's sin, degradation and godlessness. The triumph of the positive over the negative, of God's yes over his no and man's, of his order over chaos, means no abandoning of man even in the depths of his disobedience. Since God has become man in Jesus Christ and so exalted man to his side no one can be alone or without him.

From these premises Jüngel draws several conclusions. Whereas the false idea of God leads to inhumanity, a deformation and so the dehumanising of man, that of the true God in Jesus Christ leads to the true humanity of man, his exaltation and so the affirmation of his true nature as man.[35] Further, that God is with man means that he is nearer to every man than man is to himself. 'One cannot deduce from this theology a theory of an anonymous Christianity. But it does make possible the comforting certainty that even the man who is most godless and far from God, is nearer to God than he is to himself.'[36] At one and the same time God declares his own nature in man's reconciliation and in so bringing man to himself shows forth his grace. God is the God who justifies the godless and therein himself in the man Christ Jesus—in this way declares also man's true humanity.

5. CONTRA THEISM AND ATHEISM

Theism asserts the possibility that man by reason can reach, believe in and have knowledge of a Supreme Being, whereas atheism affirms that no such Being exists or can. Barth's thesis first affirms the reality of the true God revealed in Jesus Christ and in him alone and so at the same time exposes the two other false alternatives as both baseless and presumptuous. If there is only one true God, the God made known in his relation to man in Jesus Christ, then it follows that all others are false gods, idols, and that man who seeks to evade the claim and challenge of God or seeks to find God on his own is himself presumptuous, setting himself up in God's place. This is essentially Barth's argument powerfully and persuasively stated and ably interpreted by E. Jüngel.

Jüngel states that the metaphysical idea of God as the Supreme Being, the highest object of our thought, or rather that which must be beyond our thought (as Supreme), dominated both Scholasticism and the Enlightenment. He quotes Ernst Bloch as saying that this Supreme Being is 'above where man does not appear'.[37] This is precisely why he is a false god because he is not God *with* man. Paradoxically metaphysics did not think aright about God because it thought in an all too human way, i.e., it considered a God without man. It made man's hypostatized ideas and images into the reality of a god. Equally to deny God's existence is to think in a too human way because it means to take God away from man and so to leave man as his own deity—which is idolatry. In contrast Barth 'puts Jesus over against all traditional ideas of God *and* their denial in order precisely in this way to learn *to think* about God'.[38] Indeed this was the whole of his theological task, to think about the true God in contrast to all ideas about God coming from Theism and Atheism. 'Barth raises the same basic objection to both undertakings, that they do not think of God *as God* and therefore in their affirmation and denial have not affirmed and denied *God*.'[39] In simple terms they bypass the humanity of God.

The true God is the human God, the God of man, who is not simply 'Other' than man but with man in condescension and great humility. 'What marks out God above all false gods is that they are not capable and ready for this. In their otherworldliness and supernaturalness and otherness, etc., the gods are a reflection of the human pride which will not unbend, which will not stoop to that which is beneath it. God is not proud. In his high majesty he is humble.'[40] Jüngel comments: 'This is an attack on the metaphysical idea of God which could scarcely be sharper.'[41] It is also at the same time such an affirmation of God with man that it undermines Atheism as well.

Basically the assertions of Theism and Atheism are due to human pride which will not accept the humanity of God—a God self-humbled as man. Man wants himself to be as God—like the Supreme Being of metaphysics, but not like the God who identified himself with man, who suffered as man a felon's death.[42] 'The error of man concerning God is that the God he wants to be like is obviously only a self-sufficient, self-affirming, self-desiring Supreme Being, self-centred and rotating about himself. Such a being is not God. God is for himself, but he is not only for himself. He is in a supreme self-hood but not a self-contained self-hood, not in a mere divinity which is obviously presented to man in the mere humanity intended for man.'[43] In worshipping such a Being man is 'positing himself as absolute' so that 'what he thinks to see and honour and worship in himself is already the image of a false deity, the original of all false gods.'[44] Thus, 'as Luther rightly saw and said, he makes God the devil. For if . . . there "is" a devil, he is identical with a Supreme Being, which posits and wills itself, which exists in solitary glory and is therefore "absolute". The devil is that being which we can define only as independent non-being.'[45] Jüngel sums it up thus; 'According to Barth, every idea of God makes God a devil which regards God's *deity* as the *absoluteness* of his Being and does not see it as, at the same time, an eternally willed *relationship* of this Being to man.'[46] This is only correct if we substitute for the Supreme Being related to man the God and Father of our Lord Jesus Christ.

Jüngel again states that when man has an idea of God after his own image two things follow: (a) it sets the Godhead and manhood over against one another in an abstract way so that the incarnation means the end of God, God really leaving his deity behind and changing into a man.[47] A Supreme Being could not become man since there is no true reality behind the conception but an abstraction—an idol of a deified humanity. The true God, in contrast, is One who encompasses both the spheres of height and depth and does so *concretely* in Jesus Christ. 'The Godhead of the true God is not a prison whose walls have first to be broken through if he is to elect and do what he has elected and done in becoming man. In distinction from that of false gods, and especially the god of Mohammed, his Godhead embraces both height and depth, both sovereignty and humility, both lordship and service ... He does not become another when in Jesus Christ he also becomes and is man. Even —and why should we not say precisely?—in this he is God in supreme constancy.'[48] In other words, in contrast to a false abstraction which is in reality a projection of man's self-created image and so a false unity between deity and humanity (because it is a duality), the true God is revealed in concrete form in the man Jesus in unity and identity with him. The false abstraction in fact destroys the deity of God.

(b) In the second place, the metaphysical idea of God at the same time makes an abstract distinction as well as an abstract unity between God and man. This idea does not destroy the deity of God so much as his humanity. For since God's manhood is omitted God becomes inhuman, undivine, devilish.[49] God in the freedom of his action cannot possibly be identified with the Supreme Being presupposed by or unrelated to man. 'However strongly the factuality and normativeness and therefore the majesty of this Supreme Being may be emphasised, it obviously has nothing to do with the freedom of God.'[50] Rather, this Being is again the projection of man's ideas springing from the false-hood (in contrast to the pride) of man which turns the truth of God into a lie.

In contrast to all these false views Barth emphasises the reality of the true God come in the flesh, 'distinguished from all the idols imagined and fashioned by man by the fact that they are not God in the flesh but products of human speculation or naked deity, *logoi asarkoi*'.[51] In other words, it is in this relationship of God to man in Jesus Christ which he has inaugurated, carried through and maintained, which is a living reality always that we meet with, know and worship the true God and realise also the true nature of man.

Jüngel sums up the significance of the humanity of God in opposition to both Theism and Atheism by saying that these latter are in reality two sides of the one coin. 'It is of decisive moment in this thesis that the apparent opposition between Theism and Atheism is a relative one. Both, in the same way, bypass the concrete distinction between God and man and so God's real deity and man's true humanity. Theism by-passes God's deity by defining God as an absolute and independent Being but in so doing it bypasses the being of man who appears as absolutely dependent on this absolute independence. Atheism, on the other hand, bypasses man's true humanity by making *man* the being who is meant in the theistic idea of God. In this way it bypasses the true deity of God who in Jesus Christ has not revealed himself as an absolute and independent Being who posits and wills himself. Whoever thinks of God as such a Being does not think of God at all but in an all too human, i.e., in a devilish way. The apparent deifying of man has as its counterpart the making of God into a devil—and vice versa. One has to formulate it paradoxically thus. To think of God in a divine way means, for Barth, that God in his deity is human. If, on the other hand, God's deity is thought of *without man* (*Menschenlos*) then the idea of this God who is only divine is not God at all but the ideal of man estranged from himself so that man in his humanity is regarded as divine.'[52]

The only answer to these false gods, the denial of these idols, is knowledge of the true God in the humanity of Jesus Christ—the humanity of God.

Notes to Chapter 8 will be found on pp. 179–181.

CHAPTER NINE

Jesus Christ, The True Witness

Jesus Christ is *true God* in self-humiliation, the Lord as servant, and at the same time *true man* exalted to fellowship with God, the servant as Lord. As such he is our reconciliation with God. These two movements of God in Jesus Christ correspond to and embrace the kingly and priestly offices and exhaust the *material* content of reconciliation. There is, however, a third or formal aspect as well.[1] To the kingly and priestly offices there must of necessity be added the prophetic. In this Jesus Christ is not only reconciliation but at the same time revelation, exercising a prophetic office and ministry. In this aspect reconciliation 'expresses, discloses, mediates and reveals itself . . . as *the* truth'.[2] Jesus Christ is not only life, the life of his reconciling act, but at the same time *light* shining in the darkness; not only reality but also *truth*. 'It is also a movement outwards. . . . It proclaims itself as *the* truth and irrespective of its reception.'[3] Barth puts it in these terms, 'reconciliation is not a dark or dumb event, but a perspicuous and vocal. It is not closed in upon itself but moves out and communicates itself.'[4] Nor must we regard this as 'another *alongside* him; in it we are dealing with Jesus Christ *himself*'.[5] It is quite simply 'the self-attestation of Jesus'.[6] He is the true witness— the One who testifies to the truth that he is. As such he is the one Word of God, declaring, making known his reconciling being and action, as the Truth and Light of his life. As that Truth it is the basis of and takes precedence over all human knowledge of itself and is not to be identified with it. It is first real and true in itself and so objective before it is known as such.

There are several points of prime importance that emerge already in this preliminary survey.

(*a*) In this third aspect of reconciliation which is itself revelation, word and truth Barth is returning to a central theme of the *Church Dogmatics* yet, at the same time, setting it in a new context and drawing out of it new insights. He returns to the main content of the Prolegomena,[7] the doctrine of the Word of God.[8] In the Prolegomena, revelation or the Word of God is the exclusive act of God making himself known in Jesus Christ, declaring himself as Father, Son and Holy Spirit. Yet this action is not simply a *declaratory* but an *effective* act, at the same time accomplishing reconciliation.[9] Here in contrast reconciliation is seen as the total action of God in Christ, the complete and fulfilled salvation of God, whereas revelation is that same act in its outward reach, making known, proclaiming and communicating itself to men as a witness which is the Truth or Word of God. In one sense, therefore, it is the old questions that reappear and to some extent also the former answers; but in another it is—set in a different context—a new, illuminating discussion of revelation carrying it on into further understanding and fresh disclosures.

(*b*) Since Jesus Christ is the Truth, the one true Witness, the one Word of God, all other supposed sources of the knowledge of God are automatically impossible, unnecessary and so excluded. It is of deliberate and set purpose that Barth states at the beginning and as the theme of this whole section the Barmen declaration, 'Jesus Christ . . . is the one Word of God'.[10] This means again the exclusion of all natural theology.

(*c*) The fact that the reconciling life of Jesus Christ, true God and true man, is the sole truth of God which precedes and is the basis both of all other truths and of our knowledge of itself and them shows the continuing influence of Anselm on Barth. 'Here we clearly meet for the first time in a new form what sounded in our ears years ago in Barth's exposition of Anselm.'[11] Corresponding to the *Credo ut intelligam* of Anselm, Barth states that it is Jesus Christ himself in his self-giving who imparts the knowledge of himself and there is in this *a priori* a denial of any secondary source save that which he employs and uses as a further witness. Weber writes: 'Already on the first pages and then along the whole course that Barth takes one sees how decisively at this point where Jesus of Nazareth is spoken of as the "True Witness" Barth's understanding of the thought of Anselm of Canterbury as a "Proof" of the being of God is at work . . . Barth himself confirms this on page 85, after he had, for a long time, given grounds for such an expectation.'[12]

Indeed, one must say that *the* theme of this volume of the *Church Dogmatics* is Jesus Christ as his own Witness—a theme which runs throughout the whole of the *Church Dogmatics*. He declares himself in his Word, in the resurrection, in Holy Scripture, in preaching, in the Church, etc. And he alone is the source and possibility as well as the power of all declaration and knowledge of himself.[13]

Hence, Barth in his exposition does not concern himself primarily with the phenomena and fruits of the outward movement of Jesus Christ but characteristically with the root itself, its christological basis in his prophetic office.

I. JESUS CHRIST, THE LIGHT OF LIFE

The thesis which Barth proceeds to expound he expresses thus: 'That the life of Jesus Christ is as such light and his reconciling work a prophetic Word.'[14] Put otherwise this means 'that as he lives, Jesus Christ speaks for himself, that he is his own authentic witness'.[15] If we ask what the essentially simple sentence 'Jesus Christ lives' means, we receive as reply—all that he is and does. It is the life of Jesus Christ in his being and action in reconciliation. It is as risen that he lives and is the content, source and origin of faith. His life is the presupposition, basis and possibility of our life in him and our knowledge of him. It is in brief all that Barth has previously expounded of the being and action of Jesus Christ as the Lord become servant and the servant exalted to lordship in reconciliation.[16] It is so and only so that Jesus Christ lives.

This life is, therefore, not one which is self-enclosed or dumb with no relevance or meaning for us. Nor, on the other hand, does it find its expression and fulfilment in us. Nor does it receive its light and truth from elsewhere. It is of itself eloquent, giving light and so reaching out to and embracing us and all men. It is light in and of itself but not only in and for itself. It has in itself objective truth and validity, speaks to and shines in the world of darkness and is, at the same time, directed to us (*pro nobis*), for us men and for our salvation. This is the Glory of the Mediator. 'To the extent that the life of Jesus Christ as such is also light, name, revelation, truth, Logos; to the extent that glory belongs to it as such, to this extent it is his life, existence, act, work and deed, in his third and prophetic office.'[17] Put succinctly, this means that reconciliation is revelation and that each is identical with Jesus Christ. It is he who reconciles and reveals and in so doing is his own true witness.[18]

If there is a sense in which Jesus Christ is inclusively the light and word of life there is also one in which this applies to him exclusively in a way which is and can be true of no other.[19] It is here that we again see clearly the christological concentration of Barth. He discusses this in full consciousness of the fact that it can be and will be misunderstood and criticised[20] but in the full assurance that nothing else and nothing more can and must be said. For Jesus Christ is not simply one among many lights and truths, not even the best, but 'the one and only light of life'.[21] Barth expresses his position clearly in this way: 'Positively, this means that he is the light of life in all its fulness, in perfect adequacy; and negatively, it means that there is no other light of life outside or alongside his, outside or alongside the light which he is.'[22] The positive side of this Barth develops in three statements—Jesus Christ as the one and only light, as the light in its fulness and completion and as its own guarantee in his own self-testimony. The negative is the exclusion of all natural theology and the assertion that all other truths can be such only in the light of the prophecy of Jesus Christ and all other lights—those of creation—luminous only in relation to the self-revelation of his reconciliation. It is these themes which will occupy us successively in this order: (a) Jesus Christ the one and only light of life, (b) the Truth of Jesus Christ and other truths, (c) the lights of creation and the light of life, (d) the Word of God and natural theology.

2. JESUS CHRIST, THE ONE AND ONLY LIGHT OF LIFE

The claim we make for the prophecy of Jesus Christ is made for no other. It is inadmissible if applied to the person who makes this confession or to the Church or to the 'absoluteness' of Christianity.[23] It must be seen in proper perspective for 'it is a christological statement'.[24] It can be summed up thus: 'It is in the uniqueness of his works and gifts, of his being for us and to us, that the uniqueness of Jesus Christ as Lord, and therefore the uniqueness of his authority and Word, is manifested. And all this rests upon, and is guaranteed by, the fact that he is the one Lord, with unique and exclusive authority, and that he reveals himself as such. He alone who is and has life, can and does forgive, has also the "words of eternal life" (John 6:68).'[25]

Barth makes two specific statements here which are the basis for all his exclusive and unique claims for the prophecy of Jesus Christ. First, Jesus Christ is the one and only Lord as God is the one and only God. As Lord he is God, acts with his authority and power and makes his claims upon men. So Barth maintains that 'the uniqueness of the prophet Jesus Christ has its basis in that of God, and therefore, in itself'.[26] In other words, it is in the uniqueness of his divine nature that the uniqueness of his prophecy and truth lie. Since he is the final Word of God he cannot point to another to guarantee his truth but is his own guarantor, for 'what is proclaimed by God can be proved only by reference to God himself'.[27] Jesus Christ 'shares the uniqueness of God', 'is the only word which, because it is spoken directly by God himself, is good as God is, has the authority and power of God and is to be heard as God himself'.[28] Barth here combines his well-known circular argument with the deity of Christ and links these to the prophetic office of Jesus Christ.[29] This brings us to the second part of the basis, namely, that Christ's life-act is directed towards man in illuminating and transforming power. It is as such, with a claim that is total and absolute, that Jesus Christ comes to us, excluding all others, because in him we know total rescue and renewal and have no need of any other. Hence, it is his being and work for us that manifest the uniqueness of his Word and its prophetic authority. 'It is this because his life is the one and only life.'[30] No other can reconcile; he is the only Saviour whom we must trust and obey in life and in death.[31]

Not only is Jesus Christ the one and only light of life but as such he is the complete, total declaration of God about himself and man. The whole truth is enclosed in him and beside him there can be and are no other truths.[32] So Barth can sum up: 'Jesus Christ is the one and only Word of God . . . he alone is the light of God and the revelation of God.'[33]

3. JESUS CHRIST, THE TRUTH OF GOD AND OTHER TRUTHS

There are, however, according to Barth, true words spoken outside the realm of the Bible and the Church. Barth writes 'such good words may also be spoken *extra muros ecclesiae* either through those who have not yet received any effective witness to Jesus Christ, and cannot therefore be reckoned with the believers who for their part attest him, or through more or less admitted Christians who are not, however, engaged in direct confession, or direct activity as members of the Christian community, but in the discharge of a function in world society and its orders and tasks'.[34] The question now is, if this is so, how are they related to the one and only true Word in Jesus Christ attested in Holy Scripture? To the question of the relation which Jesus Christ has as Truth to these other truths, Barth has given profound thought and far-reaching answers which do not necessitate a return to any natural theology. They show that he has not neglected the question of so-called 'revelations' in the world and the nature of creation itself. 'What profound relevance it has Barth shows in an exposition which is one of the most important parts of the new half-volume. If, with his renewed emphasis on the uniqueness of the Word of God in Jesus Christ, he has again declared war on all "natural" theology, and in looking to the "light of life" has in all this turned with the same emphasis as of old against man's claim in and of himself to have an equal right to be heard, nonetheless he shows in the following that these kinds of reflections *in no way* mean a setting aside of those truths which are open to man but rather their setting up by the one Word itself.'[35] In other words, in the following significant exposition Barth answers those who claim some revelatory meaning for other truths or lights in the world on their own apart from Jesus Christ, while at the same time he shows their positive role and place as used by the Word itself. For him, while they certainly do exist, they cannot be said to rival the Truth of the one prophecy of Jesus Christ, i.e., they have no independent meaning of their own. What then is the significance of these truths in relation to the one Truth?

(a) Their Basis and Raison d'être

That there are such true words has its basis and possibility in the fact that God has reconciled the *world* to himself in Jesus Christ. His resurrection, attested in Holy Scripture, is the revelation of this cosmic deed. He has won the battle against evil and is now the victorious Lord over all. The whole world is under the dominion of the Word. We live in a reconciled universe and as a result it is co-ordinated with him, used for his purpose. This truth is of course declared to us and known by us in the biblical testimony proclaimed in and through the Church. But it does mean that '*de iure* all men and all creation derive from his cross, from the reconciliation accomplished in him, and are . . . therefore recipients and bearers of his Word. In the very light of this narrower and smaller sphere of the Bible and the Church, we cannot possibly think that he cannot speak, and his speech cannot be attested, outside this sphere.'[36] Hence, while we derive the knowledge of this possibility of true words in the world from the biblical testimony we have to 'eavesdrop in the world at large'[37] and hear the Word of Jesus Christ.

The basis and possibility of true words in the world is thus the universal sovereignty of Jesus Christ made known in the biblical testimony. Nothing can reverse or alter this great and powerful truth. The fact that in this world there is a secularism approximating to godlessness constitutes no limit to the sovereignty of this prophecy. No secularism can undo what he has accomplished in his victorious reconciliation so that we may hear 'even from the mouth of Balaam the well-known voice of the Good Shepherd . . . and it is not to be ignored in spite of its sinister origin'.[38] In the same way in 'the mixed and relative secularism' where the Gospel is in some measure known and accepted the Word of Jesus Christ is stronger than it and we may expect 'God to raise up witnesses from this world of tarnished untruth'.[39] There are and must be, therefore, true words because we live in God's world which he has reconciled to himself in his Son, in which Jesus Christ is Lord of all; he rules also *extra muros ecclesiae*.[40]

(b) Their Relation to the one Truth

If there is only one Word or Truth of God, viz, Jesus Christ, how can other true words exist and how are they related to the one Truth? It should first be made clear that these other words have no ultimate power, significance and meaning in and of themselves; 'they declare nothing of their own'.[41] Basically their relationship to the one Word of God is that he, Jesus Christ, takes and uses them and by his power makes them true words so that they bear witness to him. Or, as Barth can put it even more strongly, by his taking and using them Jesus Christ bears witness to himself through them. 'What is not doubtful and contestable is the prophecy of the Lord Jesus Christ and its almighty power to bring forth such true words even *extra muros ecclesiae* and to attest itself through them.'[42] The question, however, arises, by what criterion do we know them to be true? Barth answers that they must have three distinguishing characteristics. (*i*) 'Such words must be in the closest material and substantial conformity and agreement with the one Word of God himself . . . say the same thing . . . and are true for this reason.' (*ii*) 'Attest this one Word exactly as it is, without subtraction, addition or alteration.' (*iii*) They must be 'commissioned, moved and empowered to attest it' and to reflect and reproduce it.[43] These true words become 'parables of the kingdom of heaven'[44] through the power of the one true Word.

The one Word or Truth rests and speaks in them; while, therefore, they express it from a particular angle and standpoint, nevertheless they draw upon its fulness. But, since they have no power or capacity of themselves, that they are such truths and are known and perceived as such is in each case a miracle. These words of God, together with those of the Scripture and the Church, are all miraculous and we have 'in both cases . . . the capacity of Jesus Christ to raise up of the stones children to Abraham, i.e., to take into his service, to empower for this service, to cause to speak in it, men who are quite without any capacity of their own'.[45] This capacity which goes beyond the sphere of Bible and Church can in some cases be used even against people's own knowledge and volition. So these are not rival words to the one Word; rather 'they are true words only as they refer back to their origin in the one Word, i.e., as the one true Word, Jesus Christ himself, declares himself in them'.[46] In all this it is no new or different word that comes to us but the one and only true Word, Jesus Christ, whose self-testimony we hear in these different forms. Barth sums up as follows 'They are true words in their presupposed and implied, if not always immediately apparent, connexion with the totality of Jesus Christ and his prophecy, and therefore as they indirectly point to this, or as this indirectly declares itself in them.'[47]

(*c*) *Relation to Bible and Preaching*

A further problem arises because Barth repeats here his well-known three-fold distinction of the Word of God as spoken, written and preached.[48] Jesus Christ is the one and only true Word of God who is attested in Scripture and preaching. Does this mean then, as Weber pertinently asks,[49] that in true words outside the Bible and Church we have a fourth 'form' of the Word of God? Or, can the Scripture and the testimony of the Church be real forms of the Word if other true words are addressed to the Church and there is only one Word of God?[50]

Barth's answer is clear. There is only one Word of God and definitive testimony is given to it by the apostles and prophets in the Old and New

Testaments. Since, therefore, Jesus Christ declares himself through this testimony in a way that has binding authority for his community, preaching is bound to this and must, by the Holy Spirit, express it. One can therefore speak either of three forms of the one Word or of the one Word attested in Bible and Church. The Bible and Church stand together, the latter building on the former, and both coinciding and agreeing in an intimate way with the Word spoken in Jesus Christ. The former is, however, the definitive witness by which the Church exists. This can be called by Barth the *'normal and regular'* way in which God speaks, 'his self-disclosure by his constant address, in the power of the Holy Spirit, through the witness of his prophets and apostles and therefore by means of the biblical word'.[51] Any 'secular parable' or true words spoken outside this sphere must be 'grounded in and ruled by the biblical, prophetico-apostolic witness to this one Word'.[52] They have not an immediate or direct relation to the one Word and so cannot be called a fourth form of the Word, nor can their existence in any way exclude the Scriptures and preaching as the more direct forms of the Word. These other words which have no such immediate connexion with the Word are called by Barth *'extraordinary acts of his rule*, his free communications in the parables of the kingdom which come to it (the Church) through the general history of the world around it'.[53]

So just as their truth is not self-evident but is only true in relation to the one Word and as this comes to us in Holy Scripture through the Church, therefore it is in their agreement with the biblical testimony that these words confirm themselves as true. This is the chief criterion by which they are to be tested and judged.[54] A secondary standard of judgment is their conformity with the teaching and dogma of the Church and a third, the evidence of the good fruits they bear.[55] They cannot replace the word of the Bible but must be in 'agreement with the witness of Scripture', not in the sense of repeating single texts but as they conform with its whole content. They must be 'a good and authentic commentary sounding out the word of the Bible'.[56] One can express it thus: 'Their work will consist in leading the community at all times and places, and in all its members, more deeply into the given word of the Bible as the authentic attestation of the Word of Jesus Christ himself.'[57] In indissoluble unity with this testimony they will lead to the stimulation, encouragement and comfort of the community as well as its challenge, rebuke and call to repentance.[58] As such they will prove themselves to be genuine words. They may even lead to the discovery of what is new, to the extension of the creed but always in conformity with its source and norm.

But if, to be true words, they must affirm the biblical testimony, they also differ from it in that, unlike it, they have no 'constant and universal authority'.[59] They are no 'more than the voice of certain individual events and elements in world history'.[60] They have two characteristics, (*a*) they belong to a particular time and situation and are heard then, and, (*b*) their reception is not a matter of the whole community but only of some and perhaps sometimes even of none.[61] They cannot be given canonical or dogmatic status nor made a binding law on all. Barth does not adduce a single *specific* example.[62] The reason for this is that the christological perspective that concerns us here is not these true words in isolation but, rather, the prophecy of Jesus Christ as it evokes such true words and attests itself through them.

4. THE LIGHT OF LIFE AND THE LIGHTS OF CREATION[63]

The prophetic Word of Jesus Christ is spoken in a particular 'sphere or location',[64] viz, the world created by God which as such has its own 'lights'. Barth now proceeds to examine these further 'lights' in relation to the one light of life in Jesus Christ.

(*a*) Reconciliation and Creation

What we are dealing with here is 'in the words of Calvin . . . the *theatrum gloriae Dei,* the external basis of the covenant which conversely is its internal basis' (*C.D.,* III/1, section 41).[65] The sphere which is creation 'is the *good* work of the Creator. God sustains his creation as a good work and preserves it . . . because he is determined that in this sphere and location reconciliation shall take place.'[66] The purpose of creation is reconciliation; there to be the arena in which the prophetic Word of Jesus Christ comes to man. 'However, the doctrine of reconciliation has now to consider not only what meaning this relationship has for reconciliation but also for *creation.*'[67]

(*b*) The Lights of Creation

Creation, because it is the work of the faithfulness of the Creator, has its own features of persistency and constancy. Barth expresses it in this way: 'To the faithfulness of the Creator . . . there corresponds the persistence and constancy of the creature . . . so that he is always the Guarantor, Sustainer and Protector of his creaturely world.'[68] It is due to this faithfulness that 'the creaturely world . . . has also as such its own lights and truths and therefore its own speech and words'.[69] Thus 'this constancy has not its basis in itself. And this fact . . . it expresses in *its own* way. This speech is its self-witness.'[70] So Barth can say 'like its persistence, its self-witness and lights are not extinguished by the corruption of the relationship between God and man through the sin of man, his pride and sloth and falsehood'.[71] Nor is it interrupted by the fact of reconciliation. Nevertheless this self-witness rests on the revelation of God in Jesus Christ, 'which first uncovers and distinguishes it as the word of the *created* world, which as such is not reduced to silence'.[72] In this connexion Barth can even speak of 'revelation' and use such phrases as the 'revelation of creation' and 'primal revelation'.[73]

Thus 'the world created by God does not merely exist but also speaks to . . . man giving itself to be perceived by him'.[74] The created order is known as object by man the subject, exists not only *in re* but also *in intellectu* and so in this interaction shows its nature as cosmos. Formally this is seen in its constant and persistent features which have their relative reliability.[75] It is as it gives itself to be known and is perceived and known that the created order exists, 'hears itself speak', and so has 'created lights', 'words', 'truths'.[76] In this dialogue and reciprocity of 'the order, structure and constancy of the world created by God there is visible the *truth* of creation', and it is 'this *worldly*, not divine, truth'[77] that preserves the creation from 'the onrush of chaos'.[78] While these 'words' are not 'divine disclosures nor eternal truths'[79] yet they do 'bring illumination' and mean that the cosmos, despite the darkness of man's sin, has itself 'a measure of brightness'.[80]

(c) The One True Light and the created Lights

It is clear that in and of themselves these creaturely lights cannot attest their own truth, much less the one truth of God. 'The existence of the cosmos as the existence for one another of the intelligible and the intelligent has in itself nothing whatever to do with that of the existence of God as the Founder and Lord of his covenant with man.'[81] By this Barth does not mean that the Lord of the covenant is unrelated to the created lights but rather that they have no ultimate meaning in and of themselves; in the dialogue of the world with itself, which is its truth, 'it is not a covenant of God with man which is declared and perceived.'[82] These lights do not declare the one truth of God but rather their own *creaturely* truth. But they can only do so as the one Light shines in them and uses them in its service. The Light of Truth is the one which in its unity, totality and absolute finality both relativizes these lights and at the same time institutes and integrates them into its service.[83] It shows both their problematical nature in and of themselves and also at the same time frees and enables them to be taken up into the service of the light of life. Hence, while they now shine with their true light, they always remain 'self-attestations of creation'[84] and do not become, as in the case of other truths, self-declarations of Jesus Christ. While they have 'great practical value, force and significance'[85] in their reliability and relative validity they can be taken up and used to 'reflect the eternal light of God . . . answer his Word and . . . correspond to his truth'.[86]

Thus they are not the light of God *per se* nor in their 'revelation'. They remain creaturely servants showing by God's grace their own *created* lights. As a result 'creation can never declare itself as God does

. . . it does not know itself as God knows himself and it, but only in the limits within which it may know itself in its continuing dialogue with itself'.[87] Thus for Barth the world and its created order have a positive function to perform as the means God uses to serve the purposes of reconciliation, the sphere of his prophetic Word. As such its lights have a persistence, constancy and truth which acquire power from God to declare his glory. Despite the fact that the world is a fallen one, nevertheless 'outside the Church it is not simply darkness'.[88] What Jüngel says of Barth's interpretation of the secular order can be applied with equal truth to the light of creation in relation to the one Light. It 'speaks *of* God because God speaks *to* it and thus *enables* it to speak of itself'.[89] God uses these 'words' and 'lights' as signs and witnesses that he is the God of man, for man, faithful, trustworthy and good, since he has made all things good. He gives to these created lights the power to witness to their own light.

It is clear from the above that this exposition is entirely consistent with Barth's basic position on the relation between reconciliation, creation and man, and is but a development and drawing out of both his positive and negative conclusions in this regard. The created world and man have their place, significance and meaning in relation to and for the purpose of God's Yes of reconciliation to man. Of themselves they are not witnesses to their own truth but only become such in the light and by the power of the word, truth and light of Jesus Christ.

5. 'TRUTHS', 'LIGHTS' AND NATURAL THEOLOGY[90]

The question can no longer go unanswered; if the prophecy of Jesus Christ as the one Truth of God witnesses to itself in other 'truths' and illumines the sphere of creation to declare the glory of God, how does this relate to so-called natural theology which Barth rejects? Are these truths of the world and the lights of creation not a way of surreptitiously coming to terms with the old enemy?[91] Here we can only sketch Barth's basic attitude to revelation and natural theology and then go on to show how he views his present exposition in relation to these problems. The answer will be that he does distinguish sharply between the 'truths' and 'lights' here mentioned and natural theology.

(a) The Word of God and Natural Theology

Barth's position here has been greatly misunderstood and misrepresented. For example, his is considered primarily as a negative approach denying that man by the light of reason, nature and history can attain to God,[92] whereas what he is basically concerned to do is to affirm the truth of God in Jesus Christ. It is only in this light that the negative can be seen, properly expressed and rejected. To give it any independent treatment is to accord it an inherent importance it does not possess. W. Kreck, speaking of Barth's strict christological concentration, and the reasons for his exclusion of natural theology, writes: 'For the theological theory of knowledge this christocentric emphasis means the radical rejection of all natural theology, especially a general anthropology as the basis of theology. It is becoming increasingly clear that it was not disappointment with man or a pessimistic view of culture that was the main driving force behind this theology of crisis. Nor was Barth's concern, like Lavater, (according to Goethe), to pluck the bright feathers of all the birds of the world and put them on the one bird of paradise. It was quite the contrary. It is because we see clearly here (in Jesus Christ) who God is and who man is that such a light is shed upon man that he has no need of the muddied source of the natural knowledge of God.'[93] Barth, therefore, disputes that his task is to deny natural theology since it is a false task based on a wrong assumption, viz, that it is a true task of theology. Rather is it 'the answer to a question which is false if it wishes to be "decisive". . . . Hence it has to be rejected *a limine*.'[94] It is simply a temptation to be overcome, a serpent to be hit and killed and not to be stared at until one is hypnotised by it.[95]

The task of theology is not to affirm a way of man to God apart from Jesus Christ, but to confess and interpret the one and only way of God to man, the way he has taken in Jesus Christ. This way and word is that of reconciliation and revelation. As we have already seen, Barth interprets the clear meaning of this Word.[96] (*a*) 'Jesus Christ is the one and only Word of God . . . he alone is the light of God and the revelation of God.'[97] (*b*) Moreover, 'he is the total and complete declaration of God concerning himself and the men whom he addresses in his Word'.[98] (*c*) Finally, he 'shows himself to be the one Prophet of God'[99] in whom alone is our trust.[100] If these then are true statements of the meaning of the biblical testimony to God and his revelation in Jesus Christ, then the whole, unique, saving, self-authenticating Word of God to man is contained here and no other Word is possible or necessary. To follow after any other supposed word that claims to speak of God will be going after a false god. The one, true God has spoken of himself and only he can do so—that is enough. 'Only God can be called to witness for God . . . therefore the word of man cannot witness to the Word of God.'[101] Hence, so-called natural theology, which is no theology at all, can only be considered in order immediately to be rejected. This is not, as H. Zahrnt states,[102] to by-pass and dismiss the problem but to deal with it in the only way consonant with one's understanding and knowledge of God and man in Jesus Christ. This can be stated otherwise by Barth when he says that because of the inclusive nature of incarnation and reconciliation, i.e., because each of us is included and involved in God's action for us in Jesus Christ, 'there is nothing to justify his (man's) setting himself up over against them as the propounder of a theme *of his own*'.[103]

(b) The Word, the words and Natural Theology

Our conclusion clearly is that here in this exposition of the *Church Dogmatics* Barth has both given an answer to his critics[104] and at the same time dealt squarely with the problems involved in the relation between God, man and the world.[105] Furthermore, it is an answer which is again a firm denial that there is any place or necessity for, or any reality in, a '*theologia naturalis*'.

How then do these words differ from natural theology? Barth gives two answers. The first difference between true words in the secular sphere and so-called natural knowledge of God is that the former are taken up into the self-witness and service of the prophet Jesus Christ. But 'by way of natural theology, apart from the Bible and the Church, there can be attained only abstract impartations concerning God's existence as the Supreme Being and Ruler of all things'.[106] Such a Supreme Being cannot, however, in any way be identified with the one, only, living and true God. For Barth the truths known *extra muros ecclesiae* are, on the contrary, 'attestations of the self-impartation of the God who acts as Father in the Son by the Holy Ghost'.[107] He expresses 'no interest in what it (natural theology) *thinks* it can advance as true words concerning God and man *in general*'.[108] Thus one cannot seek 'to attribute to the human creature as such a capacity to know God and the one Word of God, or to produce true words corresponding to this knowledge'.[109] A Supreme Being reached by natural knowledge cannot speak for itself or attest itself in true words which correspond to it. Nor would it in any way conform to the biblical witness to revelation.

In the second place, that such true words can be and are spoken is due to the true God alone and is always miraculous whether in the Bible, the Church or the world outside. Natural theology speaks of man's natural ability; true theology speaks of a Word which in its work to and for man and the world, is always beyond man's capacity and so a miracle. True knowledge of God rests always on this miracle of grace and as such excludes and exposes 'natural' knowledge as that of a false god. Speaking of Calvin's views in this respect, Barth writes: 'The possibility which, according to Calvin, man in fact has, is to know and worship the gods of his own heart.'[110] So, according to Barth, between the two there is a great gulf fixed—the one leading to the true knowledge of God in Jesus Christ, the other leading to the worship of idols. The former sets the truths in their proper context in relation to the divine Word; the latter, by tearing them out of it, makes them untrue, false and a dangerous aberration.

Equally, the 'lights' of creation shine only as such in the light and by the power of the one true Light of Jesus Christ. To attribute to them as such power to witness to their own creaturely truth is to dehumanize them, when what they are crying out for is to be humanized.[111] Barth speaks in a variety of ways of the relative character of such lights when shown up by the one Word of God. Of themselves they are but 'forms', 'conditions' and 'presuppositions'[112] without binding authority. They are pointers—'into the void and the unknown'.[113] Again, he can put it in this way: 'If we do not know the whole truth, the light of life, we cannot concede that we have discovered it in one of these lights, or that we can expect the day to come when it will be seen as the one great light in all of them. We can only resist such a view.'[114] In other words, they do not testify to their creaturely truth nor to the truth of Jesus Christ. Of themselves they give no knowledge of God. They provide only 'hypotheses', 'provisional assumptions'[115] but no definitive truth with final reality. Yet they can be taken up and used to shine in their reality as true lights and so attest the divine light. In vivid and pictorial language Barth can say that the 'polyphony of creation as the external basis of the covenant' can 'when he (God) speaks his one and total Word concerning the covenant which is the internal basis of creation' evoke a symphony to which creation in turn 'in all the diversity of its voices can and will give its unanimous applause'.[116] Or again he writes 'The positive thing which takes place in the confrontation of the little lights of creation with the great light of its Creator is that they are not passed over or ignored, let alone destroyed or extinguished, but integrated in the great light.'[117] This can take place when they are known by man and used by the one Truth to declare their own creaturely truth. It is only by understanding them in this way that their real nature is seen.

Roman Catholic theologians in particular query Barth at this point. E. H. Friedmann[118] takes up the question raised by Hans Küng[119] as to whether in Barth's conception creation is dumb and cannot as God's creature testify directly to him. The answer seems to me to be quite clear; in itself it is not wholly dumb nor dark but nonetheless it cannot declare its own truth. Its 'lights' are like 'cat's eyes' which exist and have a 'light' but only shine when lit up by the light from elsewhere (a motor-car, etc.). The heavens do declare the glory of God but only in the light and by the power of reconciliation. The lights are, as it were, ready to be lit up but cannot shine in their own strength. As the one light 'shines in the cosmos, it *kindles* the lights with which the latter is furnished, *giving them the power* to shine in its own service. The latter cannot do more than become bright in this light. They cannot replace the one light and truth of the divine self-declaration.'[120] In other words they are like illuminations which have to be switched on before they can be what they are meant to be. They cannot turn themselves on nor can their light, though not without significance, be properly understood save by those who have the key to its meaning.

Friedmann asks the question how it comes about that the light shines and is known to shine. Has it a reality as such when given this light by God or does it receive it in an actualistic way ever and again? In other words, does this light once given have a permanent feature known by all, or is it something which is given and received repeatedly? He answers correctly 'an actualistic understanding of the knowledge of creation as a pure knowledge of faith in the sense that it only came into existence each time in the personally completed act of faith seems to us not to be the meaning'.[121] Or, again, 'man could read into the text of creation what could not be read out of it. But this again is not Barth's meaning'.[122] Friedmann concludes and summarizes what he believes Barth to mean as follows: 'The witnesses of creation to itself are known in the one concrete order quite apart from any express faith. It is true that faith in the one Word of God shows their dangerous ambiguity and lends them truth in this way. Though they are unclear and misunderstood they point to God as their Creator and, as signs of his glory, can be somehow known by everyone.'[123]

However, this summary, though capable of a correct interpretation, could easily be misunderstood and is only partially true. Barth seems to me to be saying three things:

(*a*) That the order of creation and the reciprocity of the known cosmos and the knowing subject man shows a constancy and a persistence which can be seen and known by all. Thus far Friedmann is right.

(*b*) The 'truth' of this can only be known by faith in the one Word of God in Jesus Christ. This 'truth' is that it is God's good creation and shines with his light. Again Friedmann has seen this clearly.

(*c*) This 'truth' of creation, its 'word', or 'light', i.e., that it is God's creation and reflects his light as Creator is, however, not known by all. This seems to be unclear in Friedmann's exposition; he tends to regard these 'lights' and 'truths' as direct rather than indirect testimony to God the faithful Creator.[124]

In looking at natural theology and creation Weber sums up thus: 'If one looks carefully one will see that Barth has exactly reversed "natural" theology. He does not devalue "nature". He gives to it in all its provisional character the word, its creaturely word. Because that happens, "Nature" is given its place as a real "creature", as God's good creation, and has the distinction of giving God the glory.'[125] There can be no clearer statement of Barth's position than this and no better testimony to the real service he has performed and to the positive achievement of his theological undertaking in response and relation to the one

Word of God and the rejection of all false, misleading, merely human and creaturely words. He has shown that 'natural' theology is in fact quite unnatural and that the truths of man and creation are only real and meaningful when used by the one Truth of God in Jesus Christ.[126]

Notes to Chapter 9 will be found on pp. 181–191.

CHAPTER TEN

Jesus Christ in Eschatological Perspective

The Coming Lord (Parousia)

Eschatology[1] has traditionally been defined as 'the doctrine of the last things', and has dealt with what happens at the 'end' of all things—the second coming, last judgment, etc. As a result it usually occupied a final chapter in the scheme of theology and was regarded as having little or no relevance for any other part. Modern thinking on eschatology has decisively altered all this and has brought it to the centre of the stage while in no way denying its significance for the final end. Indeed it has rightly argued that it is only as it is seen and interpreted in this way that its true significance for the final end can be properly affirmed. To be sure there are many and varied emphases but there has been and is a striking unanimity in underlining the centrality and importance of the doctrine. Indeed, some modern writers have put it so much in the centre that its traditional place at the 'end' has for them virtually disappeared.[2]

Karl Barth has rendered a signal service to theology by giving us an impressive, balanced and convincing treatment of the subject in contrast to many one-sided modern versions. His must be considered an outstanding exposition which does more justice than most to the biblical testimony and explains the probable relationship of the data.

Barth begins by defining what eschatology means in the New Testament. It cannot be a concept which relates 'merely to the final stage of the *parousia*. Eschatological denotes the last time. The last time is the time of the world and human history and all men to which a term is already set in the death of Jesus and which can only run towards this appointed end'.[3] By this he means that with the coming of Jesus Christ and his reconciliation accomplished and fulfilled in his death the last time has come in its fulness and has thereby set an 'end' to all other time. 'This world time was concluded by Jesus Christ in his death by the dawn of *his* time, God's time as the time of man reconciled by him to God.'[4] It is true that the 'old' man (Rom. 6:6) in his time continues and so *un*seasonably; thus the actual end of our time and history is not yet.

Notes to Chapter 10 will be found on pp. 191–195.

This indicates that eschatology has a future dimension as well which is wholly dependent on and comes from the 'End' manifest in the death of Jesus Christ. Clearly this cannot mean that it is simply Christ's 'past somehow prolonged into and determining the present',[5] but it is Jesus Christ himself who, in the power of his reconciling life, is our Future, the Coming One. We can therefore say that the eschatological perspective is based on the Christological and means quite simply the Coming Again of Jesus Christ as the One who came.

The different aspects of this perspective can now be delineated.

I. PAROUSIA IN ITS UNITY AND TOTALITY

Barth uses the term *parousia* to signify the coming again[6] of Jesus Christ, making known and effectively manifesting himself in the power of his finished work. 'The New Testament knows of only one coming again of Jesus Christ, of only one new coming of the One who came before.'[7] Yet this one event has different forms 'corresponding to the willing and fulfilment of the action of its one Subject, the living Jesus Christ'.[8] Its first form is that of the Easter event, the resurrection, its second that of the coming of the Holy Spirit and its third that of Christ's final appearing. But 'in all these forms it is one event'.[9] Nothing else happens and no one else comes but he who came. Always and in different ways it is a matter of the coming again of Jesus Christ in his unity and totality.[10] The one coming does not supplement or fill out the other. Each is the one Lord Jesus Christ in the totality of his being and action, in all he was, said and did in his life and work. So it can be said that 'for us, therefore, the resurrection and the *parousia* are two separate events. But for him they are a single event'.[11]

Yet while the three forms describe the one event in its different relationships it is the Easter event that provides the 'primal and basic pattern'[12] of the others. 'Thus, there can be no question that in all its forms the one totality of coming again does really have the character, colours and accents of the Easter event . . . is only the first if also the original form of this totality.'[13] But since we must speak of 'the last time' in relation to our time Barth can also see the three forms as commencement, middle and completion. This in no way means that the Easter event was incomplete any more than was the reconciliation accomplished in Christ's life and death. 'Nothing which will be has not already taken place on Easter day', as 'the revelation of the kingdom of God.'[14] Thus 'from the standpoint of its substance, scope and content it (the Easter event) is identical with its occurrence in the forms which follow.'[15] Each form thus participates in and brings the 'End', is an eschatological event. 'The happening of the *parousia* is thus eschatological throughout its course.'[16]

Again, it can be put in this way: it is 'the last time which *dawned* with his appearance (i.e., resurrection) . . . and the conclusion of time . . . in a definitive and general revelation'.[17] But Jesus Christ is the Lord, present also in the intervening time, the time of his community. One can, therefore, say that 'Jesus in his *coming* (i.e., final appearing) is simply the risen Jesus resuming and completing his coming and thus vindicating that beginning and promise. . . . It vaults over the interim time as well. Jesus is the Lord in this time too . . . hence even his interim time is his time and therefore fulfilled time.'[18] Thus one must say two things clearly and decisively about each form of the *eschaton*. It participates in the unity and totality of the one event, is itself fulfilment, yet has also its own distinguishing characteristics in the different relationships which Christ himself has ordained. One can therefore with caution speak of promise and fulfilment but not in the sense of a promise which is not yet complete[19] as with the relation between the Old and New Testaments. Here each promise is itself fulfilment, each in its own way contains and expresses the whole.[20] This is the testimony of the Scriptures[21] which Barth sums up thus: 'If we find in the coming of the Resurrected, his coming in the Holy Spirit and his coming at the end of the age three forms of his one new coming for all their significant differences, there need be no artificiality in explaining that these passages refer to the first and immediate form in which his coming did really begin in that generation as the Easter event and in which the two remaining forms are plainly delineated and intimated.'[22] Barth points out that the relation between the first and final forms of the *parousia* is similar to that between the death and resurrection of Jesus Christ which have an interval between. This 'forms a puzzling interval between the two great acts of God'.[23] The time of the Church is such an interval between the Ages, the first and final Coming of Jesus Christ yet is only a puzzle from our point of view. It too must be viewed as the day, the real presence of the living Lord with his people.

2. CONFIRMATION BY SOME MODERN WRITERS

There are several theologians whose treatment of this subject offers a confirmation of the basic position Barth has taken up. A. M. Ramsey[24] quotes George Milligan[25] to show that *parousia* denotes both ' "second" coming' and immediate presence with the implication of imminence. Speaking of *doxa* and *parousia* Ramsey writes: 'In expressing a future event which has already been in a sense anticipated *doxa* resembles certain other words familiar in the apostolic writings. The word *parousia*, which we are wont to connect exclusively with the second coming of Christ, does not exclude the thought of an immediate presence. . . . Similarly, those words which speak of the manifestation

of Christ are used both of a future consummation and of the original
events of the Gospel. ... These are things which the Christians await
with the conviction that what the future will bring is but the consummation of a past event and a present possession. Nor is it otherwise
with the glory. As they worship Jesus the Lord who has been exalted
into it, and as they look for the day when it is made visible, they come
to realise that it has been disclosed to them and is already near to
them.'[26]

Similarly, W. A. Whitehouse writes of the 'coming' of the Lord: 'It
happens when the Son of man lives and dies as Israel's Messiah, rises
from the dead, appears to his elect, and withdraws his physical presence
from the historical scene, having accomplished, in a mystery the end
(*Eschaton*). It is to be expected again, in a form where the veil of
mystery is lifted, at the end (*Telos*) of history. And in the interval it
happens, by what may be called an eschatological repetition, and in
virtue of the work of the *Paraclete*, when his people gather at the Lord's
appointment to meet him.'[27]

Walter Kreck writes in similar vein: 'The New Testament speaks of
the coming of Jesus Christ not only in the light of his coming once
upon a time, and the promise of his "Second" Coming, but also in the
light of his coming in the present, his self-witness by the Holy Spirit.'[28]

Further,[29] Colm O'Grady, discussing Barth's interpretation of the
Gospels and particularly of material concerning the kingdom of God,
supports him when he gives a past, present and future reference to the
one coming of Jesus Christ. He writes: 'I believe that the solution
adopted by Barth is the best, namely, that the Synoptists, and Jesus
himself, view the coming of the kingdom as one event, but one which
takes place in different forms and moments. ... Thus the texts ... cited
refer to the transfiguration, resurrection, sending of the Holy Spirit and
to the final *parousia*, for it is imminent in an anticipatory way in these
other events and even imminent in a final consummatory way in a
certain sense.'[30]

3. PAROUSIA IN ITS DISTINCTIVE FORMS

(a) The Resurrection[31]

We have already indicated the main distinguishing features of the
resurrection coming which is revelation in its basic, original and determining form. Nothing further can be or needs to be added to this
event; it is final. Here we find actualized already what will be known of
Jesus Christ in the time of the community and at the end of the ages—
the revelation of God's one, whole, final, irrevocable act of reconciliation for man and as man. 'The Easter event as the revelation of the
being and action of Jesus Christ in his preceding life and death, is his

new coming as the One who had come before.'[32] It is *the parousia* and the New Testament 'notion of the resurrection is strictly identical with the full range of content of the concept of *parousia*'.[33] The Easter event is thus the norm and criterion by which the others are to be judged and which, at the same time, gives to them their true content as well. As such it is the revelation of the glory of God.

(*b*) *The Holy Spirit*

This can be called the 'middle form of his prophecy'[34] in which Jesus Christ is the active Lord of his community. There is no vacuum[35] between Easter and the final appearing as if Jesus Christ were absent and we had to manage on our own, or as if we could only look backwards and forwards to him. He is present as the *Eschatos* in the full power, promise and presence of the Holy Spirit. 'The Spirit is the particular mode of the coming again and therefore the presence and action of Jesus Christ in the place and time between his resurrection and his final appearing.'[36] Just as the Easter history can in one sense be called 'a particular and provisional form' of revelation 'so the presence of Jesus in the Spirit, for all its fulness, can only be a pledge or first instalment of . . . his return in glory'.[37] So he is his (Christ's) presence with his people as the earnest of their inheritance of eternal life, as their sure companion on the way as well as himself being the way.[38] But he is also the hope of all men and so is universally relevant and operative. Thus this presence is a particular form of his glory.[39] Despite the riddle of our existence as reconciled but not yet redeemed we have in this form 'a day of the living Jesus Christ',[40] the very presence and saving action of the living God himself in glorious power. So it is a real presence which at the same time points forward in expectation and hope to his coming again in glory.[41] It is the manifestation of his lordship, the kingdom of God which he brings and is.[42]

If we ask why the need for this middle form,[43] why does the end not really mean the end, why not immediate redemption and consummation? The answer lies not in any necessity there is for God to redeem nor in a temporal delay in the *parousia*, but in the nature of the *parousia* itself as God's revelation of his will to reconcile and redeem man. Were it the ultimate end it would mean destruction and condemnation and not salvation. But the goodness and patience of God give time for the salvation of men and therefore for the Church and its work.

(*c*) *Final Appearing*

This is the goal of the whole divine movement, being and action. It can be summed up in the one comprehensive term, redemption.[44] While this is again the appearing of the one Lord Jesus Christ, it can be referred to as the 'definitive and general revelation'[45] in its totality and universality. The whole sweep of Barth's thought can be summed up in this way. The reconciliation of the world with God is accomplished in the life and death of Jesus Christ as atonement, revealed in the power of the resurrection, and is, by the Holy Spirit, present with men through the Church leading to man's final redemption.[46]

Barth did not have time to give us a full treatment of eschatology in its form as redemption, but he did provide sufficient material to indicate which way it might have developed. Here we can only deal with it as far as the person of Christ is concerned and not as far as it concerns ourselves. Before however doing so we ask with Barth the question why the necessity for a 'Second' Coming?[47] He answers first in the negative by showing what it is not. It is not due to 'a state of things in the time after the end of the forty days . . . which points forward to and demands a consummation . . . from the imperfection of the form of the present of the Crucified in this our own time'.[48] That there is such a limitation cannot be denied.[49] The basis of the Second Coming does not, however, lie there nor in any desire this limitation might conceivably create for its removal. For Barth on the contrary its basis is in Jesus Christ himself; there is no necessity for it but 'the free grace of God'.[50] The New Testament witness therefore is this: 'It confesses the One who was and is as the One who comes, who will come at the end of this time and all times, at the last day.'[51] Put otherwise, it was no lack felt by the community nor in the present form of Jesus Christ's presence among them that inspired their hope; 'It was the fulness of Jesus Christ himself . . . which invited and indeed summoned them to this forward looking.'[52] So Barth can say: 'The eschatological perspective in which Christians see the Crucified and Resurrected . . . is not the Minus-sign of an anxious "Not-Yet" which has to be removed, but the Plus-sign of an "Already", in virtue of which the living Christ becomes greater to them and altogether great, in virtue of which they here and now recognise in him who is the first word the final word.'[53] That they look forward to a removal of the present, temporal barrier between them and Christ leads to no lessening of their being in him; rather 'it is augmented . . . it is immeasurably deepened and enriched in its extent'.[54] It is therefore not man or his faithfulness that effects this but 'the new and conclusive act of the Giver himself proclaimed to them . . . in virtue of his grace and the fact that he is alive for evermore'.[55] Thus, to sum up, since Jesus Christ is at all times the Coming Lord the New Testament community was 'necessarily aware that he comes to us and we must go forward to him'.[56] Or again, 'they looked for him because he himself in his present as the Crucified and Resurrected as he encountered them in this time showed himself to them as the One he once was, as the One who was with them and indeed in them, but also as the One who stood before them as eternally future'.[57]

What Barth therefore is arguing is that the basis of Christ's final coming is not in his church or in man but in the revelation of Jesus Christ himself. It has no basis in ecclesiology or anthropology but exclusively in Christology—again a clear example of the Christological concentration so evident throughout the whole of Barth's theology.

Barth can sum up all that is meant by this Appearing in these words: It will be 'his general and definitive *manifestation* as *Judge, Consummator* and *New Creator* as this is promised . . . in the *near* if indefinite future'.[58] It is these different ways of viewing redemption or the Final Appearing that we now consider.

(1) *'Second' Coming*

As the One who came, was revealed and comes he will come again. He is as such our future and our hope.[59] It will be the revelation of 'his direct and comprehensive visibility for all and to all those for whom as the Son of God he became man'.[60] The New Testament community hopes for Christ's return and then and on this basis for all that this brings. It hopes for his Appearing and glory, in the visible power of God's real presence and for 'the glorification of the creature which is latent and implicit in his glory'.[61] So when we speak of Christ as our future and hope we do not mean that we have no future but rather that our future is in and with him, who brings us to glory, the true end of salvation.

(2) *Judge*

Barth warns against misunderstanding this as primarily a day of fear or as similar to a human Assize.[62] On the contrary, it is to be understood, as the Heidelberg Catechism saw it, as a source of comfort. For it is the judgment and presence of the One who has borne and borne away our sin and guilt, God's burning wrath and the severity of his punishment. It is the judgment of a God of grace. Jesus Christ is 'the Judge judged in our place'[63] who atones, declares and makes us righteous. 'For Jesus Christ really comes from heaven . . . as the Judge who anticipated the judgment for us and through whose punishment we are righteous.'[64] In short, the Judge who will come is the Saviour and Lord, 'the crucified Christ who as the Risen One proclaims and exercises the absolute sovereignty of grace'.[65]

The judgment means a final decision, viz, 'that man is justified and saved by the Son of God and without him is condemned and lost'.[66] Each will be repaid according to his work, i.e., 'the *faith* or *unbelief*' as it 'is *actually* lived out'.[67] For Christians the judgment of Christ is thus a comfort and a hope. The place to Christ's left hand may possibly remain unoccupied since on the cross God has barricaded the door of Hell.

(3) *Christus Consummator*

Barth understands this in two ways. On the one hand the time of the Church and the world has a *limit* set to it but also awaits its *fulfilment*. 'The New Testament looks forward, not merely to a better future . . . which sets a *term* to the whole time process' but also to a future which 'in its perfection includes and surpasses absolutely all the contents of time. This future will be a wholly *new order*'.[68] In other words with the second coming there is not merely an end but a consummation, perfection and fulfilment. In the whole context of Barth's Dogmatics this means the manifestation of redemption, i.e., the perfection of his reconciliation. 'Then as we read in Revelation 11:15 "the kingdoms of this *world* are become the kingdoms of our Lord and of his Christ" immediately undialectically, incontrovertibly, irresistably . . . then he will be not only the Reconciler, then he will be the Redeemer, the Saviour of the world (Titus 2:13).'[69] So the Second Coming is the fulfilment of his reconciliation in a redeemed creation—not just the end of the world but its redemption.

(4) *The New Creation*

Another way of putting this is to say that the old has passed away and all things have become manifestly new. He will come again as the New Creator. It will be 'the end and new beginning of the cosmos',[70] the 'participation in the life of this new cosmic form',[71] 'the promise of a new heaven and a new earth'.[72] The implication of this is, as William Manson has pointed out, the renewal of the cosmos and not its destruction. 'New Heavens and a New Earth signify not the final destruction or displacement of the cosmos, but its *renovation* . . . by the power of God.'[73] This can be interpreted by Barth as follows: God in Jesus Christ has at one and the same time done away with the old man and created a new, altered completely the situation between God and man; this applies equally to the created cosmos. It shares in the new creation so that we look in the coming of Christ for a new heaven and a new earth wherein dwells righteousness.[74] It corresponds to and manifests in full and effective form the character granted it in the atoning work of Christ.

(5) *Lord and King*

In all this Jesus will come as Lord and King, the One to whom we owe everything and who gives us everything.[75] He comes as the King of the Kingdom, as the one who rules by right by virtue of his being and action for man in reconciliation and his session at God's right hand. What is revealed at the resurrection, proclaimed in the Church, and manifest in his final appearing, is the exalted Lordship, the universal rule and dominion of Jesus Christ. And this is a form of his glory, the revelation of the divine grace in its fulness and scope. He is Lord of the past and of the present, 'of the cosmos no less than the Lord of his community', but as such 'he must again appear . . . in a glory which is no longer particular and transitory, but universal and permanent, embracing the whole of creation both in heaven and earth'.[76] Klappert points out that the completed reconciliation in Jesus Christ reveals the lordship of the Crucified (exalted royal man) on the one hand, but also on the other a lordship which has a teleological character as 'creative, universal execution and confirmation of the atonement, which passes through the process of a history of conflict from the beginning to a goal as yet unfulfilled'.[77] The goal is the second coming in which the lordship of the Crucified will be seen in its full glory.

(6) *The Imminence of the Parousia*

The nature of the eschatological event in Jesus Christ in its unity and totality is the reason for the *imminent* hope of the *parousia*. As such it is revelation, complete and final, making known God's time, as the content, goal and limit of all our time. Hence Barth disagrees with those who advocate a 'consequent' or 'realised' eschatology, or who believe that the Christian community or even Jesus himself was deluded and deceived. The different aspects of Jesus's coming are but moments in one and the same act. 'The theses of those who advocate a thorough-going eschatology are quite superfluous once this has been realised. There is no need to suppose that there was unforeseen delay in the *parousia*, or that hope in the *parousia* was repeatedly deferred, or that the primitive Church and even Jesus himself were disillusioned or mistaken on the subject in consequence of an exaggerated enthusiasm—a view which is so clumsy that it is surely condemned from the very outset.'[78] For since Jesus is the Last One as well as the First and since it is the same Lord in the resurrection, Holy Spirit and second coming in whom we believe, whom we love and in whom we hope, this hope is full and perfect. Because we look for One who came and comes the 'New Testament hope could only be hope for the imminent coming of the kingdom,'[79] the one whom they trusted and loved was always close at hand, standing at the door knocking (Rev 3:20). 'Would he be the One who has come, and is already present, and is trusted and loved, if he did not stand immediately at the door and knock as the One who comes and is expected? If this is the One whom we expect, we cannot expect him the day after tomorrow, but tomorrow. The termination of his coming cannot be distant, but imminent. And no dawn and progress of a new day without his coming, no continuation of time apart from the events of his new revelation, can alter this expectation in the very slightest, let alone menace or destroy it.'[80] It is no time lapse, therefore, that determines our hope but Jesus Christ the Risen Lord who came and the Spirit who is his active presence. Since he was present then and now in his fulness how can his coming be anything else but near at hand, again about to break in upon us in gracious fulfilment?

If God's time is really fulfilled in him he is always there pressing in upon us and our time, ready to bring it both to its end and perfection in himself. 'For he who is to come, is also today; each day is a day of Christ, each day a day of grace, and therefore each day a day of hope.'[81] Barth can express and sum it up in this way: 'In the New Testament "short" denotes an internal rather than an external quality. It is not related, therefore, to the few or the many years and centuries of this interval which some might feel to be long, but to the character of this interval as time which, in relation to its Whither and Whence, is only passing away ... what makes time short is not the constriction of calendar years but the actuality of his presence at the beginning and the end.'[82] The time is foreshortened (1 Cor. 7:29) because it is surrounded and pressed in on all sides by the coming Lord.[83] Hence, one must always speak of the imminence of the *Parousia*. In this connection Barth makes two points[84]

(*a*) He gives a brief discussion of the term 'short' in the New Testament (1 Cor. 7:27 and John 7:33, 12:35) where the times are, as it were, telescoped. It is by its very nature a time that must end 'but the pressure which makes it a short time is also exerted by its end, by the Second Coming of Jesus Christ in his manifestation. That he is the Lord cannot remain concealed for long',[85] but presses towards a final and full revelation. It is therefore the will and work of the Lord himself who sets a limit because he wills to be seen soon in his glory.

(*b*) The length of time until the *parousia* is unknown to us. That it is described as to come suddenly and unexpectedly indicates that 'at the hour chosen by the Lord but not previously intimated, the end will be suddenly revealed to those who wait. They can only wait for the One who will come suddenly and put an end to their time.'[86] The consequence is no idle waiting, but active work and watching in faith and hope till he comes.

Notes to Chapter 10 will be found on pp. 191–195.

Notes

NOTES TO CHAPTER ONE

1. While Barth has no Christology as such because the whole of his theology is christological he does, however, have a doctrine of God as such even though the whole of his *Church Dogmatics* could be called a doctrine of God. The reason for this is obvious. For Barth an isolated Christology would be an abstraction since it would not deal with the whole Jesus Christ in his being and action in their unity. A separate doctrine of God is, however, possible as is a separate treatment of the Trinity because in each case we are dealing with the God revealed in Jesus Christ and because in each case we are dealing at one and the same time with the whole and no mere abstraction from it.

2. *Church Dogmatics*. English translation edited by G. W. Bromiley and T. F. Torrance, Edinburgh, 1936–1969 (hereafter *C.D.*), IV/1, p. 128.

3. Jacques de Senarclens points out that Barth deals with Christology both in the narrower and the broader sense but never in isolation (See 'La concentration christologique' in *Antwort, Karl Barth zum siebzigsten Geburtstag am 10 Mai 1956*, Zürich, 1956, p. 190.)

4. *C.D.*, IV/3, 1, p. 174.

5. Ibid., p. 175.

6. Ibid.

7. 'Die Christologie bei Karl Barth und Emil Brunner' in *Das Konzil von Chalkedon* III, Grillmeier und Bacht, Würzburg, 1954, p. 618.

8. *C.D.*, IV/2, p. 79.

9. *C.D., I/2*, p. 133. Cf. *Dogmatics in Outline* (English translation), London, New York, 1949, p. 66; also T. F. Torrance 'The Place of Christology in Biblical and Dogmatic Theology' in *Essays in Christology for Karl Barth*, edited by T. H. L. Parker, London, 1956, pp. 13–14; *Theological Science*, London, 1969, pp. 216–219.

10. Cf. *C.D.*, II/1, p. 320. 'There are, strictly speaking, no Christian themes independent of Christology.'

11. Herbert Hartwell, *The Theology of Karl Barth: an Introduction*, London, 1964, pp. 15–16. See also p. 96. The quotation enclosed in the above is from H. Gollwitzer, *Karl Barth: Church Dogmatics, a Selection with Introduction*, 1957, English translation, 1961, pp. 19–20. Hartwell's quotation is correct if by 'point of departure' he does not mean a point one goes away from and leaves behind. Barth's sense is rather that the

Christology accompanies, inspires and determines the whole of theology always.

12. Ibid., p. 16. Again this is only partially true since it is Jesus Christ who reveals the Father and with the Father sends the Holy Spirit. He is the way to the Father and in and through both the Holy Spirit is known and received. See *Credo*, English translation, London, 1936, pp. 40–41, where Barth argues that it is only in and through Jesus Christ (Second Article of the Creed) that we know the Father (First Article) and the Holy Spirit (Third Article). In other words, in Barth's view the Trinity and the christological concentration are not opposites; it is in and through Jesus Christ that we know God as triune.

13. *C.D.*, IV/1, p. 17.

14. For an exposition of the meaning of the name of Jesus Christ see H. Vogel, *Christologie*, I, Munich, 1940, pp. 41–78, and *Gott in Christo*, Berlin, 1952, pp. 607–624.

15. *C.D.*, I/2, p. 10.

16. Ibid.

17. *C.D.*, IV/2, p. 105.

18. *C.D.*, I/2, p. 23.

19. E. H. Friedmann, *Christologie und Anthropologie. Methode and Bedeutung der Lehre vom Menschen in der Theologie Karl Barths*, Münsterschwarzach, 1972, p. 116.

20. By systematizing is meant pressing the content of Christian truth into a pre-conceived mould which constricts it, i.e., a form or principle.

21. Op. cit., p. 118.

22. Ibid.

23. *C.D.*, I/2, p. 25.

24. *C.D.*, II/1, p. 320.

25. *Karl Barth 1886–1968. How I Changed my Mind*. Introduction and Epilogue by John D. Godsey, Edinburgh 1969. Barth writes, 'Christian Doctrine . . . has to be exclusively and conclusively the doctrine of Jesus Christ' (p. 43). 'I should like to call it a christological concentration.' (Ibid.)

26. *C.D.*, IV/1, p. 18.

27. *C.D.*, IV/3, 1, p. 39.

28. Ibid., p. 42. Barth uses the terms 'formal' and 'material' in an unusual sense here—the former indicating simply 'who' the person is, whereas the latter fills this out in the whole history of Jesus Christ as the history of salvation.

29. Ibid.

30. Ibid., p. 46.

31. Ibid.

32. Op. cit., pp. 121–122. Cf. Günther, *Die Christologie Karl Barths, Darstellung und Beurteilung*, Mainz, 1954, p. 92; Friedmann, ibid.

33. Ibid.

34. Colin Brown, *Karl Barth and the Christian Message*, London, 1967, pp. 138–139.

35. *C.D.*, IV/3, 1, p. 175. 'I am not trying unilaterally to think through the

principle of grace to the point at which I reach the "triumph of grace" in this relationship. I should regard such a procedure as quite illegitimate.' Or again 'We are not concerned with . . . a principle, even though the principle be that of grace. We are concerned with the living person of Jesus Christ' (ibid., p. 173). This is written against the thesis of G. C. Berkouwer, *The Triumph of Grace in the Theology of Karl Barth* (English translation, London, 1956), who thinks 'the triumph of Grace' is the theme of Barth's theology. Cf., however, *C.D.*, IV/3, 1, pp. 173–180 for Barth's reply to and critique of Berkouwer. Cf. also John Baillie. *The Sense of the Presence of God* (Gifford Lectures 1961–62) London and Toronto, 1962, p. 190, and his objection to Barth's continued use of 'the name of Jesus Christ'. He writes of 'the almost parrot-like manner in which . . . he [Barth] repeats "the name of Jesus Christ" '. Baillie clearly misunderstands Barth's meaning on two counts, viz., that it is a sign pointing to a Reality and also that this Reality is filled out and given the whole content of God's revelation in Barth's christological perspectives.

36. Cf. the following: *C.D.*, II/2, p. 4. The name of Jesus Christ is not an empty title, form or figure, means or medium which God could use and discard. It points to the being of God himself in this man.

   C.D., IV/1, pp. 20–21. It is not a form or general truth to which he conforms. On the contrary he and his history are the truth from which all general truths derive and in which they have their significance.

   Ibid., p. 123. The name of Jesus Christ is not 'a formal historical or symbolical sign of the event of atonement'.

   C.D., IV/3, 1, p. 46. 'This name is not accidental or capricious. It has not merely been conferred or appended. He himself pronounces it.'

37. *C.D.*, IV/1, p. 16.
38. Ibid., p. 158.
39. Ibid., p. 16.
40. Op. cit., pp. 123–124. [Italics mine. J.T.]
41. *C.D., IV/3*, 1, p. 39.
42. Op. cit., p. 619.
43. Ibid. However, though Volk does speak of it in this way he understands it more in the way Barth himself does.
44. J. de Senarclens speaks of Jesus Christ recapitulating all reality in himself, op. cit., p. 202.
45. *C.D., IV/1*, p. 768. The expositor and critic was Hans Urs von Balthasar: *Karl Barth: Darstellung und Deutung seiner Theologie*, Cologne, 1967, pp. 253ff.
46. *The Church in the Theology of Karl Barth*, London, 1970, vol. 1, p. 79. Cf. also *The Church in Catholic Theology: Dialogue with Karl Barth*, London, 1969. Vol. 2, p. 339, where O'Grady writes that Barth's, 'theology of "response" and "reflection" must be broadened to include a theology of participation, of "sub-operation" and "mediation" '. This, however, is precisely what Barth has all along fought against—man sharing in a semi-independent way in the saving act of God in Jesus Christ, and so contributing to some extent to his own salvation.

47. Cf. Friedmann, op. cit., p. 123, n. 352, for a summary of the names of the criticis:

　　H. G. Pöhlmann, *Analogia Entis oder Analogia Fidei? Die Frage der Analogie bei Karl Barth*, Göttingen, 1965.

　　L. Vilette, *Foi et Sacrament*, II: *De Saint Thomas à Karl Barth*, Paris, 1964.

　　R. Prenter speaks of a 'Christomonistic Universalism' in 'Karl Barth's Umbildung der Traditionellen Zweinaturenlehre in lutherischer Beleuchtung', *Studia Theologica*, II, 1957, p. 73.

　　E. Brunner, *The Christian Doctrine of God, Dogmatics*, vol. 1, English translation, London, 1949, p. 234.

　　H. Bouillard, *Karl Barth* II/2, *Parole de Dieu et existence humaine*, Paris, 1957, p. 293, thinks Karl Barth's theology has the appearance of Christomonism.

　　E. H. Amberg, *Christologie und Dogmatik*, Berlin, 1966, p. 73, is against the polemical slogan, Christomonism.

　　G. Gloege, 'Zur Versöhnungslehre Karl Barths' in *Theologische Literaturzeitung*, 1960, p. 184, asks of Barth's Dogmatics how it can avoid becoming speculative Christosophy and end up as gnosis?

　　Friedmann believes that Barth tries to defend himself against monistic dangers and quotes *C.D.*, IV/3, 2, p. 713 where, speaking of the hidden nature of the revelation of Christ in the world, he can say that it does not mean that Christ merges with world events. 'This would be Christomonism in the bad sense of that unlovely term' (in einem üblen Sinn dieses ohnehin unschönen Begriffs).

48. Wolfhart Schlichting, *Biblische Denkform in der Dogmatik. Die Vorbildlichkeit des biblischen Denkens fur die Methode der 'Kirchlichen Dogmatik' Karl Barths*, Zürich, 1972, pp. 277–278.

49. Cf. *C.D.*, IV/2, p. 536.

50. Op. cit., p. 278. The quotation here is from *Die Christusgemeinde und ihr Herr*, Berlin, 1967, p. 7.

51. *Christologie und Dogmatik*, p. 93. See Schlichting, ibid., p. 279.

52. *C.D.*, IV/1, p. 123.

53. Ibid., p. 122.

54. Ibid., p. 127.

55. Ibid., p. 128.

56. Ibid., p. 124. [Italics mine. J.T.]

57. Ibid., p. 125.

58. Ibid., pp. 126–127.

59. Ibid., p. 138. [Italics mine. J.T.] Barth follows the more strictly christological sections with other doctrines which are always intimately related to them—the doctrine of sin which is not known apart from but only in the light of Christ. In relation to the deity of Christ, God's humiliation it is *pride*; in relation to the humanity of Christ, man exalted to God it is *sloth*; and in relation to Jesus Christ as God-man, the Truth, it is *falsehood*.

　　Further, reconciliation is applied and made real by the work of the Holy spirit, first in the Church or community, in the *gathering* of men awakened to the divine verdict of justification, then in the *upbuilding* of this community which follows the divine direction of sanctification and finally in the *sending* of the community in the enabling power of the divine promise.

Then come the individuals in the community as they are awakened to *faith*, quickened in *love* and enlightened in *hope*.

For this massive and symmetrical conception of Dogmatics see *C.D., IV/1–IV/3*, 1, 2.

60. Cf. Wolfhart Pannenberg, *Jesus—God and Man*, English translation, London, 1972, p. 34. Heinz Zahrnt, *The Question of God*, English translation, London, New York, 1969, p. 94, believes it is the Pre-Existence of Christ.

W. Künneth, *Die Theologie der Auferstehung*, Siebenstern-Taschenbuch, 1968, p. 143.

Cf. also Berthold Klappert's critique of these in *Die Auferweckung des Gekreuzigten, Der Ansatz der Christologie Karl Barths im Zusammenhang der Christologie der Gegenwart*, Neukirchen, 1971, pp. 87–88, n. 3.

61. See in particular for the basis of these statements, *C.D.*, IV/1, pp. 283ff, The Verdict of the Father, and *C.D.*, IV/2, pp. 364ff, The Direction of the Son. But cf. also *C.D.*, I/2, p. 122, where this is already clearly set out in the Prolegomena. There, in the context of revelation, the Easter story is central. 'From the Easter story, the passion story is of course inseparable. In it takes place the hidden work of Jesus Christ which is subsequently revealed and believed in his resurrection . . . What happens in this life and passion of Christ is thus the concrete content of the revelation which takes place in the event of Easter.' At this particular point in the *Church Dogmatics* the incarnation is seen as 'the presupposition of this work and event' but it is from the event itself that this is known and interpreted.

62. Op. cit., pp. 85ff, section 6. 'The Unity of Person and Work in the reconciliation on the cross.'

63. *C.D.*, IV/1, p. 126. According to Klappert this unity of person and work is directed against two wrong ways of viewing this whole question. (1) Subordinating the person to the work and having a purely functional Christology. (2) Isolating the person from the work in favour of an ontology of Christ's being. The former is mainly directed against Bultmann and the latter against the form of traditional Christology (op. cit., p. 90).

64. *C.D.*, IV/1, p. 126.

65. Ibid., p. 133.

66. Op. cit., p. 93.

67. Ibid., pp. 93–94.

68. *C.D.*, IV/1, p. 133.

69. Klappert, op. cit., p. 94.

70. *C.D.*, IV/1, p. 133.

71. Ibid., pp. 133–134.

72. Op. cit., pp. 97–98. Klappert sums up Barth's intention and achievement in this way 'With this bracketing of person and work, the interpretation of the person by the work and vice versa, Barth reaches back

behind orthodoxy to the Reformation and behind the Christology of the early Church to the New Testament.' Ibid., p. 99.

73. Ibid., p. 88.
74. *C.D.*, I/2, p. 122, where he speaks of it as the 'presuppositions' of the life and passion of Christ.
75. Ibid., p. 23.
76. *C.D.*, III/2, p. 337. Cf. O'Grady, op. cit., vol 2, p. 64, who underlines this.
77. Otto Weber, *Karl Barths Kirchliche Dogmatik*, Neukirchen, 1967, pp. 200–201.
78. Cf. *C.D.*, IV/2, pp. 36–116 in particular.
79. Op. cit., p. 85f. Friedmann thinks that Barth's new emphasis, in which he unites so many aspects in one, is in danger of pushing out the incarnation as a real event at the beginning of the earthly life of Jesus. Op. cit., p. 242. This is similar to the actual result of Klappert's position but is completely false, as will be shown.
80. *C.D.*, IV/1, pp. 157–210.
81. *C.D.*, IV/2, p. 42.
82. Op. cit., pp. 88–89.
83. *C.D.*, IV/1, pp. 157–210, 211–283, and 283–357.
84. Op. cit., p. 229.
85. Ibid.
86. *C.D.*, IV/2, pp. 20–21. [Italics mine. J.T.]
87. Klappert, op. cit., p. 97; Geyer *Einfuhrüng in die Theologie K. Barths*, W.S., 1969/1970.
88. *C.D.*, IV/2, pp. 105–113.
89. Ibid., p. 105. [Italics mine. J.T.]
90. Ibid. Colm O'Grady, op. cit., vol. 1, p. 134, comments: 'With this Barth would wish to be less abstract or static and more actual and soteriological than the scholastics and at the same time, less soteriological and more ontological than the Reformers.'
91. Klappert, op. cit., pp. 96–97.
92. *C.D.*, IV/2, p. 109.
93. Cf. Pannenberg, op. cit., pp. 121–122, who believes that, though there are early traces of a functional Christology in the New Testament it can never be separated from an ontological reference. See also R. H. Fuller. *The Foundations of New Testament Christology*, London, 1965, pp. 247–250, where he criticises Oscar Cullmann's functional Christology and opts for an ontological one which, like Barth's, is dynamically related to the divine action. He writes 'Action implies prior being—even if, as is also true, being is only apprehended in action.' (Ibid., p. 248.)
94. H. Hartwell, op. cit., p. 36. Cf. *C.D.*, I/2, p. 170, where Barth speaks of the necessity of two sides or aspects of Christology, a static-ontic and a dynamic-noetic, yet it is always the latter which gives significance and meaning to the former. Hence Barth interprets God not simply as a being in himself and for himself but as One whose being in himself is known from and in his action for us. This again links on to the *Logos ensarkos* idea where the Son is not a disincarnate Logos but is always enfleshed, directed and related to man in reconciliation.

The above view is also a criticism of the older theology where the actualism was seen at the beginning (Incarnation) and the end (Atonement) with a static place in between. Moreover the relationship between the Logos and the two natures and between the two natures themselves was also regarded in static terms.

E. Jüngel, *Gottes Sein ist im Werden, Verantwortliche Rede vom Sein Gottes bei Karl Barth, Eine Paraphrase.* Tübingen, 1965, p. 90, n. 61, points out that Barth does not think of God's being as action without the idea of it having 'stability'. In him the two are one so that Jüngel can say 'the alternative static-dynamic is superseded by Barth just as is that of ontology-personalism'. (ibid.)

Schlichting, op. cit., pp. 162–176, gives a full discussion of the charge of actualism brought against Barth especially that of Panactualism by Pöhlmann (op. cit., passim). That there is an actualism cannot be denied but that his theology is all actualism must be. In particular Schlichting points to God's faithfulness, his being and election in Jesus Christ, the nature of man and creation and the new creature in Christ as pointing to the stability of God's being. Schlichting concludes that Barth does not contest that there are static features in the biblical view of God. He writes 'side by side with places that have an actualist sense are others which praise God's unchanging faithfulness, which know human nature in sin and grace as continuous, and which understand man's being in Christ as trustworthy', p. 171.

95. *C.D.*, IV/2, p. 109. [Italics mine. J.T.]
96. It would be impossible here to do anything more than touch upon Barth's view of history in relation to the incarnation and atonement. Briefly, however, it can be called 'truth in the form of a story that is told' and it includes three aspects. (*a*) It is the story of God in his movement to man, in becoming man in Jesus Christ. (*b*) It is the story of the movement of Jesus's life as such from its beginning to its climax in the cross and resurrection and of the reconciliation and revelation wrought and made known there. (*c*) Since it is God who is active here in reconciliation this is analogous to, reflects and has its basis in the inner life of God, which is a history of the divine relationships of Father, Son and Holy Spirit. Cf. *C.D.*, IV/1, pp. 157–158; *C.D.*, IV/3, 1, pp. 179ff. Reconciliation as a history; *C.D.*, IV/1, pp. 7–9, 208, the Trinity. Cf. also E. Jüngel, op. cit., pp. 88–89, n. 52, where he points out that Barth recalls the abandoned term Urgeschichte (primal history) to signify the history of God with man. *C.D.*, II/2, pp. 8–9.
97. Cf. e.g., *C.D.*, IV/2, p. 658f.
98. Ibid., p. 110f.
99. W. Pannenberg, op. cit., p. 33. That Pannenberg's interpretation is right is queried by Klappert, op. cit., p. 4.
100. Ibid., p. 33.
101. Ibid., p. 35.
102. *The Christian Doctrine of Creation and Redemption, Dogmatics,* vol. 2, English translation, London, 1966, p. 322.
103. H. Volk, op. cit., p. 663, believes Brunner's later work is less

decidedly Chalcedonian than his earlier and so is a falling away from his previous truer emphasis.

104. Op. cit., pp. 3–5.

105. *C.D.*, I/1, p. 356, where he speaks of a 'respect for its (not absolute but relative) authority'. Cf. *C.D.*, I/2, pp. 654–655; *C.D.*, IV/2, p. xi; *Credo* English translation, London, 1936, pp. 179–183. Eberhard Jüngel, op. cit., p. 22, n. 26.

106. *C.D.*, IV/2, p. 108.

107. It is, however, also clear in his attitude to the Reformers and post-Reformation theology both Lutheran and Reformed.

108. Op. cit., p. 638. Cf. O. Weber, op. cit., p. 245: 'Barth represents the theology of Chalcedon. There is no doubt about that.'

109. *C.D.*, IV/1, p. 133.

110. Ibid., p. 127.

NOTES TO CHAPTER TWO

1. In reply to a question about the relation between incarnation and the Person and Work of Christ in reconciliation Barth states ' "Incarnation" is here used as a summary word including the whole of "christological doctrine". It is a tactical use. I had to deal with Christology even in *Prolegomena*, because Christ is the Word of God. I could not anticipate the whole doctrine of reconciliation, but an extract in so far as the doctrine of reconciliation is revelation.' (*Karl Barth's Table Talk*, ed. J. D. Godsey, Edinburgh, 1963 (*Scottish Journal of Theology Occasional Paper No. 10*) (hereafter *T.T.*), p. 61. This is the reason why Barth here follows more closely the traditional schema of subject, object and predicate whereas later he begins with the event of reconciliation. Nevertheless, even here while the schema is different the starting point is the same. It is for this reason that one can without great difficulty quote passages from the *Prolegomena* (*C.D.*, I/1 and *C.D.*, I/2) side by side with those from the doctrine of reconciliation (*C.D.*, IV/1 and *C.D.*, IV/2).

2. *C.D.*, I/2, pp. 122ff.

3. Cf. Heppe, *Reformed Dogmatics*, English translation, London, 1950, p. 411; Heinrich Schmid, *Doctrinal Theology of the Evangelical Lutheran Church*, English translation, Minneapolis, 1961, pp. 270ff; *Westminster Confession of Faith*, VIII/I. The Lutherans distinguished between a universal or general will by which God's grace is directed to all men and a special grace or will which is directed towards all who will believe. In the Reformed tradition, it is linked to a limited atonement. This is quite contrary to Barth's view.

4. Cf. also more modern treatments like Emil Brunner, *The Mediator*, English translation, London, 1949, pp. 303ff; Heinrich Vogel, *Christologie* I, Munich, 1940, p. 79f, and *Gott in Christo*, Berlin, 1952, pp. 624ff, where Vogel speaks of a relative as well as an absolute basis of the incarnation. The former does not mean that there is a basis or even necessity in man's sin but that it is related to sinful humanity (for

us men and for our salvation). Barth makes no such distinction; for him the absolute basis is supreme though it does, at the same time, include the relative as well.

5. *C.D.*, II/2, p. 157. Here it is clear that election, incarnation and reconciliation are intimately and indissolubly related to one another.

6. Ibid., pp. 94, 158, 162.

7. Ibid., pp. 161ff.

8. Cf. H. Hartwell, op. cit., p. 106; see *C.D.*, II/2, p. 94.

9. *C.D.*, IV/2, pp. 42–43.

10. *C.D.*, II/2, p. 177.

11. *C.D.*, I/1, pp. 473–474; *C.D.*, I/2, pp. 34–35; *C.D.*, IV/1, pp. 200–204; *C.D.*, IV/2, pp. 43–45.

12. *C.D.*, IV/1, pp. 200–201.

13. Ibid., p. 203; cf. Emil Brunner, *The Mediator*, p. 311. 'The obedience of the Son is not the obedience of an historical personality, but the presupposition on the basis of which this personality could become historical.'

14. Op. cit., p. 233.

15. *C.D.*, IV/2, p. 44.

16. Cf. Heppe, op. cit., p. 414. Not 'the divine nature (common to the three persons of the Trinity) but the person of the Logos' was incarnate. They immediately add, of course, 'the Word existing eternally in the form or nature of God'. Schmid, op. cit., p. 303.

17. *C.D.*, I/2, p. 33.

18. Ibid.

19. Ibid., pp. 33–35, 133 and *C.D.*, IV/2, pp. 40–43.

20. *C.D.*, IV/2, pp. 43–44.

21. Ibid., p. 45.

22. *C.D.*, II/2, p. 158.

23. *C.D.*, IV/1, p. 48. [Italics mine. J.T.]

24. 'The Covenant in the Theology of Karl Barth.' *Scottish Journal of Theology* (hereafter *SJT*), vol. 17, No. 2, June 1964, p. 196.

25. Ibid., p. 197. Thomas Aquinas (*Summa Theologica* Part III Questions I–XXVI, English translation, London, 1924, p. 12) disagrees with those who believe that the incarnation would have taken place apart from human sin and writes 'Since everywhere in the Sacred Scripture the sin of the first man is assigned as the reason of the incarnation, it is more in accordance with this to say that the work of the incarnation was ordained by God as a remedy for sin; so that, had sin not existed, the incarnation would not have been.' But he adds, 'And yet the power of God is not limited to this; even had sin not existed, God could have become incarnate.' In other words Aquinas does not entirely exclude it as a possibility but regards it as improbable. Calvin (*The Institutes of the Christian Religion*, Book II, Chapter 12, 1, English translation, London, 1949, p. 401) implies the necessity of incarnation had man not sinned on the basis that man in his innocence and lowliness could not 'penetrate to God without a Mediator'. Otto Weber, *Dogmatik* II, Neukirchen, 1959, p. 174, is against such a view.

26. Op. cit., p. 234. Klappert puts this point in this way 'Within reconciliation . . . the following moments and aspects are to be distinguished (1) The Freedom aspect (the *Proseity* of God as Being in
relationship). (2) The Eternity aspect (the eternal self-determination of
God as a Being *pro se* to a Being *pro nobis*). (3) The Reaction aspect (the
pro nobis of reconciliation on the cross as the revelation of the reaction
of the Judge and Lord of the Covenant to sin and the sinner). (4) The
Realization aspect (reconciliation is, in its form as reaction, at the same
time decisively the fulfilment of the original will of God)' (Ibid., p. 235).
In this respect while one can speak of God's original will for man
nonetheless it is in practice fulfilled in God's gracious condescension
and reconciliation in Jesus Christ as at the same time a reaction to man's
sin. Klappert puts it in this way. It is 'the carrying out of the eternal
covenant will of God . . . and its confirmation in view of the reaction
to the incidence of sin'. (Ibid, p. 236.)

27. *C.D.,* I/2, p. 122.

28. *C.D.,* IV/2, p. 40; cf. *C.D.,* I/2, pp. 125–126. This is one reason why
Barth is loth to apply the term sacrament to Baptism and the Lord's
Supper. See for a discussion of this *C.D.,* IV/4, pp. 108ff and p. 161.

29. *C.D.,* I/2, p. 126. That the incarnation is a mystery is in line with both
the Lutheran and Reformed dogmaticians who speak of it as 'a high
and holy mystery beyond the grasp of human understanding (1 Tim.
3 : 16)' (H. Heppe, op. cit., p. 410; Schmid, op. cit., p. 303).

30. *C.D.,* I/2, p. 124. See also pp. 172–173.

31. Ibid., p. 122. Cf. Heppe, op. cit., p. 424, who quotes Alting as follows:
'The conception of Christ is distinguished by three acts which are
expressed by the one name *incarnation*. These are (1) The formation, (2)
the sanctification, (3) the assumption of the human nature.' This is not
exactly identical with Barth's but does contain two identical elements,
viz., sanctification and assumption. Cf. Schmid, op. cit., p. 303, who
gives a similar definition.

32. *C.D.,* I/2, p. 37.

33. Cf. *C.D.,* IV/1, pp. 157ff.

34. *C.D.,* I/2, pp. 37–38.

35. *C.D.,* IV/2, pp. 40–41.

36. Ibid., p. 40, 'God did indeed become man, not to be driven into a
corner by his own work, but rather in the sovereignty of his suffering,
death and resurrection to establish his Lordship over all creatures—and
within the world' (Von Balthasar, op. cit., p. 183).

37. Ibid., p. 42.

38. *C.D.,* I/2, pp. 135–137.

39. *C.D.,* IV/2, p. 45.

40. See *The Christian Faith*, English translation, edited by H. R. Mackintosh
and J. S. Stewart, Edinburgh, 1928, p. 368. Cf. *C.D.,* I/2, p. 134.

41. *C.D.,* IV/2, p. 37.

42. Ibid.

43. Ibid.

44. Ibid., p. 41. [Italics mine. J.T.]

45. *C.D.*, I/2, p. 33.
46. Ibid., p. 136.
47. Ibid.
48. Ibid.
49. H. Volk, op. cit., p. 622.
50. Roman Catholic apologists (e.g. H. Volk, op. cit., p. 637; Colm O'Grady, op. cit., vol. 2, pp. 67–68) deny that in praying to the sacred heart of Jesus they are abstracting the humanity from the divinity and thereby ascribing to it divine qualities. Their intention is to worship 'the man Jesus because the divine Person is indivisibly joined to the concrete man Jesus'. The relationship is maintained 'in the Catholic understanding of the hypostatic union. . . . In this way the creature is not deified but its concrete unity in the person of the *Logos* is presupposed and claimed.' (Volk., ibid., p. 637.) Similarly O'Grady (op. cit., pp. 67–68) writes 'Because we admit the ontological sanctification of Christ's human nature, as the consequence and realization of its personal unity with God, and because we admit this human nature's instrumentality in the work of reconciliation, we also assert the legitimacy and necessity of rendering the homage of adoration to, for example, Christ's physical heart. Not to a physical heart in itself, in abstraction from the divine person, but to the physical heart of the man Jesus of Nazareth which never *is* in abstraction from him. God's divine love is manifested and bestowed in the human love of his physical heart . . . Karl Barth's rejection of devotion to the sacred heart is a confirmation of his monophysite tendency in the explanation of Christ's work of reconciliation.' Barth grants that Roman Catholic dogma does not intend any separation of divinity from humanity in the person of Christ. What he does rightly oppose nevertheless is a false understanding of the humanity of Christ at this point. He puts it in this way: 'the objection is that by direct glorification of Christ's humanity as such the divine Word is evaded and camouflaged. For when we are speaking of Jesus Christ, this Word does not possess its human-ness as an "object of manifestation" alongside Itself. It is God's revelation to us in its human-ness . . . Where it is made such an object, recollection of the really intended "material object" is a belated reservation void of force.' (*C.D.*, I/2, p. 138.) In other words Roman Catholicism ascribes to the humanity of Jesus a direct revelatory power it possesses only in and through the Word and so in this way at this point substitutes the creature for the Creator. The charge of monophysitism levelled by O'Grady against Barth cannot be sustained since the humanity is not absorbed by the deity. Barth asserts, however, that only the divine can reveal but does so in and through his union with the human. So the union of the Word and the flesh is real in the Person of Jesus Christ; it is here that God reveals himself in his action, in history, in the incarnation. But Barth must always insist that this flesh, this history takes its existence, power and meaning from the Word, has significance in and through it alone and not vice versa or in a semi-independent way.

51. *C.D.,* I/2, p. 147.
52. Op. cit., p. 628.
53. *C.D.,* I/2, pp. 36–37.
54. Ibid., p. 149. Cf. Heppe, op. cit., p. 414. 'In particular the incarnation of the Logos is not to be thought of as though he had inwardly united himself with a ready-made self-existent human being. Rather the person of the Logos of God took the nature of man or humanity up into its subsistence in such a way that without detriment to its divine existence it entered the human mode of being and condition.'
55. Heppe also speaks of the Reformed dogmatician's view of Christ's humanity as '*an individuum*, an exposition of human nature in individual form. (Op. cit., p. 417.)
56. 'The Atonement and the Oneness of the Church', *SJT.,* vol. 7, no. 3, September 1954, pp. 249–250. Quoted again in *Essays in Christology for Karl Barth* edited by T. H. L. Parker, London, 1956, p. 16. Cf. for a full discussion of this subject H. M. Relton, *A Study in Christology*, London, 1917, passim. He states his aim as a 'wish to demonstrate the value of *Enhypostasia* for modern Christology' (Ibid., p. xxxi).
57. *C.D.,* I/2, p. 163.
58. *C.D.,* I/2, pp. 164–165; Cf. *C.D.,* IV/2, p. 49. See for a similar criticism of this teaching D. M. Baillie, *God was in Christ. An Essay on Incarnation and Atonement*, reprinted Faber, London, 1969, pp. 85–93. Baillie, however, (I believe mistakenly) wishes to dispense with the *an-* and *enhypostasia* altogether.
59. Ibid., p. 164.
60. The most controversial modern re-interpretation of this theologou-menon has come from Friedrich-Wilhelm Marquardt in his book *Theologie und Sozialismus. Das Beispiel Karl Barths* (Munich, 1972, pp. 265–275), under the title 'The *assumptio carnis* and the "species man"' (Gattung-Mensch). Briefly his thesis is that Barth's socialist views (Marzist-Leninist theory-praxis) has deeply influenced his theology and that this is seen (among other places) in the *an-* and *enhypostasia*. The Son of God in assuming our humanity became, not merely an individual man but the species man. In this way Barth (according to Marquardt) extends 'the "christological" anhypostasy to an "anthropological" enhypostasy of the collective "*genus man*".' (H. Hartwell, article review, *SJT*, vol. 28, no. 1, 1975, p. 68.) The meaning of this is far from clear but what is certain is that it is not what Barth intends. (See for a full discussion of this subject, Hermann Diem, 'Die Christologie Karl Barths in der Sicht von Friedrich Wilhelm Marquardt', *Kerygma und Dogma*, July 1974, pp. 145–153.)

What Marquardt is rightly concerned to maintain is the universal significance of the incarnation in Barth's inclusive christology. The latter position can be stated in this way that since God became man in Jesus Christ, all men are ontologically related to him and so are virtually and potentially his whereas believers are actually and practically so (cf. *C.D.,* IV/2, pp. 59ff). What Marquardt seems to be doing is reading back these truths into the incarnation rather than (as with Barth)

deducing them from it. In particular the following objections may be
raised to this procedure:

(a) Since *an-* and *enhypostasia* are terms of relationship any expansion
destroys this, endangers both sides and so makes the incarnation
meaningless (Diem, op. cit., p. 153).

(b) For Barth and traditional theology the *humanum* assumed is 'simply
the potentiality of being in the flesh' (*C.D.*, I/2, p. 149). Moreover,
in Jesus Christ it was an individual man that the Son of God
became. Marquardt changes this individuality of the man Jesus into
a collectivist species man and so substitutes anthropology for
Christology. This is, as Diem remarks, (op. cit., p. 148) to stand
Barth on his head and to reach the goal aimed for, that of a natural
theology.

(c) As Hartwell points out (op. cit., p. 68) there is considerable confusion here because, according to Marquardt, Jesus is not himself
the *genus man*. But in some sense he must be, otherwise Marquardt's
claim loses all validity.

61. *C.D.*, I/2, p. 150.

62. Ibid., pp. 151ff.

63. *C.D.*, I/2, p. 40. 'Italics mine. J.T.] The early Church, according to
Barth, felt that these statements concerning Christ's humanity could not
be held together with those of the sinlessness of Jesus. Both Luther and
Calvin and later Reformed teaching held that it was not convenient for
the Son of God to be united with our sinful human nature—so there
was an understandable but nonetheless unjustifiable reserve. This was
only altered in the last century with Gottfried Menken in Germany and
Edward Irving in Britain. (Ibid., p. 154.) See for a good summary of
this position A. B. Bruce, *The Humiliation of Christ*, Edinburgh, 1876,
pp. 266–276. Menken's views are summarised by Bruce and are almost
identical with those of Barth.

The critics believe that this theory impairs the sinlessness of Jesus and
means attributing to him original sin. (See A. B. Bruce, op. cit.,
pp. 271ff and H. R. Mackintosh, *The Doctrine of the Person of Jesus Christ*,
Edinburgh, 1912, pp. 277ff.)

Does the assumption of fallen humanity imply sin in Christ? What
is the biblical witness? There can be little doubt that in this regard
Menken, Irving, Barth and others are right as over against the long
weight of ecclesiastical tradition and exegesis. Those passages adduced
by Barth as testimony to this view (see *C.D.*, I/2, p. 152, e.g. Rom. 8: 3,
2 Cor. 5: 21; Gal. 3: 13; Mt. 27: 38 etc.) are much more readily interpreted in this way than in the other. There is also clear testimony in the
New Testament to the sinlessness of Jesus. These two strands, though
logically hard to reconcile are yet clearly discernable and point to the
mystery, paradox and meaning of the incarnation. To that extent
Menken, Irving and their modern successors are right on the one hand
to point to the reality of Christ's identity with us in our fallen nature
and yet, on the other hand, to recongise in it his real holiness, sanctification and sinlessness by the Holy Spirit.

64. *C.D.*, I/2, p. 160. Cf. *C.D.*, IV/2, p. 42. See also Heppe, op. cit., p. 414.
65. Ibid., p. 161. See Heppe, op. cit., p. 431 where *unio personalis* or *immediata* (direct) in the person of the Logos is distinguished from *unio mediata* (indirect) of the two natures which is mediated by the Holy Spirit.
66. Op. cit., p. 633.
67. Ibid., p. 634.
68. *C.D.*, IV/2, p. 65.
69. Ibid., p. 51.
70. Ibid., p. 52.
71. *C.D.*, I/2, p. 163.
72. *C.D.*, IV/2, pp. 51–52.
73. *C.D.*, I/2, p. 164.
74. Ibid., see also *C.D.*, IV/2, p. 67.
75. *C.D.*, IV/2, p. 52. Cf. *C.D.*, I/2, p. 171.
76. *C.D.*, I/2, p. 164.
77. Ibid., p. 162.
78. *C.D.*, IV/2, p. 52. Cf. T. F. Torrance, *Theological Science*, p. 216, where he writes that the hypostatic union is 'the unique togetherness of God and man in Christ which is normative for every other relationship between man and God'.
79. Op. cit., p. 310.
80. *C.D.*, IV/2, p. 53.
81. Ibid., p. 54.
82. Ibid., p. 58. Barth (ibid., pp. 52–58 following Heppe, op. cit., pp. 430–432) shows how these analogies are incapable of being used here. (*a*) The union cannot exist as Father, Son and Holy Spirit (co-essential) i.e., it is not a unity in the twofold form of the same being or essence but of dissimilars. (*b*) It is not a special existence of the union between God and all things as in creation and providence. (*c*) It is not like the union of man and wife i.e., of two self-existing persons. (*d*) It is not like chemicals and their properties, e.g. glowing iron and heat. (*e*) It is not like form and substance or any other antithetical objects which are mutually necessary and complementary. (*f*) It is not like the unity of body and soul for the latter does not assume the former and so give it existence. (*g*) Nor is it like the *unio sacramentalis*, the concurrence of inward and outward, of the thing signified with a sign. (*h*) Finally it is not to be explained by the *unio mystica* i.e., the experience of grace. It is here that Donald Baillie went astray since he thought he saw the indwelling of Christ in believers as a suitable analogy in this regard. But the indwelling of the divine by grace in human life and the consequent union is an indwelling which others also experience, not a unique union incomparable in nature and meaning that in the existence of this man alone we meet with the living God as our Saviour. It is quite different to say this man is indwelt by God through grace and this man is God himself in person. (See Baillie, op. cit., pp. 114–118. Cf. *T.T.*, p. 51, where Barth also criticizes Baillie.)
83. Ibid.
84. Ibid., p. 61.

85. Ibid., p. 63.
86. Ibid.
87. Ibid., p. 64.
88. Ibid.
89. Ibid.
90. Ibid., p. 65.
91. Barth states two conditions which must be strictly observed in these relationships. (*a*) The movement is from the divine to the human which is determined by it and only so in the opposite direction. (*b*) There is thus no simple correspondence between the two, i.e., while God became man, man did not become divine (*C.D.*, IV/2, pp. 70–72).
92. *C.D.*, IV/2, pp. 73ff.
93. This states that the human nature became partaker of the divine nature in some of its qualities, e.g. omniscience, omnipotence, etc., but as O. Weber partinently remarks 'The "temple" in which the Godhead of God "dwells" does not need to be "defied" in order to be able to receive the Godhead'. (*Karl Barths Kirchliche Dogmatik. Ein Einführender Bericht*, Neukirchen, 1967, p. 246.)
94. *C.D.*, IV/2, pp. 84ff.
95. Ibid., p. 88.
96. Ibid.
97. Ibid., pp. 104ff.

NOTES TO CHAPTER THREE

1. It was carried out with an impressive insight, comprehension and learning by one of the greatest of them: Johann Gerhard, *Loci Theologici* IV, *Caput* V. *De Divina Christi Natura*, Tübingen, 1764, pp. 373–420. Four kinds of 'proofs' were usually adduced: the divine names, the divine honours, the divine works and the divine attributes. Cf. Heppe, op. cit., pp. 123–124; Schmid, op. cit., p. 299; Gerhard, op. cit., pp. 374–375. Gerhard adds a fifth: divine worship; his list then reads; *Dictus, cultus, opus, confessio, munera quinque haec divinam Christi naturam mox tibi monstrant.* These were all applied to Christ in Holy Scripture, point to and prove his personal divinity. Accordingly, 'the Son is not created or made by God or adopted by grace or because of merit. He is God the Son according to his nature and is therefore true *autotheos*, like the Father and Holy Spirit'. (Heppe, op. cit., p. 125.)
2. E. Brunner, *The Christian Doctrine of Creation and Redemption, Dogmatics*, English translation, vol. 2, London, 1966, p. 342.
3. J. K. S. Reid, *The Authority of Scripture*, London, 1957, p. 201. See also the whole section, pp. 194–233, for a full discussion of the teaching of Barth and Brunner on Holy Scripture.
4. 'The fact that God's revelation is contained in this book does not mean that the texts of this book are a revelation as such.' K. Barth, 'The Christian Understanding of Revelation' in *Against the Stream, Shorter Post-War Writings*, English translation, edited by R. G. Smith, London,

1954, p. 217. Cf. also John Baillie, *The Idea of Revelation in Recent Thought*, London, 1956, pp. 34–35.

5. *C.D.*, I/1, p. 124.

6. *C.D.*, I/2, p. 462.

7. Ibid., p. 463. Barth puts it in this seemingly paradoxical way, 'we distinguish the Bible as such from revelation' as human words, but 'the Bible is not distinguished from revelation' (ibid.), as the Word of God spoken to man. 'Therefore, where the Word of God is an event, revelation and the Bible are one in fact, and word for word one at that'. (*C.D.*, I/1, p. 127.)

8. *Karl Barth's Doctrine of Inspiration* quoted by Colin Brown in *Karl Barth and the Christian Message*, London, 1967, p. 32.

9. H. R. Mackintosh, *Types of Modern Theology*, London, 1937, p. 290.

10. P. T. Forsyth, *The Person and Place of Jesus Christ*, London, 1946, p. 115.

11. Ibid., pp. 159ff.

12. John Baillie (op. cit., pp. 32–33) has shown that 'what God reveals to us is himself and not merely a body of propositions about himself'.

13. *C.D.*, I/1, pp. 124–135. *C.D.*, I/2, pp. 1–202. W. Pannenberg (op. cit., p. 127, n. 28) has rightly pointed out that 'the understanding of God's revelation as self-disclosure, self-revelation, is almost universal in contemporary Protestant theology'. He goes on to state that 'the patristic idea of a substantial presence of God in Jesus has become accessible in our century from the perspective of the problem of revelation, insofar as revelation implies identity of essence' (ibid., p. 132).

14. *C.D.*, IV/1, pp. 301ff. *C.D.*, IV/2, pp. 141ff and 298ff. *The Knowledge of God and the Service of God*, English translation, London, 1938, p. 87f.

15. *C.D.*, IV/3, 1, pp. 38ff.

16. *C.D.*, I/1 and *C.D.*, I/2.

17. Jüngel, op. cit., p. 29. Cf. *C.D.*, I/1, p. 361.

18. *C.D.*, I/1, p. 127. John Baillie's translation in *The Idea of Revelation in Recent Thought*, p. 35.

19. Ibid., p. 349. Cf. T. F. Torrance, *Theology and Church. Shorter Writings by Karl Barth*, English translation, London, 1962, Introduction, p. 25: 'Revelation, as Calvin had taught, is God speaking in Person.' Torrance points out (ibid., pp. 24–27) that for Barth, revelation has three aspects. (*a*) It is an *act* of God, a dynamic event indicating the transcendence and freedom of God. (*b*) It is the very Being and Person of God himself that is revealed and 'not just something *of* himself, not just something *about* himself, but very God himself' (ibid., p. 25; [Italics mine, J.T.]). (*c*) It is a 'rational event, for in revelation God communicates to us his Word and conveys to us his Truth' (ibid., p. 27). Hence theology is the human *ratio* which corresponds to and seeks to express the objective rationality of the divine Word in Jesus Christ.

20. Ibid. 'Jesus Christ is for Barth neither "the final revelation", as R. Niebuhr holds, nor "the crown of revelation", as W. Temple claims, but *the* revelation.' H. Hartwell (op. cit., p. 70).

21. One cannot however deal with revelation in this limited sense alone

but must see it in its whole context and wider implications. It is therefore clearly one of the important Christological perspectives in Barth's theology.

22. *C.D.,* I/1, p. 368. [Italics mine. J.T.] Cf. p. 339. 'God reveals himself as the Lord' is a simple analytical and not a synthetic statement. According to John McIntyre (*The Shape of Christology*, London, 1966, p. 158) Barth interprets 'analytical' to mean that in revelation 'the distinction between form and content cannot be applied'. This means 'that whereas in other circumstances an alteration of form would entail an alteration of content, or the possibility of alteration of content, in the case of revelation, the fact that God exists in the form of a man does not entail any change in his nature . . . from all eternity. The content remains identical in the two situations; otherwise we would be obliged to deny the occurrence of revelation' (ibid.). This is correct as far as it goes since when God became man in Jesus Christ (or to adopt the term used here, revealed himself in Christ) there was no change in his nature but he took a new form, that of man without ceasing in any way to be true God. However, McIntyre is not right when he implies that Barth may create the impression that by examination of the statement on revelation, namely, that God was in Christ we can then, by this anlaysis, affirm the deity and that the Son is consubstantial with the Father. Clearly, as McIntyre says, the transition from revelation to the recognition of *God* in Christ and to that of the Son being co-essential with the Father 'is itself the subject of revelation and not the result of analysis' (ibid.). Barth would not in any way dispute this.

McIntyre raises a further important point in relation to Barth's use of what he calls the 'revelation model', namely, that he combines with it the 'two-nature model' of Chalcedon. The revelation of God in the Person of Christ is of One who is true God and true man in their unity. This is also clearly linked to Barth's strong emphasis on God being known (revealed) only in and through the humanity of Christ in reconciliation (*C.D.,* IV/1 and *C.D.,* IV/2). McIntyre concludes 'My own feeling is that if the revelation model is to be made to work in our time it has to take this form, and not the form which Brunner and the earlier Barth had favoured' (ibid., p. 161). What he means by this is that in the earlier form of Barth's doctrine there is a tendency to underestimate the historical nature of the revelation of God in Jesus Christ, 'a residual element of Kierkegaardian scepticism' (ibid., p. 157). There is some truth in this though it should be pointed out that revelation is never isolated from reconciliation and this is always connected with the words and deeds, the life and death of Jesus of Nazareth.

23. Ibid., p. 353. [Italics mine. J.T.]
24. Ibid., p. 363.
25. Ibid.
26. Ibid.
27. Ibid., p. 371.
28. Op. cit., p. 100.
29. *C.D.,* I/2, p. 1.

30. Barth on Revelation, *SJT*, vol. 13, no. 4, Dec. 1960, pp. 372ff.
31. Ibid., p. 373. [Italics mine. J.T.]
32. *C.D.*, I/1, p. 371.
33. Ibid.
34. Ibid.
35. Op. cit., p. 282.
36. *C.D.*, I/1, p. 369.
37. Jüngel, op. cit., pp. 30–31.
38. *C.D.*, I/1, p. 133.
39. Op. cit., p. 373.
40. Jüngel, op. cit., p. 31.
41. *C.D.*, I/1, p. 362.
42. Ibid., p. 342.
43. Ibid., pp. 353–354.
44. Ibid., p. 358.
45. Ibid.
46. Ibid., p. 346.
47. Ibid., p. 340.
48. Op. cit., p. 157.
49. *C.D.*, I/1, pp. 383–399.
50. Ibid., p. 385.
51. Ibid., pp. 384 and 385.
52. Ibid., p. 359.
53. Op. cit., p. 372.
54. *C.D.*, I/1, p. 358. Cf. pp. 350–351. Barth distinguishes between God's self-interpretation in revelation and illustration which is the human and illegitimate attempt to find a creaturely analogy to the Trinity (*C.D.*, I/1, p. 396 and *T.T.*, pp. 46–47).
55. Ibid., p. 390.
56. Ibid., pp. 391–392. See also for a detailed discussion of this Jüngel, op. cit., pp. 16–27, with the significant title '*The vestigium trinitatis* as a hermeneutical problem.' By this he means that by giving sole place to revelation at the beginning of Dogmatics and by placing the doctrine of the Trinity where Scripture normally stands Barth is making 'a *hermeneutical* decision of the utmost revelance' for the whole content and form of the *Church Dogmatics*. Cf. *T.T.*, pp. 48–49, where Barth states that revelation as event is the 'epistemological concept', the 'critical principle' of the *Prolegomena* and so of the Dogmatics as a whole.
57. Ibid., p. 363.
58. Ibid., p. 372.
59. Ibid., p. 368.
60. Jüngel, op. cit., p. 30.
61. *C.D.*, I/1, p. 362.
62. Ibid., p. 369.
63. Ibid.
64. Ibid., p. 373. [Italics mine. J.T.]
65. Ibid., p. 350. Inner worldly realities now unknown may one day be 'revealed' and so become known by man and completely unveiled.

Their hiddenness is only relative; God's however is complete and absolute.

66. Ibid., p. 374.
67. Ibid., p. 373.
68. Ibid., p. 378.
69. Ibid., p. 379.
70. Ibid., p. 381.
71. Op. cit., p. 32.
72. *C.D.*, I/1, p. 381.
73. Op. cit., p. 373.
74. Op. cit., p. 281. John Baillie, op. cit., p. 64, writes in a similar way 'It is not as if all who experience these events and happenings find in them a revelation of God . . . we must therefore say that the receiving is as necessary to a completed act of revelation as the giving. It is only so far as the action of God in history is understood as God means it to be understood that revelation has place at all. The illumination of the receiving mind is a necessary condition of the divine self-disclosure.' Cf. P. T. Forsyth, op. cit., p. 149, 'The finished work of Christ was not finished till it was got home.'
75. Ibid.
76. *C.D.*, I/2, pp. 1–25.
77. Ibid., pp. 203–242. F. W. Camfield, *Revelation and the Holy Spirit, An Essay in Barthian Theology*, London, 1933, p. 88, puts it convincingly in this way 'Revelation in order to be revelation, cannot be objective merely; it must be subjective as well. Only in being subjective can it be seen as objective.' Cf. however Hartwell's (op. cit., p. 107) more critical questions at this point where he partially answers himself.
78. Cf. Aloys Grillmeier, *Christ in Christian Tradition*, English translation. New revised edition, London and Oxford, 1975, p. 76f. It was associated chiefly with a Jewish Christian group which eventually separated from the main-stream of Christianity.
79. *C.D.*, I/1, p. 460.
80. Ibid., p. 461. This follows the general lines of Docetism.
81. Ibid., p. 462. Cf. *T.T.*, p. 53, for a further brief statement of these views. T.F. Torrance, *Theological Science*, pp. 45–46, sums up these two heretical christologies in this way 'In *Docetic* Christologies we see that we cannot take the way of deduction, beginning with a particular idea of God and then finding that fulfilled or confirmed in Jesus Christ, only then to relegate the actual humanity of Jesus to a place of ultimate unimportance compared to the idea of the Christ or of God as brought to light through him. In *Ebionite* Christologies we see that we cannot take the way of induction (at least as "induction" is usually understood), beginning with the manhood of Christ and seeking to rise towards God as the goal or end of man's thought, only then to end up in the idealizing of man himself. As against both of these erroneous ways of procedure we begin positively with God himself meeting us in Jesus Christ, giving himself to us. . . .'
82. Ibid., p. 464.

83. Ibid.
84. Ibid.
85. *C.D.*, I/2, p. 13.
86. Ibid., p. 14. It is lacking at the beginning of Mark, in Acts in the *Kerygma* except Acts 10, 36ff; it is seen at the climax of John 20: 28, but not in the Synoptic parallels.
87. E. Brunner, *The Christian Doctrine of Creation and Redemption, Dogmatics*, vol. 2, p. 346.
88. Ibid., p. 348.
89. *C.D.*, I/2, p. 21. [Italics mine. J.T.]
90. *C.D.*, I/1, p. 474.
91. Jüngel, op. cit., p. 33, n. 83, points out that 'within the trinitarian chapters (of the *Church Dogmatics*) about God the Father, God the Son and God the Holy Spirit in each instance God is spoken of in his "revelatory function" as Creator, Reconciler and Redeemer and then in his mode of being as eternal Father, eternal Son and eternal Spirit'.
92. *C.D.*, I/1, p. 474. Cf. P. T. Forsyth, op. cit., p. 112. Interpreting Mt. 11: 27 he writes 'surely the Father and the Son here are both absolute terms. . . . *The* Father in his holy eternity is meant. And with such a Father the Son is *correlative*. . . . If the one is an eternal Father the other is a co-eternal Son'.
93. T. F. Torrance, *Karl Barth, An Introduction to his Early Theology, 1910–1931*, London, 1962, p. 100, writes of Barth 'He distinguished his position sharply from the romantic impressionalistic theologies which like to think of the divine revelation as the impartation of life rather than as the communication of truth.' As Torrance indicates, this is mainly directed against 'Herrmann's insistent idea that revelation ist nicht lehre' (ibid., n. 2). See *Theology and Church*, p. 248f. In contrast to Barth, Herrmann tried to accept the deity of Christ but rejected the traditional dogma associated with it; cf. W. Herrmann, *The Communion of the Christian with God*, English translation, London, New York, 1913, pp. 57ff.
94. *C.D.*, I/1, p. 475. This seemingly tautological statement is very typical of Barth's whole approach to theology and derives from the biblical thought form as interpreted by Anselm. He uses what one might call the circular argument. One cannot evaluate or judge whether or not Jesus Christ is the Son of God from a position outside revelation, reconciliation and faith which could claim neutrality or scientific objectivity. This would make us the judges of One who is Lord and God. It would also be purely subjective and unscientific since it would fail to understand and estimate aright the nature of its object. The only position from which to know, understand and evaluate is from within the circle enclosed by revelation and faith. This alone is true scientific objectivity which respects, is obedient to and follows the nature of its object—God the Son as he comes into our human nature revealing, reconciling and known by faith.
95. Ibid., pp. 475–476.
96. Ibid., p. 476. [Italics mine. J.T.]

97. J. Moltmann, *The Crucified God*, English translation, London, 1974, p. 240, points out that Barth follows 'the Cappadocians in distinguishing between the immanent Trinity and the economic Trinity. God is "beforehand in himself" everything that he reveals in Christ. God corresponds to himself'. Moltmann goes on to support the view of Karl Rahner that the distinction is inappropriate since God's relationship to us is not merely an analogy or image but *is* the Trinity even though it comes in the form of grace. Barth would, to my mind, wish to say both, namely, that God is as he reveals himself. He is both triune *per se* and a correspondence to it in his relation to us. Barth's later views in the doctrine of reconciliation come closer to those of Rahner though they do not coincide.

98. *C.D.*, I/1, pp. 476–477. P. Melanchthon's phrase was '*hoc est Christum cognoscere, beneficia eius cognoscere, non . . . eius naturas, modos incarnationis contueri*' (Loci Communes 1521), quoted by Barth (ibid.).

99. Ibid., p. 480.

NOTES TO CHAPTER FOUR

1. As the Editors of the English translation point out (*C.D.*, IV/1, p. vii) both words 'reconciliation' and 'atonement' are used to translate the one German word *Versöhnung* though reconciliation is the more central and the more widely used term. One cannot fully agree with John McIntyre (op. cit., p. 165) that 'Barth shifts the emphasis from revelation to reconciliation' as the *Church Dogmatics* proceeds. This is partially true. On the other hand revelation to be effective must be reconciliation and reconciliation to be known must be revelation.

2. *C.D.*, IV/1, p. 3. In von Balthasar's lyrical appraisal of Barth he speaks of the doctrine of election as the 'very heart of Barthian theology' (op. cit., p. 187). This does not necessarily contradict Barth's own statement here since God's election is most manifest in reconciliation.

3. Ibid., pp. 22–66. For excellent summaries of this section see Colm O'Grady, op. cit., vol. 1, pp. 130–132; Hans Küng, *Justification, The Doctrine of Karl Barth and a Catholic Reflection*, English translation, London, 1964, pp. 20–28; J. L. Scott, 'The Covenant in the Theology of Karl Barth', *SJT*, vol. 17, no. 2, June 1964, pp. 182–198; G. W. Bromiley, 'The Doctrine of the Atonement', *SJT*, vol. 8, no. 2, June 1955, pp. 176–177.

4. Ibid., p. 33. Jer. 31: 31ff; 32: 38ff.

5. Ibid., p. 47.

6. Barth's is, therefore, very definitely and distinctively a *theologia crucis*. This does not mean that other terms applied to his theology, e.g. that of the Word of God or Revelation are now inapplicable. Rather the cross and resurrection are God's word and revelation as the climax and content of his reconciling action. This is an emphasis being made increasingly by modern German theologians, notably Jürgen Moltmann in his recent book *The Crucified God*, pp. 20–154. See also Moltmann,

'Gesichtspunkte der Kreuzestheologie heute', *Evangelische Theologie*, vol. 33, no. 4, July/August 1973 (hereafter *Ev.Th.*), p. 346, for a list of recent writers (Catholic and Protestant) on this central theme.

7. I cannot agree with T. H. L. Parker in his booklet *Karl Barth*, Eerdmans, Michigan, 1970, p. 115, that 'the casting of the doctrine of the Mediator in terms of the Prodigal Son is unconvincing and even perverse'. I believe that, contrary to Parker, Barth has made a convincing case for its use.

8. *C.D.*, IV/2, pp. 21–25.

9. *C.D.*, IV/1, pp. 157–210. The parallel to this in *C.D.*, IV/2, pp. 20–154, is 'The Homecoming of the Son of Man'.

10. *C.D.*, IV/2, p. 21.

11. Ibid., p. 23.

12. There is a parallel to this manner of thought in P. T. Forsyth in a sermon entitled 'The Empire of Christ: The Emigration of the Divine' preached in the City Temple, London, as long ago as 8th May, 1900. See *Peter Taylor Forsyth, Director of Souls. Selections from his practical writings*, compiled and edited by Harry Escott, London, 1948, pp. 58–59.

13. *C.D.*, IV/1, pp. 158–159. This is no new thought in Barth's *Church Dogmatics*. Already in *C.D.*, I/2, he sees the incarnation as God's act of freedom in crossing the very real boundary between himself and us and thereby showing himself to be the true God. It is a boundary which is no obstacle to God, puts no limitation on him in his act of revelation. 'His nature as God compared with our nature as men, his nature as Lord, Creator, Reconciler and Redeemer compared with ours as creatures and sinners doomed to die, does not limit him in such a way that, in spite of all, he cannot be God within the sphere indicated by this nature of ours. His majesty is so great that even in the lowliness of this God-existence of his in our sphere, even when identical with one of the realities of our cosmos which meet us, and precisely in the midst of this lowliness, it can still be majesty, indeed in that very way it can show itself to be majesty.' (Ibid., p. 31.)

14. Ibid., p. 159.

15. Op. cit., p. 123.

16. *C.D.*, IV/1, p. 211.

17. Ibid., p. 160.

18. Ibid.

19. Op. cit., pp. 139–140.

20. *C.D.*, IV/1, pp. 211ff.

21. *C.D.*, II/2, p. 511. [Italics mine. J.T.] Here we see clearly the relationship between Gospel and Law which is such a distinctive feature of Barth's theology. The Lord who reconciles at the same time claims man for his obedience. 'The one Word of God is both Gospel *and* Law' (ibid.) but in this irreversible order.

22. Op. cit., p. 140.

23. *C.D.*, IV/1, p. 160. 'Son of David' and 'Son of Man' are omitted in the English translation. Again Klappert shows that the uniqueness of Jesus

as qualitatively Other is reflected in a great variety of ways in the Gospels. He names seven: (1) Jesus's call to discipleship, (2) 'I say unto you', (3) Forgiveness of sins, (4) 'My Father' and 'your father'. (5) 'Abba', (6) 'Amen' before the 'I say unto you'. (7) The claim to exercise an authority only God has (op. cit., p. 145). Cf. also *C.D., I/1,* pp. 458–460.

24. *C.D., IV/3,* 1, p. 73.
25. *C.D., IV/1,* p. 161. In saying this Barth is affirming different strata of tradition in the New Testament but denying that they differ in their estimate of and testimony to Jesus Christ. This is an assertion which is questioned by many New Testament scholars today. Klappert (op. cit., pp. 145–146) believes that scriptural quotations used by Barth (*C.D., IV/1,* pp. 160–164) come from later strata of the tradition and, however, correct, are in themselves insufficient to prove the point, i.e., the deity of Christ from the earliest strata. He himself, however believes that Barth's basic contention is correct but has to be defended otherwise than he (Barth) does. This could be done by pointing to the nature of the earliest strata—the Son of Man, *Mari* and *Kyrios* traditions and showing how, directly or indirectly, they do testify clearly to the true deity of Jesus Christ. For the Son of Man passages see Klappert (ibid., pp. 102–130) and for *Mari* and *Kyrios* pp. 140–141. Klappert (ibid., p. 143, n. 15) points out that the identification of the heavenly Father, his kingdom come on earth, and Jesus of Nazareth 'is for Barth an indirect confirmation of his thesis of the primitive Christian insight of the deity of Jesus quite apart from the christological titles in the narrower sense'. (Cf. *C.D., II/2,* p. 687f; *C.D., IV/2,* pp. 161, 197).
26. Ibid., pp. 161–162.
27. Ibid., p. 163.
28. Ibid., p. 162.
29. Ibid., p. 163.
30. Ibid., p. 162.
31. Ibid., p. 161.
32. Ibid., pp. 163–166. Here one can see clearly that already in his doctrine of reconciliation Barth combines in one the three aspects traditionally separated—the deity of Christ (true God), the humiliation of Christ (first 'state'), and the atonement on the cross (priestly office).
33. Op. cit., pp. 151–164.
34. *Gottes Sein ist im Werden,* pp. 97ff.
35. This is brought out by Berkouwer (op. cit., pp. 124ff), and by Jüngel, '. . . keine Menschenlosigkeit Gottes, . . .', *Ev.Th.,* vol. 31, no. 7, July 1971, pp. 376–390.
36. Op. cit., pp. 152–154.
37. Ibid., p. 152.
38. *C.D., IV/1,* pp. 161–166.
39. Ibid., p. 164.
40. Ibid., p. 165.
41. Op. cit., p. 154.
42. Kähler, *Theologische Bücher,* 2, 1956, p. 60, as cited by Klappert (op. cit.,

p. 156). Barth here uses the analysis of Formgeschichte in his interpretation.

43. *C.D.*, IV/2, p. 250. [Italics mine. J.T.]
44. *C.D.*, IV/1, p. 199.
45. Op. cit., p. 159.
46. However correct this is Barth speaks frequently in this section of the incarnation and does not oppose it to a *theologia crucis*. Cf. *C.D.*, IV/1, pp. 174, 177, 179, 184, 185, 192.
47. *C.D.*, IV/1, p. 177. [Italics mine. J.T.]
48. Ibid., p. 186; see also pp. 159, 191. Cf. *C.D.*, IV/4, p. 146; Barth's sense of irony comes out here where he takes a term he himself had earlier popularised, viz., 'Wholly Other' and uses it against his opponents who support a 'natural' knowledge of God.
49. Ibid., p. 176. Cf. Moltmann, *The Crucified God*, p. 205, for a view reflecting Barth's. Barth in no way suggests that the opposite of what we deem to be divine is divine. There is no such direct revelation in the humanity of Jesus and his humiliation on the cross. Humanly speaking it is and remains a thing of shame. For Barth, it is the mystery and miracle of God who by his revelation in the resurrection in the power of the Holy Spirit makes himself known as the One who was humbled in our humanity, in the 'flesh' and particularly on the cross.
50. Ibid.
51. Berkouwer, op. cit., p. 126.
52. *C.D.*, IV/1, p. 130.
53. Ibid.
54. Ibid., p. 166.
55. Ibid., p. 167.
56. Ibid., p. 166.
57. Ibid. See also pp. 167, 168 and 176.
58. Ibid., p. 170.
59. Ibid., pp. 167–168. See also p. 175.
60. Ibid., p. 169.
61. Ibid., p. 171.
62. Ibid., p. 175.
63. Op. cit., p. 167.
64. *C.D.*, IV/1, p. 184. [Italics mine. J.T.]
65. Ibid., p. 177. The next section will deal with the obedience of the Son to the Father which is 'the mystery of the inner being of God as the being of the Son in relation to the Father' (ibid., p. 177). These two inter-related moments Barth deduces from Mt. 11: 25–30, and its parallel in Lk. 10: 21–24. The action of Jesus in the world revealed to the 'babes' and 'foolish' in the midst of apparent failure is that of the omnipotent God. He does this in obedience to the Father as the omnipotent One who alone can reveal God.
66. Ibid., pp. 180–183.
67. Barth briefly touches on the *Kenosis* theology of seventeenth-century Lutheranism, i.e., of the Giessen and Tübingen schools. The Lutherans all held to the fullness of the deity in Jesus Christ but taught a com-

munication of some of the divine attributes to the humanity of our Lord. Yet they also taught a *Kenosis* in the state of humiliation, i.e., some form of a self-emptying of the divine qualities in the human Jesus. Giessen, following Martin Chemnitz, taught a partial abstention from use by the man Jesus, but Tübingen, following J. Brenz, taught not just abstention but a concealment of the attributes which were nonetheless used. A decision in favour of Giessen was given by the *Decisio Saxonica*, 1624, followed by the greater part of Lutheran orthodoxy. Barth regards this decision as surprising, for while Tübingen did tend to Docetism, the Giessen theory of a divine majesty and glory only partially used is far more questionable, 'is . . . logically and theologically an impossible one, an inner contradiction'. (*C.D.,* IV/1, p. 182.)

The Giessen teaching was, according to Barth, the basis for the later nineteenth century *Kenosis* theory which had great vogue both in Germany and in Britain. There were three main forms of this teaching. One, a partial or complete abstention on the part of the Logos from the use of the divine attributes while on earth—a self-limitation of God in the incarnation (Sartori). These were then regarded as being resumed again at the resurrection. The second form (Thomasius) was the retention by God the Son in the incarnation of the essential attributes of deity (love, truth, holiness) but the giving up of the so-called relative attributes (omnipotence, onniscience and omnipresence)—those by which God is related to the world. The third and more subtle form favoured by many British theologians (among others P. T. Forsyth, H. R. Mackintosh and Charles Gore) spoke not of a giving up of certain qualities or attributes but of their contraction to potency only. Side by side with a *Kenosis* they also taught a *plerosis*, a self-realisation of Jesus Christ, a resumption of all that was contracted or held in potency only—a form of self-fulfilment.

Barth believes that these forms of Kenoticism are wholly mistaken and are a real breach with traditional teaching since God cannot in any way cease to be God. The common presupposition of all 'schools' of the Church is that 'the Godhead of the man Jesus remains intact and unaltered'. (ibid., p. 183).

68. *C.D.,* IV/1, p. 184.
69. Ibid. J. Moltmann quotes C. Schmitt, *Politische Theologie*, II, 1971, p. 116, as showing that the origin of the phrase 'God against God' ('Gott gegen Gott') is Catherine of Siena. 'Gesichtspunkte der Kreuzestheologie heute', *Ev.Th.,* vol. 33, no. 4, July–August 1973, p. 352.
70. Ibid.
71. Op. cit., pp. 175ff.
72. *Christologie*, I, pp. 181–192. Cf. *C.D.,* IV/1, p. 185.
73. Ibid., p. 189.
74. Ibid., p. 192.
75. *C.D.,* IV1, p. 185.
76. Op. cit., p. 194.
77. *C.D.,* IV/1, p. 185. According to Klappert (op. cit., p. 177) Berkouwer

(op. cit., p. 309) does not distinguish between the Seinsparadox rejected by Barth and the Gerichtsparadox accepted by him.

78. Op. cit., p. 195.

79. *C.D.*, IV/1, p. 185. Cf. H. J. Iwand in *Diskussion um Kreuz und Auferstehung*, edited by B. Klappert, p. 290, and G. Gloege, 'Gott in Wiederspruch', *Theologische Literaturgeitung* (hereafter *Th.LZ*), 1951/2, p. 89.

80. *Credo*, p. 93.

81. *C.D.*, IV/1, p. 185. [Italics mine. J.T.] O. Weber (*Dogmatik*, II, p. 182) questions whether theology can be pursued without the use of paradoxical statements and says, in contrast to Barth, 'the centre of Christology is paradox'. Klappert (op. cit., p. 180) comments on this that there is no material difference between Barth and Weber since the latter also rejects the Seinsparadox in God. He quotes H. Schröer (*Denkform*, p. 151) as saying: 'With Barth the idea of mystery obviously plays the central role that paradox formerly did.' On the other hand, Barth makes many statements that have indeed a paradoxical structure and nature.

It is obvious, however, that the idea of a paradox, cleft or disunity (Entzweiung) in the being of God is not dead. It has recently been revived by J. Moltmann (*Ev.Th.*, op. cit., pp. 351–353). Moltmann's views show a new awareness of the place of the cross as basic to Christian faith and theology and is a strong confirmation of Barth's emphasis, *theologia crucis*.

Moltmann begins with the God-forsakenness of Jesus Christ on the cross. Since he is God the Son we must therefore speak of disunity between the Father and the Son—'God against God'. Moltmann believes that the gulf is absolute on the cross but is overcome in the mutual self-giving of the Father and the Son in the power of the Holy Spirit. Hence he seeks to formulate a trinitarian theology of the cross.

Moltmann's statements are provocative and somewhat one-sided. Basically he puts the matter on its head by beginning with a division and then seeking to overcome it. Moreover, he tends to isolate one aspect of the cross, that of God-forsakenness, from all the others. One must, however, begin (as Barth does) with the fact that the true God in his being as triune is revealed precisely in the humiliation and contradiction of the cross. But this shows God at peace, at one already and particularly in this act. It reveals both that he is one and triune. It is from this point of view that one should then examine the relation of Father and Son in the work of the cross rather than starting with the supposed disunity and antimony. If this is so one cannot speak so baldly, as Moltmann does, of a 'God against God'.

Two further criticisms have rightly been levelled against Moltmann at the discussion of his paper at Grafrath bei Fürstenfeldbruck, October 12th–14th, 1972 (see *Ev.Th.*, op. cit., pp. 338–339). He fails to distinguish clearly between the Father and the Son (e.g. the title of his work *The Crucified God*) in relation to the death of Christ and to see the subordination of the Son to the Father which dominates the New Testament witness (W. Schrage, E. Schweizer, F. Hahn). Secondly, he tends to make the death of Christ constitutive of his deity rather than the revelation and definition of it. His approach thus 'conceals the danger of absorbing God in the event or process in which he becomes what he is' (ibid., p. 339). There are obvious points of contact here with Process theology. Cf. also Moltmann, *The Crucified God,* pp. 241ff.

82. Ibid., p. 186.
83. Ibid.
84. Ibid. [Italics mine. J.T.]
85. Ibid., p. 187.
86. Cf. *C.D.,* I/2, pp. 1–44, where Jesus Christ the Objective Reality of Revelation is the basis of Jesus Christ the Objective Possibility of Revelation.
87. Op. cit., p. 180.
88. *C.D.,* IV/1, p. 192.
89. Ibid., p. 195.
90. Klappert, op. cit., p. 185.
91. *C.D.,* IV/1, p. 194.
92. Ibid., p. 195.
93. Ibid.
94. Ibid., p. 204.
95. Ibid., p. 203.
96. Ibid., p. 195.
97. Ibid., p. 199.
98. Op. cit., p. 184. Here again Barth uses the indirect method of argument and the way of analogy. The human Jesus in his obedient humility is not as such the divine nature and obedience but is necessarily analogous to it since it is the human correspondence to the being of God himself. It is this direction downwards in the being of God that makes the self-humiliation on the cross possible. Barth is naturally speaking here of the eternal obedience of the Son to the Father to whom he is subordinate yet with whom he is equal and one.
99. *C.D.,* IV/1, p. 195.
100. Ibid., p. 199.
101. Klappert, op. cit., p. 186.
102. *Critique of the Idea of the Obedience of the Son.* Several criticisms of this view have been made.

(*a*) Otto Weber (op. cit., pp. 181–184) feels that the 'below' is so strongly taken up into the 'above' that the history of Jesus Christ as earthly history is too easily regarded as a mere documentation of what precedes it. Klappert (op. cit., p. 188) answers this by saying that Barth does not 'speak of an eternal self-humiliation of God, of an eternal history of the condescension on the cross'. He contends that in various places Barth speaks of this as a new act of God which 'is not to be put into the shade or weakened by this reference to its inter-trinitarian background'. (*C.D.,* IV/2, p. 42.) He writes 'Barth begins with the contingency of God's being in the crucified—something that is very far removed from the idea of the earthly event of the condescension of the Son of God on the cross as a mere documentation or epiphany of the eternal, inter-trinitarian history of God. In him we have to do with God himself; in him God reveals himself as the One he is. If reconciliation reveals God himself on the cross as Father and Son, a being in the subordination and unity of this relationship then this corresponds to God. This last which is ultimate, the condescension of the Son of God in its contingency on the cross corresponds to the first, the inner history of God, without simply being identical with it or its mere epiphany' (Klappert, op. cit., p. 189).

(b) G. C. Berkouwer (op. cit., p. 304) states that 'when Barth speaks of . . . an "obedience of God" . . . he exceeds the boundaries of the *revelation* which we have in Christ', and so is purely speculative. This, however, begs the question in what way it does so. Barth believes that he has a strong scriptural basis to support him, that the God revealed in Jesus Christ, in his humiliation and cross, is a God in whom obedience is not a foreign but an inalienable and quite indispensable element. (For the Scriptural basis see *C.D.*, IV/1, pp. 190–194.) The obedience of Jesus Christ to the Father's will is not simply that of a man but as such is a reflection of the inner nature of the deity. In this way it is an integral part of revelation and no mere theosophism.

(c) Walter Kreck ('Die Lehre von der Versöhnung', Zu Karl Barth, *Kirchliche Dogmatik*, IV/1 and IV/2, *Th.LZ.*, 1960/2, p. 89) asks the question: 'Why has one to speak of an "above" and a "below", of a kind of subordination in the being of God? Does it perform the service it ought? . . . Must the humiliation . . . of Christ have its basis analogically in God himself? Is it not enough to say that the true God is such a love as is revealed in Christ's humiliation . . . instead of using analogy in this consequential way?'

To this Klappert replies by quoting Barth himself when he says that God's relation to what is outside himself, to creation, mirrors the relation which he has as triune within himself. His love expresses the will of his Being. Just as the creature (below) depends upon the Creator (above) so this corresponds to the nature of the love of God. It is not an undifferentiated love but a loving being in an inner relationship of 'above' and 'below' without in any way denying the equality of the modes of being. Klappert concludes 'It is only recourse to the inter-trinitarian Being of God, only this inter-trinitarian analogising . . . which can express the love-character of reconciliation' (op. cit., p. 191. Cf. E. Jüngel, *Gottes Sein ist im Werden*, p. 113f). It is, in other words, the love of God based on and expressed through the obedience of the Son as we see it on the cross. This is what the *love* of God has revealed him to *be*.

Barth's views (in many ways a novelty in the history of dogma—a personal remark made to me by Professor E. Jüngel, Tübingen) find a significant anticipation and confirmation in P. T. Forsyth's *Marriage: Its Ethic and Religion*, London, 1912, p. 70. Speaking of the Being of God he says: 'Now the nature of that God is Father, and Son and Holy Spirit. Father and Son co-exist, co-equal in the spirit of holiness, i.e., of perfection. But Father and Son is a relation inconceivable except the Son be obedient to the Father.

'The perfection of the Son and the perfecting of his holy work lay, not in his suffering, but in his obedience. And as he was eternal Son, it meant an eternal obedience; for the supreme work of Christ, so completely identified with his person, could not be done by anything which was not as eternal as his person.

'But obedience is not conceivable without some form of subordination. Yet in his very obedience the Son was co-equal with the Father; the Son's yielding will was no less divine than the Father's exigent will. Therefore, in the very nature of God, subordination implies no inferiority.' This has profound implications for personal relations in the family and the Church as well as for society, as Forsyth indicates. 'There is an obedience bound up with the supreme dignity of Christian love, so that where most love is, there is also most obedience' (ibid., p. 71).

NOTES TO CHAPTER FIVE

1. Otto Weber, *Karl Barths Kirchliche Dogmatik*, p. 212.
2. B. Klappert, *Die Auferweckung des Gekreuzigten*, p. 195. [Italics mine. J.T.]
3. Klappert (op. cit., pp. 194–195), states three things Barth's exposition of the atonement means: (*a*) The *pro nobis* is not to be interpreted simply as an existential-ontological *pro me*. It is the *world* that God reconciles with himself in Jesus Christ so that the '*pro me* is a function and moment of the *pro mundo*' (p. 195). (*b*) This section of the *Dogmatics* has its basis and presupposition in the preceding, i.e., in deity of Jesus Christ and is its necessary consequence. It is for this purpose that the Son of God became man. But 'these questions, according to Barth, cannot be exchanged' (p. 195). They are there in this irreversible order. (*c*) The relation between them is not that of an historical sequence of Incarnation and cross but that of two aspects of the one event both related to the cross.
4. Again Klappert (ibid., pp. 196–197) points out that the title Barth uses here—Jesus Christ as Judge—is consistent with the earliest stratum of the New Testament tradition, the Son of Man as Lord and Judge of the world, though Barth himself does not directly relate it to this tradition.
5. 'The fourfold answer describes not only the four essentials of the New Testament doctrine of the atonement but at the same time retails the four *termini* of traditional Christology: (*a*) the Judge, (*b*) Representative (*c*) Satisfaction (*d*) Righteousness.' (Klappert, op. cit., p. 198—this is a verbal statement of Prof. W. Krecks.) These are, of course, recast and filled out in a fresh way by Barth and are not simply repeated.
6. Klappert, op. cit., p. 198.
7. *C.D.,* IV/1, p. 235. [Italics mine. J.T.]
8. O'Grady, op. cit., vol. 1, p. 139, states 'This means that God's activity takes the place of man's in the work of reconciliation. "For us" means solely "in our place" (an unsere Stelle). He (Barth) insists so repeatedly

on the divine activity that he leaves no place for the cooperating activity of Christ's human nature.' This is at once both a misinterpretation of Barth and an indication of the gulf between the Reformed and the Roman teaching on the place of the human nature of Christ in the incarnation and the atonement. The atonement is all God's work (*God was in Christ reconciling*: 2 Cor. 5: 19), but since God and man are one in Jesus Christ his action is in and through the human nature assumed in the incarnation. In Barth's theology the human nature of Jesus Christ is not set aside or ignored. It does not, however, play the semi-independent, sub-operative role in atonement that O'Grady believes and therefore to a secondary degree co-operates in Christ's redemptive activity. This is wholly contrary to the biblical and Reformed teaching and to this extent it is God alone, but God in Christ who is active. For this reason one must reject O'Grady's position since it endangers the sovereign grace of God, and exemplifies clearly the chief barrier still existing between Evangelical and Roman Catholic Dogmatics.

9. *C.D.*, IV/1, p. 231.
10. Ibid., pp. 224ff.
11. Ibid., p. 217.
12. Ibid., p. 219.
13. Ibid., p. 225.
14. Ibid., p. 232.
15. Ibid., p. 238.
16. Ibid., p. 231. See also pp. 219–220, 231–233, 400–403, 445–453.
17. Ibid., p. 451.
18. Ibid., p. 220.
19. Ibid.
20. Ibid., p. 232.
21. Ibid.
22. Ibid., p. 233. [Italics mine. J.T.] The one who does this is both true God and true man.
23. Op. cit., p. 200.
24. Klappert, ibid., pp. 200–201, speaks of this as a 'correction and new interpretation of the traditional, doctrinal "picture of Christ in the preaching of the late Middle Ages which shows him as Judge" ' (E. Wolf, 'Die Christus verkundigung bei Luther', in Peregrinatio, *Studien zur reformatorischen Theologie und zum Kirchenproblem*, 1962, vol. 1, p. 38). Cf. *Dogmatics in Outline*, English translation, London, 1960 Reprint, p. 134, where Barth quotes the Heidelberg Catechism, Question and Answer 52, which speaks of Christ as Judge as a 'comfort' whose coming I await 'with my head erect' 'who before yielded himself to the judgment of God *for me* and took away all malediction from me' [Italics Mine. J.T.]. On this Barth comments: 'A different note is struck here, Jesus Christ's return to judge . . . is tidings of joy' (ibid.).
25. Klappert, ibid., p. 200.
26. *C.D.*, IV/1, p. 217. Cf. *Dogmatics in Outline*, p. 135.
27. Ibid., p. 216. Klappert (op. cit., p. 201) points out that the same

teaching is found in the New Testament idea of Jesus as Son of Man and Judge of the world, 'whose function is primarily to forgive sins (Mark 2: 10). This is seen in his right of disposal over the Sabbath which was created by God for man (2: 28), in his fellowship at table with tax-gatherers and sinners (Matthew 11: 19), in gathering the elect (Mark 13: 26ff), in giving himself for the many (10: 45), Who as such is judge (8: 38; Luke 12: 9), Who comes to judge the world (Matthew 25: 31)'.

28. Ibid., p. 222.
29. Ibid., p. 235.
30. Ibid.
31. Ibid., pp. 237–238.
32. Ibid., p. 264. Cf. pp. 235, 239. Own translation.
33. Ibid., p. 226. See p. 238.
34. Ibid., p. 238.
35. Ibid., p. 227.
36. Ibid., p. 239.
37. Ibid., pp. 239–240.
38. Ibid., p. 236. Colin Brown (op. cit., p. 134) questions Barth and disagrees with him at this point. 'What Barth seems to have done is to misconstrue the universal significance of Christ. Barth has made him the universal object of judgment. The New Testament depicts him as the universal criterion of judgment. . . . To all he is Judge. But only to those who receive him, who are in Christ, is he judged in their place.'
But this is an even less acceptable position than Barth's for two reasons. (*a*) If Christ's substitutionary atonement is only for those who are 'in Christ', Brown must hold to a limited atonement. Christ died only for the elect. For the New Testament, on the contrary, Christ's judgment, which he accepted in becoming sin for us is as universal as the atonement. (*b*) Brown fails to distinguish between the judgment Christ bore for us on the cross and the judgment we await at the end. Barth does not deny the possibility of some being excluded at the last.
39. Ibid., p. 237.
40. Cf. Klappert, op. cit., pp. 205–206.
41. *C.D.*, IV/1, p. 492.
42. Ibid.
43. Ibid., p. 500.
44. Ibid., p. 403; cf. p. 406.
45. Ibid., p. 405 and p. 492.
46. Ibid., p. 406.
47. Ibid., p. 404.
48. Ibid., p. 405.
49. O. Weber, *Dogmatik*, II, p. 346.
50. This is Barth's answer to those who, like George S. Hendry, *The Gospel of the Incarnation*, London, 1959, p. 127, criticise the concept of substitution which seems to remove man together with his sin. Cf. for a view similar to Barth's, James D. G. Dunn, 'Paul's Understanding of the Death of Jesus' in *Reconciliation and Hope*, edited by Robert Burke

(Eerdman, Michigan), 1974. Dunn writes: 'His [Jesus's] death was the end of fallen man, the destruction of man as sinner. But only those who, like the offerer of old, identify themselves with the sacrifice, may know the other half of the chiasmus, the life of Christ beyond the death of sin, the righteousness of God' (ibid., p. 137).

51. There are three conclusions to be drawn from this: (*a*) Jesus Christ reveals what we are—sinners—by being what we are in our place. (*b*) Jesus Christ reveals what we are by taking our sin—a sin that remains ours—upon himself, bearing it and so forgiving it. (*c*) Jesus Christ reveals what we are by bearing away what we are so that we are no longer sinners but righteous in and through him. (*C.D.,* IV/1, pp. 240–242).

Klappert points out (op. cit., pp. 205–208) that Barth deepens and corrects three traditional ideas of the atonement in this section. (*a*) Since one cannot separate sin as a thing from the sinner who commits it, it is we in our totality who are condemned as sinners. Christ is our representative, takes the place of the sinner and does not simply remove an obstacle, 'sin', but the sinner. This is 'a christological-personal understanding of substitution'. It represents a deepening of the view of atonement as the simple removal of sin to that of personal relationships. (*b*) At the same time there is also 'a correction of an idea of substitution which is orientated to guilt and punishment, *meritum* and *imputatio*' (ibid. p. 207). Sin is not something which can be weighed and punished like a thing, nor can it be removed by merit imputed to us; it is personal and as such is personally borne and borne away by Jesus Christ, and so there is atonement. (*c*) Again it is a critique of Socinianism which regards the work of Christ as primarily exemplary, showing us an obedience we have to follow. Barth, on the contrary, argues that man himself, needs to be judged, helped, and saved.

One can compare here John Rodgers's (*The Theology of P. T. Forsyth,* London, 1965, pp. 287–288) exposition of Forsyth's doctrine of the atonement with Barth's. They show considerable similarity.

52. *C.D.,* IV/1, p. 244.
53. Klappert, op. cit., p. 209.
54. *C.D.,* IV/1, p. 235.
55. Ibid., p. 238.
56. Ibid., pp. 244–245.
57. Op. cit., p. 210.
58. *Jesus, God and Man,* pp. 245ff. Cf. Klappert, op. cit., pp. 210–214 for the following.
59. Pannenberg, ibid., p. 245. [Italics mine. J.T.]
60. Ibid.
61. *Exegetica. Aufsätze zur Erforschung des Neuen Testaments,* edited by E. Dinkler, 1967, p. 453.
62. *Exegetische Versuche und Besinnungen,* II, 1964, p. 55f.
63. *New Testament Studies,* 1961/2, p. 207.
64. Klappert, op. cit., p. 212.
65. Op. cit., p. 245.

66. *New Testament Theology*, Vol. I, *The Proclamation of Jesus*, English translation, London, 1971, pp. 276ff.
67. Op. cit., pp. 212–213.
68. Ibid., p. 286.
69. Ibid., p. 288.
70. *C.D.*, IV/1, p. 245; cf. ibid., p. 225, where Barth speaks of 'obvious reminiscences' in the Gospel records and also passages which are palpably '*Vaticinia ex eventu*'.
71. Ibid., p. 244.
72. Ibid., p. 245.
73. Ibid.
74. Ibid., p. 237.
75. Ibid., p. 245.
76. Ibid., pp. 245, 246 and 265.
77. Ibid., p. 246.
78. Ibid.
79. Ibid., pp. 246–247.
80. Ibid., p. 251.
81. Ibid.
82. Klappert, op. cit., p. 217. 'This is the centre of Barth's doctrine of reconciliation.' Ibid., p. 216.
83. Jüngel, *Gottes Sein ist im Werden*, p. 99. Cf. *C.D.*, IV/2, pp. 84–85, where Barth says 'it is only the pride of man, making a god in its own image' (ibid., p. 84) that could not accept this. This presupposition affected the Christology of the early Church and Reformed and Lutheran orthodoxy. 'This presupposition was a Greek conception of God, according to which God was far too exalted for . . . his incarnation and therefore the reconciliation of the world and himself, to mean anything at all for himself, or in any way to affect his Godhead' (ibid., pp. 84–85). For Barth, on the contrary, the divine immutability is so interpreted that, while it does not mean a change in God, it can envisage and encompass his suffering as man and with and for man. G. C. Berkouwer (op. cit., pp. 297ff) gives a lengthy critique of Theopaschitism (the idea of the suffering of God) in ancient and modern theology and rejects its premises. He sees it, however, as an attempt to affirm and preserve the unity of the person of Jesus Christ over against Nestorianism but as an attempt which fails.

　　Jürgen Moltmann, 'Gesichtspunkte der Kreuzestheologie heute', *Ev.Th.*, vol. 33, no. 4, July/August 1973, pp. 353–363, takes the opposite point of view and as a result is much closer to Barth. He is critical of the *apatheia* theology of antiquity for its static concepts which influenced Christian thought and speaks rather of *Patricompassianismus*, thereby indicating opposition to the kind of Theopaschitism of the 'God is dead' theology and acceptance of a limited view of the suffering of God in the context of the Trinity. See also Moltmann, *The Crucified God*, pp. 267ff. J. S. Whale, *The Impassibility of God*, Cambridge, 1926, passim.
84. *C.D.*, IV/2, p. 357. Cf. David Jenkins, *The Glory of Man*, S.C.M., London, 1967, p. 106f, who argues, along the same lines as Barth, that

the traditional belief in the unchangeableness of God can be allied to that of his compassion and suffering.

85. Op. cit., p. 101.
86. Op. cit., p. 218.
87. *C.D.*, IV/1, p. 254.
88. Ibid., p. 255.
89. Ibid., p. 253. Barth is prepared to say that Jesus Christ suffered our punishment but only in the sense outlined above. It is therefore only in this limited way that his 'substitutionary' theory of the atonement can be regarded as 'penal'.

Again it should not be thought that because he is critical of Anselm Barth minimises or disagrees with the idea of the wrath of God. God's wrath is the burning fire of his love (*C.D.*, IV/1, p. 393) which cannot brook opposition and rebellion but must destroy it as evil. At the same time this judgment is unto salvation.

90. Ibid., pp. 254–255. In this section Barth not only reinterprets Anselm but also introduces another aspect of the atonement—again a divine work, viz., the *Christus Victor* aspect. His satisfactory work is the triumph of God's grace over man's sin.
91. Ibid., p. 256.
92. Ibid.
93. Ibid.
94. Op. cit., p. 222.
95. Ibid., p. 223.
96. *C.D.*, IV/1, p. 257.
97. Ibid.
98. Ibid., pp. 257–258.
99. Ibid., p. 258.
100. Op. cit., pp. 223–224.
101. *C.D.*, IV/1, p. 273.
102. Ibid., p. 275.
103. Ibid., pp. 275–283.
104. It would be impossible here to enter into a full discussion of the many differences between Barth and Bultmann on the atonement. For a full discussion the reader is referred to B. Klappert (op. cit., pp. 264–272). Here only one point will be mentioned. Barth is against both the more extreme and the more guarded statements of Bultmann in this respect. On the one hand he is against the idea that Jesus Christ first has significance as he comes in the *kerygma* and finds obedience among his hearers. On the other hand Bultmann has clearly stated that the significance of the event of salvation does not depend on my decision. Nonetheless he does not clearly base the significance for us on what is significant, i.e., on the objective reality of Jesus Christ the Reconciler. In contrast Barth makes the latter the sole basis and criterion of the former. It is precisely at this point that one of the main differences between Barth and Bultmann emerges.

Another way of putting this is that for Barth the once for all event of reconciliation on the cross implies and includes an historical event. It is not to be understood as giving content to existential-ontological structures derived from elsewhere, i.e., a pre-understanding nor as being realised only in the repeated word of proclamation.

NOTES TO CHAPTER SIX

1. *C.D.,* III/2, p. 43.
2. Ibid, p. 44.
3. H. Hartwell, op. cit., p. 123.
4. *C.D.,* III/2, p. 52.
5. Ibid., p. 57.
6. Ibid., p. 58.
7. Barth devotes a whole section to this—Jesus as whole man (*C.D.,* III/2, pp. 325–344)—in which he shows that soul and body are one in him in a relationship made real by the Holy Spirit.
8. Cf. Heinrich Vogel, *Gott in Christo,* pp. 657–671, where he distinguishes between the two. Real man is man both as natural and as fallen. True man is man as the image of God in full fellowship with God showing his glory. This is very similar to Barth's position.
9. *C.D.,* III/2, p. 209.
10. For a similar view see Walter Kasper, *Jesus der Christus,* Mainz, 1975, pp. 231ff.
11. For a brief summary of this section, see Stuart D. McLean, 'The Humanity of Man in Karl Barth's Thought', *SJT,* vol. 28, no. 2, 1975, pp. 127–134.
12. John A. T. Robinson, *Honest to God,* S.C.M., London, 1963, pp. 64–83.
13. In a previous section (*C.D.,* III/2, pp. 55–71) Barth spoke of Jesus as man for God, i.e., man in whom God's work of grace is fully accomplished, who wholly serves his purposes of reconciliation. Barth calls this his divinity, meaning thereby the unique origin and divine determination of this man, his union and identity with God.
14. *C.D.,* III/2, p. 209.
15. Ibid., p. 210.
16. Cf. McLean, op. cit., pp. 128–130.
17. *C.D.,* III/2, p. 214.
18. Ibid., p. 215.
19. Ibid., p. 216.
20. Ibid.
21. The biblical basis Barth gives for this interpretation is that of the two-fold law of God—for God and the neighbour (Mk. 12: 29–31, and par). Jesus in his humanity for others (love to man) corresponds to, is analogous with his being for God (love to God).
22. *C.D.,* III/2, p. 217.
23. Ibid.
24. Ibid., p. 218.
25. Ibid.
26. Ibid., pp. 218–219.

27. Ibid., p. 219. Cf. *T.T.*, p. 57, where Barth writes, 'image has a double meaning: God lives in togetherness with himself (the Original), then God lives in togetherness with man (first Image), then men live in togetherness with one another (a second Image)'. Cf. McLean, op. cit., p. 132. *Imago dei* is therefore to be understood as being in relationship which as such is a correspondence to God himself. Barth has here modified his previous idea of the image as God's likeness in man destroyed by the Fall. Now it is this interpersonal relationship in Jesus Christ and between people which reflects the unity and tri-unity of God himself.

28. See *C.D.*, IV/1, pp. 192–204. Cf. Chapter 4 above.

29. *C.D.*, III/2, p. 219.

30. Ibid.

31. Ibid.

32. Ibid., pp. 219–220.

33. Ibid., p. 220.

34. 'Die Möglichkeit theologischer Anthropologie auf dem Grunde der Analogie', *Ev.Th.*, vol. 22, no. 10, October 1962, pp. 541–542.

35. J. Y. Lee ('Karl Barth's use of Analogy in his Church Dogmatics', *SJT*, vol. 22, no. 2, June 1969, p. 150) writes, 'Barth's *analogia relationis* presupposes the *analogia entis* in so far as the latter is based on a dynamic and living ontology'. This, however, is to make the distinction between Barth and Roman Catholicism the simple one of a static or dynamic ontology whereas the real differences is christological, i.e., whether the relationships between God and man are wholly based on the divine revelation in Jesus Christ or have also a partial basis elsewhere. Others who wrongly think as Lee are: O'Grady (op. cit., vol. I, p. 95), Von Balthasar (op. cit., p. 175f), and A. B. Come (*An Introduction to Barth's Dogmatics for Preachers*, London, 1964, p. 147).

36. A. B. Come, op. cit., p. 147.

37. This interpretation of the cross as the integrating factor of the earthly life of Jesus and so the key to the meaning of his existence was pointed out originally by E. Jüngel (*Parrhesia. Karl Barth zum achtzigsten Gerburtstag am 10 Mai 1966*, Zürich, 1966, p. 82f) and is taken up and used extensively by B. Klappert, *Die Auferweckung des Gekreuzigten* (see p.160). Cf. *C.D.*, IV/2, p. 131, where Barth speaks of the 'history and existence' of Jesus and 'the integrating factor that he has risen again from the dead'.

38. Chapter 4.

39. *C.D.*, IV/1, pp. 157–210.

40. *C.D.*, IV/2, p. 24. The elder brother represents man who rejects Jesus Christ as God the Son humbled and Son of Man exalted.

41. Ibid.

42. Ibid., p. 29.

43. Ibid.

44. Ibid., pp. 29–30.

45. Ibid., p. 30.

46. Ibid.

47. Ibid.
48. *C.D.*, I/2, p. 156.
49. *C.D.*, IV/2, p. 30.
50. In the succeeding exposition *C.D.*, IV/2, pp. 31–154, Barth discusses three further aspects of this exaltation (1) In the divine election of grace. (2) In the incarnation and resurrection. (3) In the union and communion of God and man in Jesus Christ, i.e., in the hypostatic union and the communication of grace.
51. See *C.D.*, IV/2, pp. 154–264.
52. *C.D.*, IV/2, p. 250. [Italics mine. J.T.] This clearly goes back to and reflects the strong influence of the thought of Martin Kähler on Barth's whole attitude to the Gospel records. See Daniel L. Deegan, 'Martin Kähler: Kerygma and Gospel History', *SJT*, vol. 16, no. 1, March 1963, p. 58.
53. Ibid., p. 133.
54. Ibid., p. 299.
55. Op. cit., p. 315f. In this Barth combines the true humanity of Jesus with his exaltation and his kingly office.
56. *C.D.*, IV/2, p. 141; see also pp. 254 and 256.
57. Klappert, op. cit., p. 315. Cf. *C.D.*, IV/2, p. 291. 'His resurrection revealed him as the One who reigns in virtue of his death, from the cross (*regnantem in cruce*).'
58. *C.D.*, IV/2, p. 290.
59. Ibid., p. 292.
60. Ibid.
61. Cf. Gustaf Aulen, *Christus Victor*, English translation, London, 1965, where he sees this as the classical statement of the atonement. This is saying too much but it is nevertheless a very central and significant aspect.
62. Barth argues (*C.D.*, IV/2, pp. 255–258) that this emphasis on the cross as already Christ's victory is in line both with the Gospels and the Pauline epistles. In the former the cross is the climax of their witness and in John is both glorification and exaltation, while in Paul the significance of the life of Christ is concentrated on the cross in the light of the resurrection. J. L. Blair ('The Relation of the Incarnation to the Atonement', *SJT*, vol. 16, no. 1, March 1963, p. 70), while agreeing with this in general, states that 'oftener the victory is identified with the resurrection and exaltation'.
63. *C.D.*, IV/2, p. 132.
64. Ibid., p. 290.
65. Ibid., p. 295.
66. Ibid.
67. Ibid.
68. Ibid., p. 296.
69. Op. cit., pp. 236ff.
70. *Grundfragen der Dogmatik, Einführung in die evangelische Theologie*, vol. 3, Munich, 1970, pp. 84ff, 96ff, 277–279.
71. Op. cit., pp. 368–377.

72. Ibid., p. 86.
73. Ibid., p. 87.
74. Ibid. Klappert (op. cit., p. 374) agrees with Kreck when he summarizes Barth's position thus: 'The coincidence of the humiliation of the Son of God and the exaltation of the man Jesus on the cross includes . . . the temporal succession of the *exinanitio* (humiliation) of the Son of God on the cross and the *glorificatio* (exaltation) of the man Jesus in the resurrection.'
75. *C.D.,* IV/2, p. 139.
76. Op. cit., p. 279.
77. Ibid., p. 87.
78. Ibid., p. 279.
79. Op. cit., pp. 240–241.
80. *C.D.,* IV/2, p. 117.
81. Op. cit., p. 240.
82. Ibid.
83. Ibid., p. 242.

NOTES TO CHAPTER SEVEN

1. In each of the three parts of Volume IV of the *Church Dogmatics* Barth first sets out what God has done in Jesus Christ in reconciliation. He has revealed himself in the self-humiliation of the Son on the cross and so atoned (IV/1). He has exalted man in Jesus Christ to fellowship with himself (IV/2) and as the God-man he bears witness to himself as the light of life (IV/3). Barth then proceeds to speak of the subjective realization of this in man and in the world. But before doing so he shows that the transition from Christ's life to ours is not an obvious reality or truth. Whence do we know that what God has done in Christ includes, concerns, and is applicable to us? The answer is in the power of the resurrection and by the Holy Spirit. The transition is therefore not something that we can make but which God does in this way. Hence we have in IV/1 'The Verdict of the Father' (pp. 283–357), i.e., on the work of the Son in the awakening; in IV/2 'The Direction of the Son' (pp. 264–377) in the exaltation of man in the resurrection; and in IV/3, 1 'The Promise of the Spirit' (pp. 274–367) in which comprehensive treatment is given to the resurrection and the work of the Holy Spirit.

2. In an exhaustive survey Klappert has sought to show that for Barth the awakening is related primarily to the Son of God humbled on the cross whereas the resurrection is particularly associated with the man Jesus exalted and so reigning from the tree. In general terms this is correct but it should not be made as exclusive as Klappert does. In John D. Godsey's review of Barth's *Church Dogmatics* ('The Architecture of Karl Barth's Church Dogmatics', *T.T.*, pp. 1–12) Barth himself replied to Godsey 'Very good, but perhaps you have been more consistent than the work itself! I see more complexities—even contradictions!' (ibid.,

p. 12)—One needs to have a similar reservation in regard to Klappert.

3. *C.D.*, IV/1, p. 303. Own translation.

4. Ibid.

5. The difference is very much obscured in the English translation by failure sufficiently to distinguish between these two.

6. *C.D.*, IV/1, p. 304. It is again obvious how in his interpretation of the awakening and the resurrection Barth keeps close to the formula of Chalcedon. For it is as 'very God and very man that he (Jesus Christ) is worthy of the divine gift of new life' (ibid.). Cf. *C.D.*, III/2, p. 448.

7. Cf. Klappert, op. cit., pp. 291–293.

8. Cf. *C.D.*, III/2, pp. 447ff.

9. Cf. Klappert, op. cit., pp. 291ff.

10. *C.D.*, IV/1, pp. 301–304. Cf. Klappert, op. cit., pp. 293–294.

11. Klappert, op. cit., p. 294.

12. *C.D.*, IV/1, p. 300.

13. Ibid.

14. Ibid. Barth clearly follows K. H. Rengstorff closely here (so Klappert, op. cit., p. 294). Klappert quotes Rengstorff (*Die Auferstehung Jesu*, p. 27) as follows 'Right up to the burial of Jesus is history . . . a history in which, as in all other history, human thoughts, plans, possibilities, influences and powers work themselves out. It forms in whole and in part a section of human history. But with the burial of Jesus this kind of history comes to an end. In what follows man has no part in causing it. The sphere in which it happens lies outside of human possibilities; it is the realm of God, his exclusive domain.'

15. Ibid. By this Barth means two things: (*a*) It cannot be proved by historical argument or deduced from historical causes or known as 'the result of human will and activity' (*C.D.*, IV/1, p. 301). It is God's act alone. (*b*) However, it really took place at a particular time and place and so can be historically dated and given a particular locality. Hence we cannot simply say, as is the tendency of the Bultmann school, that Christ's connection with history ended at the cross.

16. Ibid., p. 301. [Italics mine. J.T.]

17. Ibid.

18. Op. cit., p. 298.

19. Ibid., p. 301. Barth is here polemicising against Bultmann. Both see the cross and resurrection in their unity as an eschatological event where God acts for man's salvation. Bultmann, however, sees the resurrection largely as the reverse side of the cross, i.e., as showing its meaning. He writes, *'faith in the resurrection is really the same thing as faith in the saving efficacy of the cross,* faith in the cross as the cross of Christ'. (*Kerygma and Myth*, vol. 1, edited by Hans Werner Bartsch, English translation, London, S.P.C.K., 1953, p. 41.) The two—cross and resurrection—merge and are realized in the *kerygma*.

For Barth on the contrary the saving nature and divine revelation of the cross are only real and true because the awakening is a real event and a new act of God with objective reality and content. According to Barth there is a differentiated relationship between the cross and the resurrection. The cross is a negative action with a positive purpose whereas the resurrection reveals this purpose but has always this negative event as its presupposition (*C.D.*, IV/1, pp. 309ff).

20. Klappert, op. cit., p. 299.
21. Ibid., p. 302.
22. *C.D.*, IV/1, p. 303.
23. *Credo*, p. 98.
24. Ibid., p. 91.
25. *C.D.*, IV/1, p. 303. Own translation.
26. *Gott in Christo*, pp. 739ff.
27. Op. cit., p. 303.
28. Klappert (op. cit., pp. 301–305, n. 19) shows that Barth has modified his views on this point and queries the correctness of his final conclusion. He sets out the following five views:

   (*a*) Jesus Christ was awakened in his humanity but arose in his divinity (*Credo*, pp. 91, 98, 100). H. Vogel (*Christologie*, I, p. 741) also mentions this view.

   (*b*) Awakening and resurrection are interchangeable terms for the same event, the former, the act of God the Father, the latter that of the Son (*C.D.*, III/3, p. 440; H. Vogel, op. cit., p. 739f).

   (*c*) The awakening is the act of the Father (the Son, passive) and the resurrection the (active) revelation of the Son to the disciples (*C.D.*, IV/1, p. 303). This is the position Barth finally accepted thus rejecting or modifying the two earlier views (*a*) and (*b*) above.

   (*d*) Others regard the two terms as interchangeable (Vogel and Weber) but Vogel (op. cit., p. 739f) sees them nonetheless as passive and active respectively, whereas Weber (*Dogmatik* II, p. 89) sees both terms as basically passive in meaning. Klappert agrees with this.

   (*e*) Klappert agrees with Barth that awakening indicates the passive and leads to the appearances in this irreversible order but believes that the Son is passive in both awakening and resurrection.

29. *C.D.*, IV/1, p. 303; Gal. 1: 1; Rom. 6: 4, where the Subject is God the Father.
30. Ibid.
31. Ibid., p. 304.
32. Ibid.
33. Ibid.
34. Ibid.
35. Ibid.
36. Op. cit., pp. 305–306.
37. Ibid., p. 307.
38. *C.D.*, III/2, p. 448.
39. *C.D.*, IV/1, p. 301.
40. Ibid., p. 176. This last phrase is omitted in the English translation.
41. Klappert, op. cit., p. 298.
42. Retrospective means that from the vantage point of the resurrection one can look back and see the truth of his being, life and action as a whole. What Pannenberg means by retroactive is far from clear. It does

not mean that the resurrection makes Jesus divine or noetically confirms our knowledge that he is so but rather confirms and establishes the pre-Easter claims of Jesus that he is one with God. In other words these claims have an ontic basis and reality in the resurrection and without it would not be true (*Jesus, God and Man*, pp. 136–137).

43. There were of course 'preliminary manifestations of glory'; 'anticipatory exceptions' (*C.D.*, III/2, p. 449; *C.D.*, IV/1, p. 301; *C.D.*, IV/2, p. 141), e.g., Baptism (*C.D.*, III/2, p. 479), Transfiguration (*C.D.*, III/2, p. 478), signs, miracles of Jesus (*Dogmatics in Outline*, p. 102), confession of Peter (*C.D.*, IV/1, p. 301), Jesus's word before the Sanhedrin (*C.D.*, III/2, p. 503; *C.D.*, IV/2, p. 137). Klappert quotes Schniewind who states that 'careful historical research must meet traces of this epiphany for, where its traces disappear, historical work is invalidated'. Klappert himself writes: 'But the pre-Easter history of Jesus remains, according to Barth, basically, therefore, limited to these anticipatory exceptions. This is because the awakening as the exemplary revelation has the completed self-humiliation of the Son of God on the cross as a real form of revelation *sub contrario* as its presupposition' (op. cit., p. 297). Hence in this light the previous life of Jesus is, as a whole, genuine revelation. Jüngel (*Unterwegs Zur Sache*, Theologische Bemerkurgen, Munich, 1972, pp. 139–140, n. 34) believes that Barth modified his earlier views by stating that revelation was only 'latent' in the previous life of Jesus. He quotes Barth on the resurrection as follows: 'He (Jesus Christ) moves out from the *latency* of his being and action of yesterday and from the *inoperativeness* of his power, appearing to the disciples . . . declaring himself, making known his presence, and what had been accomplished in him for all men and for the whole created order, putting it into effect.' (*C.D.*, IV/3, 1, p. 291. [Italics mine. J.T.])

44. *C.D.*, III/2, p. 449.
45. See *C.D.*, IV/2, pp. 133, 154, 252, 285–287, 297.
46. Ibid., p. 285.
47. Ibid., p. 133.
48. Ibid.
49. Ibid., p. 131–134.
50. Ibid., p. 134. Cf. p. 140 for a similar definition.
51. Ibid., p. 133.
52. Ibid., p. 141.
53. Ibid., p. 142.
54. Ibid., pp. 132–133. [Italics mine. J.T.] Cf. Klappert, op.cit., pp.316–317.
55. Ibid., p. 142. [Italics mine. J.T.]
56. Op. cit., p. 316.
57. Ibid., p. 322.
58. Ibid.
59. *C.D.*, IV/2, p. 154.
60. Op. cit., p. 322. Cf. *C.D.*, IV/2, p. 153. Jesus exalted to the Father meant that he was 'placed as man at the side of God, in direct fellowship with him, in full participation in his glory'.
61. *C.D.*, IV/2, p. 144.

62. Ibid., pp. 144–145.
63. Ibid., p. 145. In this connection Barth points to the Emmaus story and the breaking of bread, to the similarity to the Lord's Supper and the feeding of the five thousand (*C.D.,* IV/2, p. 145). The physical touching is also important where 'He gave himself to be known by them as the Crucified' (ibid.)—a specific repudiation of Docetism (*C.D.,* III/2, p. 448). 'It is the fact that the Risen Christ can be touched which puts it beyond all doubt that he is the man Jesus and no one else' (ibid.). So Barth speaks not of a merely spiritual resurrection or of a transformed bodily presence but of a bodily and real presence of the man Jesus with his own after his rising from the dead.

For Barth, then, these bodily manifestations are no mere embarrassing accretions, 'the progressive materialisation of the appearances of Jesus' (James Denney, *Jesus and the Gospel,* London, 1909, p. 143), but real pointers to his true humanity. Denney, while not accepting completely the argument against such manifestations, draws a line at the eating and drinking of Jesus and states: 'Eating is a function which belongs to the reality of this life, but not to that of immortality; and there does seem something which is not only incongruous but repellent in the idea of the Risen Lord eating' (ibid., p. 146). Barth seems to be able to combine this conception with that of a change of form in the being of the Risen Lord.

64. *C.D.,* IV/3, 1, p. 311.
65. Ibid.
66. Ibid., p. 312.
67. *Credo,* p. 100.
68. Ibid. [Italics mine. J.T.]
69. *C.D.,* IV/3, 1, p. 312.
70. Myth is not adequate to describe this event but 'saga' and 'legend' are (*C.D.,* IV/1, p. 336).
71. *C.D.,* IV/1, p. 336; cf. pp. 333ff for fuller treatment of this point. See also Klappert, op. cit., pp. 325ff. This is contrary to the view of Rudolf Bultmann that the resurrection is not an historical event but is primarily the rise of the faith of the first disciples in the crucified Lord. However, it is probably fairer to Bultmann to say, as does Weber, that 'neither Bultmann nor Barth . . . want to deny the reality of the resurrection, i.e., of the fact of the Risen Lord' (op. cit., p. 83).
72. *Dogmatik,* II, p. 88.
73. Ibid.
74. *C.D.,* IV/3, 1, p. 310.
75. Ibid., p. 311.
76. Ibid., p. 312.
77. Ibid., pp. 311–312.
78. Ibid., p. 312.
79. Ibid. (Italics mine. J.T.]
80. Ibid., p. 313.
81. Ibid., p. 312.
82. *C.D.,* III/2, p. 443, where Barth quotes Bultmann as saying that the

event of Easter is 'the rise of faith in the risen Lord, since it was this faith which led to the apostolic preaching' (*Kerygma and Myth* 1, English translation, p. 42). To this Barth replies: 'This will not do. Faith in the risen Lord springs from his historical manifestation, and from this as such, not from the rise of faith in him' (ibid., p. 443; cf. *C.D.*, IV/1, p. 341).

83. *C.D.*, IV/3, 1, p. 312; cf. *C.D.*, III/2, p. 448.
84. Ibid.
85. Ibid.

NOTES TO CHAPTER EIGHT

1. For a fuller discussion of this subject see the present writer's article 'The Humanity of God in the Theology of Karl Barth', *SJT*, vol. 29, no. 3, 1976, pp. 249–269.
2. *The Humanity of God*, English translation, London, 1961, p. 42.
3. *C.D.*, II/2, p. 7.
4. Ibid., p. 110.
5. For an excellent summary and interpretation, to which I am much indebted, see Eberhard Jüngel '... keine Menschenlosigkeit Gottes...', *Ev.Th.*, vol. 31, no. 7, July 1971, pp. 376–390.
6. *C.D.*, II/2, p. 7.
7. *The Humanity of God*, p. 43.
8. Jüngel, op. cit., p. 382.
9. *The Humanity of God*, p. 44. This extract is a succinct summary of the greater part of Barth's *Church Dogmatics*.
10. Jüngel, op. cit., p. 387.
11. Jüngel, *Unterwegs zur Sache, Thesen zur Grundlegung der Christologie 2*, 284, Munich 1972, p. 289.
12. Jüngel, ibid., p. 290.
13. *The Humanity of God*, p. 44.
14. Jüngel, '... keine Menschenlosigkeit Gottes...', op. cit., pp. 380ff, and 384ff.
15. *The Humanity of God*, p. 45.
16. *C.D.*, II/2, pp. 6–7.
17. Ibid., p. 5.
18. Jüngel, op. cit., p. 382.
19. *C.D.*, II/2, p. 6.
20. Jüngel, op. cit., p. 384.
21. *C.D.*, IV/1, p. 66.
22. *C.D.*, IV/2, pp. 100–101.
23. Ibid., pp. 93–94.
24. *The Humanity of God*, p. 46.
25. Ibid., p. 47.
26. Ibid. It does not mean that God would not be God without man or that he has any need of him to fulfil his own being. 'It is not as though God stands in need of another as his partner, and in particular of man, in

order to be truly God' (p. 47). He would be and is sufficient in himself and no lonely God without man and the universe. However, he has chosen to be the God of man.

27. Ibid., p. 48.
28. Ibid., p. 49.
29. Op. cit., p. 384.
30. Jüngel, ibid, p. 388.
31. Cf. *C.D.*, IV/1, pp. 478–513, 'The Fall of Man'.
32. *C.D.*, II/2, p. 317.
33. Ibid.
34. *C.D.*, IV/1, pp. 480–481.
35. Op. cit., p. 388.
36. Ibid., p. 389. The theory of 'anonymous Christianity' teaches that 'all men of goodwill . . . "somehow" belong to the Church'. (Hans Küng, *On Being a Christian*, English translation, London, 1977, p. 98.) Küng, like Barth rejects this but it has been popularised by Karl Rahner and A. Röper (see Küng, ibid., p. 617).
37. Ibid., p. 378. See n. 4, *Atheismus im Christentum*, Frankfurt, 1968, p. 98.
38. Ibid., p. 380.
39. Ibid., p. 381.
40. *C.D.*, IV/1, p. 159.
41. Op. cit., p. 384.
42. Ibid., p. 385.
43. *C.D.*, IV/1, p. 422.
44. Ibid.
45. Ibid.
46. Op. cit., p. 386.
47. Ibid., p. 385.
48. *C.D.*, IV/2, p. 84.
49. Jüngel, op. cit., p. 386.
50. *C.D.*, IV/3, p. 448.
51. *C.D.*, IV/2, p. 101. Otto Weber (*Dogmatik*, II, pp. 142–143) agrees with Barth at this point. His position could be put like this. Let us suppose, he says in effect, that the eternal Logos is conceived as a *Logos asarkos*. What are the consequences? It means 'that we are to think of the Son of God "in himself", apart from the man Jesus' (ibid., p. 143), that our conception of God or the Trinity is to that extent divorced from the incarnation. We would know a God *in abstracto* but not God *in concreto* since we would begin not with the event of God's self-revelation but with a pure being of God. Moreover, God's action in Christ would be one episode amongst others and not an event of permanent and eternal significance affecting all men. The best that we can say of a *Logos asarkos* is that it is a limiting concept. W. Pannenberg, *Jesus, God and Man*, p. 394, n. 65, is in full agreement with both Weber and Barth at this point.

If this is the view of traditional Christology it is rightly criticised since such a *Logos asarkos* would be a speculation, would in fact be, as Barth states, an idol, the original of all the false gods that men worship. That there are such tendencies in the traditional view cannot be denied. However, as we have seen, the *Logos asarkos* of traditional doctrine was regarded as a consequence of the *Logos ensarkos*. It is from the word in the flesh that we know the eternal Word in himself. To that extent Weber's critique can only be partially accepted. It can, however, be wholly accepted, as can that of Barth and Pannenberg if by *Logos asarkos* is meant an attempt to know a God apart from Jesus of Nazareth. According to the biblical witness no such God exists.

52. Jüngel, op. cit., p. 387.

NOTES TO CHAPTER NINE

1. *C.D.,* IV/3, 1, p. 7.
2. Ibid., p. 8.
3. Colm O'Grady, op. cit., vol. 1, p. 159.
4. *C.D.,* IV/3, 1, p.8.
5. Otto Weber, *Karl Barths Kirchliche Dogmatik,* Neukirchen, 1967, pp. 284–285.
6. *C.D.,* IV/3, 1, p. 11. Otto Weber, *Dogmatik II,* Neukirchen, 1962, p. 276f, points out correctly that this truth is not effected by the Holy Spirit but demonstrated and confirmed to us by the Spirit. Cf. *C.D.,* IV/2, p. 39.
7. This is affirmed by Hans Küng, *Justification. The Doctrine of Karl Barth and a Catholic Reflection,* London, 1964, English translation, p. 331: 'Barth . . . has broadened and deepened the position adopted in the Prolegomena.' 'With this guiding principle, making reconciliation equivalent to *revelation,* the problem of the Prolegomena is obviously taken up again in relation to the prophetical office of Christ.' (Ibid.)
8. *C.D.,* I/1 and *C.D.,* I/2, cf *C.D.,* IV/3, 1, p. 114. This view is in contrast to those like Emil Brunner ('A New Barth', *SJT,* vol. 4, no. 2, June 1951, pp. 123–135) who maintains that in later volumes Barth has changed his position or has left behind the idea of the Word of God. There is a unity and continuity in Barth's work and a return to the beginnings here which at the same time goes on to new, enriching insights and perspectives. See the following who agree with this view:
   C. O'Grady, op. cit., vol. 1, p. 43.
   G. C. Berkouwer, *The Triumph of Grace in the Theology of Karl Barth,* English translation, London, 1956, p. 10.
   H. Urs von Balthasar, *Karl Barth: Darstellung und Deutung seiner Theologie,* Cologne, 1967, pp. 34 and 69ff.
   H. Bouillard, *Karl Barth,* vol. 1. *Genèse et évolution de la théologie dialectique,* Aubier, Paris, 1957, pp. 120, 262.
   W. Schlichting, 'Sozialismus und biblische Denkform', in *Ev.Th.,* vol. 32, no. 6, November/December 1972, p. 595.
   E. H. Friedmann, *Christologie und Anthropologie. Methode und Bedeutung der Lehre vom Menschen in der Theologie Karl Barths,* Münsterschwarzach, 1972, p. 40 writes: 'One can indeed state that today Barth's theological

development can and may be seen neither as linear nor as discontinuous; rather it appears a complex matter, influenced by many historical circumstances, confrontations and new insights within which nevertheless a definite road, once entered upon, is maintained.' In other words— and with this judgment I agree—there is a continuity in Barth's thought from first to last especially from 1932 onwards, yet there are within this unity, modifications from time to time.

9. *C.D.,* I/1, God the Son, God as the Reconciler, pp. 457–474. See especially p. 468 where revelation and reconciliation are one.

10. *C.D.,* IV/3, 1, p. 3. First article of the theological declaration of the Synod of Barmen, 31st May 1934. Cf. *C.D.,* II/1, pp. 172–178, for a commentary on it. The relevant words are 'Jesus Christ, as he is attested to us in Holy Scripture, is the one Word of God, whom we have to hear and whom we have to trust and obey in life and in death.

We condemn the false doctrine that the Church can and must recognise as God's revelation other events and powers, forms and truths, apart from and alongside this one Word of God.'

This was meant positively to affirm the truth of the Gospel and negatively to speak a word against 'a definite and new form of natural theology, namely, by the demand to recognise . . . in the form of the God-sent Adolf Hitler, a source of specific new revelation of God, which, demanding obedience and trust, took its place beside the revelation attested in Holy Scripture' (*C.D.,* II/1, p. 173). It was also against natural theology as such as seen in the previous two centuries where it was believed on all sides that God revealed himself not only in Jesus Christ but 'in reason, in conscience, in the emotions, in history, in nature, and in culture and its achievements and developments' (ibid.) Barth's position is that this is a denial of revelation and that to give even the slightest place to natural theology is to undermine true theology and strike at the roots of revelation. For natural theology soon ceases to claim a subordinate and seeks the whole place. Barth believes that the position taken up at Barmen owed its power not primarily to any theologians or Church group but to the miraculous Word of God, which is Jesus Christ himself (ibid., p. 176). Humanly speaking, however, Barmen owed more to Barth than to any other theologian. (See Karl Barth, *Fragments Grave and Gay*, edited with a Foreword and Epilogue by Martin Rumscheidt, English translation, London and Glasgow, 1971, pp. 71–72.)

11. Weber, *Karl Barths Kirchliche Dogmatik*, p. 285.

12. Ibid., p. 283.

13. Also in this connexion Barth follows the basic insight of Calvin foreshadowed in the early Church of the three-fold office of Jesus Christ as prophet, priest and king. 'He is not only high priest and king, but is also as such the prophet. In this discussion Barth joins himself to Calvin but he goes beyond the "limits" of Calvin's doctrine and especially the orthodoxy that succeeded him' (Weber, bid., p. 285). Barth is particularly critical of Lutheran teaching which tended to obscure the third

aspect or merge it into one of the others or make the priestly the prime one (*C.D.*, IV/3, 1, p. 6).

This prophetic work of Christ is the christological basis of the Church's missionary task. The modern era since the Reformation has been marked by a turning away of the world from the Church, yet at the same time the freeing of the Church to turn to the world in a great variety of ways—mission, service, etc. Church history is thus a subsidiary testimony to Holy Scripture which challenges us 'to pay particular attention to the character of reconciliation as revelation' (ibid., p. 38) to the prophecy of Jesus Christ as the basis of our witness to all. This can be summed up thus: 'Jesus Christ speaks to this people with the intention and commission that it for its part should speak to the world' (ibid., p. 18; see also p. 154). If we look at the missionary history of this century and the last 'its only final explanation is the fact that the reconciliation of the world accomplished in Jesus Christ does actually have the character of revelation, of the Word of God demanding expression. . . . This being the case, it is surely no accident that on the very threshold of this new period of Christianity Calvin should rediscover the doctrine of the *munus Christi propheticum*' (ibid., p. 38). This is the basis for the latter part of this Volume IV/3, 2, the Church sent as a light and witness into the world. (See pp. 681ff.) 'The Holy Spirit and the Sending of the Christian Community.'

14. *C.D.*, IV/3, 1, p. 86. The Scripture reference is to John 1: 4f, 'His life is the light of men.'

15. Ibid., p. 46.

16. Ibid., pp. 39–45 and 105–106.

17. Ibid., p. 48. Barth describes this eloquently in various ways and from different angles (*a*) as light proceeding from himself and no-one else, (*b*) as a declaration and expression of his own inward self, (*c*) as the revelation of his salvation history, (*d*) as the proclamation of his truth as Mediator and (*e*) as the Word which corresponds to and expresses his reality (ibid., pp. 46–47).

18. It is at this point that Barth discusses the relationship of the Old Testament prophets to the theme expounded here, i.e., Jesus Christ as the one true Prophet. The differences can be put thus: (1) They speak the word; he is the Word. (2) They speak to Israel; he to the nations. (3) They prophesy by pointing to a fulfilment; he is that fulfilled covenant between God and man. (4) They are God's messengers; he is the Mediator. They are, therefore, not adequate types of Christ, only *the whole history of Israel* can be and is such. Barth then shows how this history properly prefigured and so witnessed to Christ in these four ways. Ibid., pp. 49–71.

19. Cf. P. T. Forsyth, *Missions in State and Church*, London, 1908, p. 206, in a sermon entitled 'The Exclusiveness of Christ'. 'We have our whole converse with God in him always. There is none other like him [Jesus Christ], none beside him, none above him in our relations with God.' Forsyth quotes Hort (*Hulsean Lect.*, p. 160) with approval: 'The *exclusiveness* of Christ is in truth but another name for the absolute

universality of his kingdom combined with its absolute *unity*' (ibid., p. 204).

20. Op. cit., pp. 88–90. The main objections are that it is presumptuous and so is intellectually obscurantist, morally arrogant, politically intolerant and disruptive.

21. Ibid., p. 86.

22. Ibid.

23. Ibid., pp. 90–91.

24. Ibid., p. 91.

25. Ibid., p. 110.

26. Ibid., p. 109. Cf. p. 90, and also *Credo*, English translation, New York, 1936, pp. 39–50.

27. Ibid., p. 105.

28. Ibid., pp. 96 and 98.

29. By this is meant that only by God is God known. No one is adequate to measure or understand him. We have no place outside of his self-revelation by which to judge him. Hence he authenticates and proves himself. But since Jesus Christ is this self-revelation he is God's Word to us. So we argue from God to God in this circle enclosed by Jesus Christ who discloses God's nature and action as a saving Word spoken to all men.

30. Ibid., p. 87.

31. Cf. Weber, op. cit., p. 289. 'He is the one Word which brings salvation and takes man out of his darkness into light.'

32. *C.D.*, IV/3, 1, pp. 99–103. In this connection, therefore, there are four things that are excluded. (*a*) Since he is the whole truth he needs no completion by others. (*b*) Since he alone is Lord he has no rival to challenge him. Such a one would be superior to, equal or identical with him in irreconcilable contradiction. (*c*) Since he is the one true Word, no synthesis between him and others is possible, whether Mary and the Church (Roman Catholicism), or general revelation (natural theology), or human self-understanding (Bultmann). These are in fact the three great misunderstandings of the faith opposed by Barth in *C.D.*, IV/3, 1. (*d*) His prophecy cannot be transcended by any other either in the content of its declarations, the depth of its truth, the urgency of its demands or the wisdom it imparts.

33. Ibid., p. 97.

34. Ibid., p. 110.

35. Weber, op. cit., pp. 289–290.

36. *C.D.*, IV/3, 1, p. 117. See p. 116 for a summary of this point, and *C.D.*, IV/1, pp. 157–158, for the idea that every man owes his creation and existence to the fact of God's reconciliation, and that this salvation history is the basic history of every man.

37. Ibid., p. 117. Barth can put this point otherwise and say that because God has bound himself to man in Jesus Christ there may be 'a godlessness of man (eine Gottlosigkeit des Menschen) but according to the word of reconciliation there is no non-humanity of God (keine Menschenlosigkeit Gottes)', p. 119. Own translation. God is the God

of all men and does not leave himself without a witness. A reconciled world of which we know on the basis of the biblical testimony may be expected to have some 'revelations' of its truth, give intimations of its real character but only in the power and light of the one and only life of Jesus Christ, the Reconciler.

38. Ibid., p. 119.
39. Ibid., p. 121.
40. Ibid., pp. 110, 125, 135.
41. Ibid., p. 111. Cf. pp. 113, 118, 123.
42. Ibid., p. 135. Cf. p. 122.
43. Ibid., p. 111.
44. Ibid., pp. 112, 114, 117, etc.
45. Ibid., p. 118.
46. Ibid., p. 123.
47. Ibid.
48. Ibid., p. 114. Cf. *C.D.*, I/1, pp. 98–135, and *C.D.*, I/2, pp. 457ff.
49. Op. cit., p. 291.
50. Barth modifies his position in relation to the first half-volume of the *Church Dogmatics* by speaking of the Bible and the Church as 'witnesses' to the one Word. (Cf. *C.D.*, I/2, p. 457f.) So there is only one Word of God attested in Scripture and Church yet also using other words outside to bear the same witness.
51. *C.D.*, IV/3, 1, p. 130. [Italics mine. J.T.]
52. Ibid., p. 115.
53. Ibid., p. 130. [Italics mine. J.T.] See also pp. 131 and 133.
54. Ibid., pp. 125ff.
55. Ibid., pp. 126 and 127. In relation to dogma these words will lead the members of the community 'more deeply into the *communio sanctorum* of all ages which is attested in these documents' (ibid., p. 127). In the case of the good fruits one will have to discern the spirits whether men are, by such words, led to greater freedom, uplift and unity, etc. (ibid., p. 128).
56. Ibid., p. 126. Cf. p. 130.
57. Ibid., p. 134.
58. Ibid., pp. 128 and 129.
59. Ibid., p. 130.
60. Ibid., p. 131.
61. Ibid., p. 133.
62. Ibid., p. 135. He does, however, give *general* examples in pp. 123 and 125. Two only need be mentioned. Such a true word may speak of 'the goodness, peril, triumph and future glory of the divine work of creation' (ibid., p. 123). It will in general be seen in its isolation and abstraction, but, in the light of Christ, will show these elements in the truth and unity 'of the divine work of creation which is enclosed in Jesus Christ, executed in him and directed towards him' (ibid.). The same is true of the many acts of goodness 'warm readiness to understand and forgive' (ibid., p. 125) seen outside the Church. These do not of themselves form a point of contact for man in relation to grace but

they are pointers whose 'truth' is shown in the revelation in Jesus Christ.

63. For an excellent summary of this section in Barth see E. Jüngel, *Gottes Sein ist im Werden*, Tübingen, 1966, pp. 19–21. See also E. H. Friedmann, op. cit., pp. 143ff.

64. *C.D.*, IV/3, 1, p. 151. See also pp. 137, 152–153.

65. Ibid., p. 137.

66. Jüngel, op. cit., p. 19, n. 26. To be sure, reconciliation and creation exist neither in the antithesis of a dualism which would mean estrangement or actual hostility nor in a monism which would mean that they both derive from a superior truth. *C.D.*, IV/3, 1, pp. 151–152.

67. Ibid.

68. *C.D.*, IV/3, 1, p. 138.

69. Ibid., p. 139.

70. Jüngel, op. cit., p. 20, n. 26.

71. *C.D.*, IV/3, 1, p. 139.

72. Jüngel, op. cit., p. 20, n. 26.

73. *C.D.*, IV/3, 1, p. 140. These refer back to earlier expressions of Paul Althaus. However, they are clearly used in a quite different sense from that of Althaus and from what is usual in Barth. Moreover, they play no significant role in his later exposition. They are to be understood, as Jüngel clearly shows, as the 'lights' or 'revelation' of creation, given their light and power as creaturely phenomena by the one true light of life, Jesus Christ.

74. Ibid., p. 141.

75. Ibid., p. 142. To this extent these aspects of the cosmos can be grasped without faith and are known to all. Barth points out that there are six general features common to the 'lights' of the cosmos (ibid., pp. 142–150).

(1) 'The simple one of existence. . . . The existence of the cosmos which makes itself known for the cosmos which knows and *vice versa*' (p. 143).

(2) This expresses itself in the rhythm in which this essential co-existence and inter-relationship take place—a rhythm which is dynamic and multiform and which is repeated ever and again.

(3) The cosmos exists in a series of inner contraries, polarities or antitheses, e.g., light and darkness, etc.

(4) It exists in the context of natural and spiritual laws which confirm its constancy.

(5) As 'summons and invitation to the active ordering and shaping of things, and therefore to a step into freedom' (p. 147).

(6) Finally, there is the unfathomable mystery that runs through all creation, the question of its ultimate meaning, goal and truth.

In all these forms of light we see the truths of the cosmos but not any of them or all of them together can speak their own word of truth or be the revelation of God. It is God's Word alone that can disclose 'what the creature itself cannot disclose as its truth, namely, that it is creature, the creature of God, but no more' (pp. 149–150). Thus while Barth speaks of creation as the sphere of reconciliation he at the same time gives it its relative but important place with its rich variety and meaning. Cf. *C.D.*, III/1, passim.

76. Ibid., p. 141.
77. Jüngel, op. cit., p. 20.
78. *C.D.*, IV/3, 1, p. 141.
79. Ibid.
80. Ibid.
81. Ibid., p. 151.
82. Ibid., p. 143.
83. Ibid., pp. 154–164.
84. Ibid., p. 153.
85. Ibid., p. 163.
86. Ibid., p. 164.
87. Ibid., p. 162.
88. Weber, op. cit., p. 293.
89. Jüngel, op. cit., p. 21.
90. For Barth's views on natural theology in the *Church Dogmatics* see *C.D.*, I/1, pp. 147ff, 219, 448, 540; *C.D.*, I/2, pp. 123, 263ff; *C.D.*, II/1, pp. 76ff, 85ff, 162ff, 215ff, 453; *C.D.*, IV/1, pp. 79ff; *C.D.*, IV/2, pp. 100ff.
91. See Otto Weber, op. cit., pp. 290–291. 'One must ask again whether . . . this does not imply . . . "natural theology"?' (ibid., p. 293). He states that this question will scarcely fail to be asked by Roman Catholic Dogmatics. For a full discussion of the question of a 'natural knowledge' of God see Otto Weber, *Dogmatik I*, pp. 219–251. John Baillie, *The Sense of the Presence of God* (Gifford Lectures 1961–62), London and Toronto, 1962, pp. 168–188. Baillie shows that there have been three kinds of argument used to support natural theology. First, that of an intuitive awareness of the divine as in the Stoics. Secondly, *a posteriori* 'proofs' by way of observation and reasoning. These were the well-known five ways of demonstrating the existence of God, first put forward by Plato and Aristotle and then brought to greater precision and integrated into his system by St Thomas Aquinas. Finally there is the view advocated by Emil Brunner not of a natural theology but of a general revelation given in nature, conscience and history. Of the latter it may be asked if the very uniqueness of the biblical revelation does not at once exclude this possibility? Of the former two one may query, as Barth does repeatedly, whether the 'god' or 'gods' so arrived at as Supreme Being or *Summum bonum*, etc., have anything to do with the God and Father of our Lord Jesus Christ?
92. Emil Brunner's views in *Natural Theology*, comprising 'Nature and Grace' by Professor Dr Emil Brunner and the reply 'No' by Dr Karl Barth, English translation, London, 1946, p. 74.
93. 'Zur Eröffnung der Barth—Ausstellung in Bonn am 1.2.1971', *Ev.Th.*, vol. 31, no. 6, June 1971, p. 327. Cf. Jacques de Senarclens, 'La concentration christologique' in *Antwort: Festschrift zum 70 Geburtstag von Karl Barth*, Zürich, 1956, p. 198. He writes, 'Barth's rejection of natural theology is not a polemical *parti pris*, a kind of contempt for the world

and men, a pure negation. It is the result of an attitude that is entirely positive, the complement of an affirmation; Christ is risen, in him God has done all things needful.'

94. *Natural Theology*, p. 128. Cf. pp. 74 and 123.
95. Ibid., p. 76.
96. *C.D.*, IV/3, 1, pp. 96–109 and pp. 154–164.
97. Ibid., p. 97.
98. Ibid., p. 99.
99. Ibid., p. 104.
100. Cf. H. Hartwell, *The Theology of Karl Barth: An Introduction*, London, 1964, pp. 48–53, who makes the same three points in almost identical terms. T. H. L. Parker, 'Barth on Revelation' *SJT*, vol. 13, no. 4, December 1960, pp. 376–378, has given a good summary of Barth's position, i.e., of the positive bases from which he rejects all natural theology. The three bases correspond exactly to the three points (*a*), (*b*) and (*c*) in my text. (1) 'Natural theology is denied . . by the affirmation of the uniqueness of Jesus Christ as God's self-revelation.' God reveals himself only in him; in him alone is God known. (2) 'Natural theology is denied . . . by the affirmation of the completeness and sufficiency of the revelation of God in Christ.' God reveals himself to us fully in Jesus Christ. To seek to know God apart from him is thus both unnecessary and impossible. (3) 'Natural theology is denied . . . by by the affirmation of the reconciling character of revelation.' The total deliverance wrought for us by Christ's reconciling act reveals our total inability to lift ourselves up to God or know him as he is. The denial of natural theology is but the obverse of a total reconciliation of us by God in Jesus Christ.
101. *Natural Theology*, pp. 124–125. Cf. p. 118, where Barth gives the Scriptural evidence that it is so, viz., all and fully from God alone. Mt. 7: 14, 18: 3; John 3: 3, 5: 24; 1 John 3: 14; Rom. 8: 10; 2 Cor. 4: 16; Col. 3: 9f; Eph. 2: 5; 2 Tim. 2: 11, etc. Barth is aware of the fact that other passages (e.g. Psalm 19, Romans 1 and Acts 17) seem to point to an independent natural theology. However, he argues that this would be in direct contradiction to the main witness of the New Testament that God is known only in his revelation in Jesus Christ. Cf. *C.D.*, II/1, pp. 99ff. For a contrary view see Bouillard, op. cit., pp. 119ff and especially pp. 128–129.
102. *The Question of God: Protestant Theology in the Twentieth Century*, English translation, London and New York, 1969, p. 59. Quoted with apparent approval by E. H. Friedmann, op. cit., p. 85.
103. *Natural Theology*, p. 104.
104. Weber, op. cit., p. 290, writes: 'In this connexion one would not be far wrong in seeing Barth's answer to the numerous questions that have been put to him not only in Germany or in Zürich but also in Utrecht.' In other words, he is concerned with the question how one relates creation, man and their words to the Word of God.
105. As H. Hartwell clearly puts it 'Jesus Christ, (is) the key to the understanding of God, the universe and man.' Op. cit., p. 96.

106. *C.D.*, IV/3, 1, p. 117.
107. Ibid.
108. Ibid. [Italics mine. J.T.]
109. Ibid., p. 118. See also p. 121. Cf. *Natural Theology*, pp. 94, 117, 121 and 124.
110. *Natural Theology*, p. 107. See p. 119. Whether this corresponds exactly with Calvin is disputable. There can, however, be no doubt that this is how Barth himself interpreted him and understood the matter.
111. *C.D.*, IV/3, 1, p. 148.
112. Ibid., p. 155.
113. Ibid., p. 156.
114. Ibid., p. 159.
115. Ibid., p. 163.
116. Ibid., pp. 159–160.
117. Ibid., p. 156.
118. Op. cit., p. 151.
119. Op. cit., p. 330.
120. *C.D.*, IV/3, 1, p. 153. [Italics mine. J.T.]
121. Op. cit., p. 151.
122. Ibid., pp. 151–152.
123. Ibid., p. 152.
124. A further interpretation of this section has been given by G. Koch. 'In view of the activity of Jesus Christ in "true words" of extraordinary men outside the Church which in "an unlikely and inconceivable way", yet "in reality", are witnesses to Christ Karl Barth has renewed the early Church teaching on the *Logos spermatikos*' ('Gotteserkenntnis ohne Christus', *Ev.Th.*, vol. 23, no. 11, November 1963, p. 584). Koch refers to one place where Barth expressly uses the term. (*C.D.*, IV/2, p. 725.) In this, however, Barth is simply using it in an illustrative and descriptive way and is not giving it a specific meaning in relation to the ancient Church or the Word of God. Jüngel rightly rejects this as a proper interpretation of this section of the *Church Dogmatics* (op.cit., p. 21, n. 26).

What is the *Logos spermatikos*? W. Köhler (*Dogmengeschichte, Von den Anfängen bis zur Reformation*, Zürich, 1951, pp. 60–61) points out that this idea was a form of natural theology used by the Apologists and particularly Justin Martyr. A logos existed and governed all history but in the ancient world was only known in seed form (a *logos spermatikos*) that came to fruition and full form when the Word (Logos) became flesh. Christ is the fulness of the Logos, a part of which is to be found in creation. The reasonable (*logikos*) existed before Christ but is only fully found in him. But because it existed in part all who lived 'reasonable' lives according to the Logos were Christian. (Cf. Grillmeier, op. cit., p. 91f.)

This is, however, natural theology with a vengeance and is quite different from anything that Barth teaches in relation to the 'true words' or 'lights' of creation. The *Logos spermatikos* speaks of a 'word' that is natural to and inheres in the world. Barth speaks of 'true words' as being given power to witness to the one Word by that Word itself and this ability is a miraculous act. Nothing could be in greater contrast to the views of the Apologists than those of Barth.

125. *Karl Barths Kirchliche Dogmatik*, p. 294.

126. Both G. Koch (op. cit., p. 584) and F. W. Marquardt (*Theologie und Sozialismus, Das Beispiel Karl Barths*, Munich, 1972, p. 263) accuse Barth of bringing back 'natural theology' into his Dogmatics. This is based on a remark made by Barth on 12th October 1960 to representatives of the Brüdergemeinde in Basle: 'Later I brought in the *theologia naturalis* via Christology.' But H. Diem, 'Die Christologie Karl Barths in der Sicht von F. W. Marquardt', *Kerygma und Dogma*, July 1974, p. 143, shows that this is simply untrue since Barth's statement is a repetition of one made by him in the Barth-Thurneysen correspondence 1914–1925 in *Revolutionary Theology in the Making*, English translation, London 1964, pp. 161–162 and p. 176. It is clear that Barth means that Christology is the key to the understanding of nature, i.e., man, nature and creation are seen and known as they are in the light of Jesus Christ alone. There is no place here for an independent *theologia naturalis*. A. Szekeres, 'Karl Barth und die natürliche Theologie', *Ev.Th.*, vol. 24, no. 5, May 1964, pp. 229ff, fully agrees with this verdict.

There are two other questions Barth takes up which should also be briefly alluded to here.

(*a*) *The Place of Religion.* Religion (including the Christian) is, according to Barth, the human attempt to reach a god and worship him. Revelation, on the other hand, both *abolishes* this false religion of the natural man and at the same time by the justification and sanctification of man by grace *elevates* religion to its true nature. The truth or falsity of religion and religions outside the Christian sphere must be judged by this standard. Since Jesus Christ is Lord of all in reconciliation we may expect true words from any sphere yet they can be known as such only in and through the same Lord.

There is, thus, a dialectic or polarity between revelation and religion. The former both makes known true words in this sphere and at the same time unmasks the false claims of religion as such. 'Other religions are caught up in the economy of salvation, as refractions of the Light, and as potential recipients of the promise of the Spirit (the positive side of the dialectic), but because they have turned away from the Light, and given an absolute status to religion, the Gospel is still as relevant to their sinful condition as it is to the Christian Church where revelation is open to a similar distortion (this is the negative side of the dialectic)' (J. H. Veitch, 'Revelation and Religion in the Theology of Karl Barth', *SJT*, vol. 24, no. 1, February 1971, p. 20. Cf. *C.D.*, I/2, pp. 280–361, *The Knowledge of God and the Service of God*. Gifford Lectures, English translation, London, 1938, p. 21. H. Hartwell, op. cit., pp. 89–91).

(*b*) *The Question of Dialogue.* Barth believes in the possibility and necessity of dialogue between the Church and the world. Its basis is in the fact that by Christ's reconciliation all men are potentially and virtually his, are converted to God. Dialogue will thus have as its aim the leading of those who do not know what they already are in Christ to this true knowledge. The criterion of dialogue will be revelation and not unbelief since the latter does not correspond to man's real nature as revealed in réconciliation. Only the Holy Spirit making clear to man the meaning of revelation and bringing home to him reconciliation can suffice. Neither natural theology nor apologetics can help or lead men to faith; it is truth alone that wins converts.

Therefore, to take natural theology and its false presuppositions seriously is to do a disservice to man in dialogue. If it is the common starting-point and faith is masked, unbelief may be led to certain possibilities which are not real faith and so be deceived. On the other hand unbelief may defend itself against this false theology and feel it has won a victory. The result will be a hardening through pride or through finding a false object of faith which is not true faith.

Barth insists that the other partners must be treated seriously, even if their unbelief cannot, and they must receive sympathetic understanding. However, as with mission 'they will not be allowed to exercise any pressure on the Gospel but . . . this will be opposed to them in all its radical uniqueness and novelty, with no attempt at compromise or at finding a point of contact and the like. Missions are valueless and futile if they are not pursued in strict acceptance of these two presuppositions, and therefore with a sincere respect and yet also an equally sincere lack of respect for the so-called religions'. (*C.D.*, IV/3, 2, p. 875.) See for the above *C.D.*, II/1, pp. 91ff; *C.D.*, IV/3, 1, 191ff.

NOTES TO CHAPTER TEN

1. For Barth this is a further elaboration and implication of the Prophecy of Jesus Christ (*C.D.*, IV/3, 1, pp. 323–324) as well as an interpretation of his doctrine of Time (see particularly *C.D.*, III/2, pp. 485–511) and of the significance of the resurrection generally (*C.D.*, IV/1, pp. 318ff).

2. This can be seen in R. Bultmann, *History and Eschatology*. The Gifford Lectures, Edinburgh, 1957, where the eschatological event is the cross and resurrection. The end is not the Second Coming but what happens in Jesus Christ and to the individual in relation to the kerygma. In contrast to a consummation in Christ at the end Bultmann views it as an event culminating in existential decision here and now, a *nunc aeternum*. See also C. H. Dodd, *The Parables of the Kingdom*, London, 1936. In Dodd eschatology is 'realized' in the life and death of Jesus and does not await any future consummating event.

3. *C.D.*, IV/3, 1, p. 295. It can only be understood in relation to Jesus Christ. 'Strictly speaking, there are no "last things", i.e., no abstract and autonomous last things apart from and alongside him, the last One.' (*C.D.*, III/2, p. 490. Cf. M. Kähler, *Dogmatische Zeitfragen*, II, Leipzig, 1908, p. 490, who writes: 'Indeed we do not know a number of last things but only a "Last" Person, who can only be this because he is also "first".')

4. *Credo*, p. 118. 'In the cross of Christ that time, with all its past, present and future possibilities, is in its totality concluded and become past.' (Ibid.)

5. *C.D.*, III/2, pp. 485–486.

6. Cf. O. Weber, *Karl Barth's Kirchliche Dogmatik*, p. 299, who uses the same words and so replaces Barth's own title 'The Promise of the Spirit' (*C.D.*, IV/3, 1, pp. 274ff) with 'The Coming Again of Jesus Christ by the Spirit'. W. Kreck, *Die Zukunft des Gekommenen, Grundprobleme der Eschatologie*, Munich, 1966, p. 83, queries the correctness of Barth's use of the term *parousia*. Nevertheless he agrees with Barth's general position. He writes, 'What Barth says here can scarcely be supported by the New Testament use of the term. It would, however, be difficult to deny that the New Testament does speak of a threefold coming of Jesus Christ.' Cf. O. Weber, *Dogmatik*, II, p. 750, for a similar verdict.

7. *C.D.*, IV/3, 1, p. 293.

8. Ibid.

9. Ibid.

10. Ibid.

11. *C.D.*, III/2, p. 490. Here Barth uses *parousia* for the final appearing, whereas in *C.D.*, IV/3, 1, pp. 293ff, it is consistently used for the one coming of the Lord in all three forms.

12. *C.D.*, IV/3, 1, p. 293.

13. Ibid., p. 294. 'The Easter event is the original because the first eschatological event' (ibid., p. 295).

14. *C.D.*, III/2, p. 489.

15. *C.D.*, IV/3, 1, p. 293.

16. Ibid., p. 296.

17. *C.D.*, III/2, pp. 486–487. [Italics Mine. J.T.]

18. Ibid., pp. 489–490. [Italics Mine. J.T.]

19. This is the tendency and weakness of Jürgen Moltmann's book *Theology of Hope*, English translation, New York, 1967.

20. Barth points out that these eschatological perspectives are analogous to the doctrine of the Trinity (*C.D.*, IV/3, 1, pp. 294 and 296). There is a three in one and one in three. Each is the whole, yet each is distinguishable from the others and has different emphases. There is a kind of *perichoresis*, a mutual indwelling, because it is the one God and Lord who is active in his unity and totality and differentiated relationship in each form of the *parousia*.

21. For the biblical testimony cf. *C.D.*, III/2, pp. 493–511; and O'Grady, op. cit., vol. 1, p. 343. Barth gives three reasons why the Scriptures so speak:

(*a*) The Old Testament witnesses to God's kingship now and still to come.

(*b*) Jesus himself looked forward to a future event and moved towards it. The kingdom was hidden in his presence and pressed for its revelation. This took place in the resurrection.

(*c*) The testimony of the Spirit who is presence but promise as well.

22. *C.D.,* IV/3, 1, p. 295. B. Klappert, *Die Auferweckung des Gekreuzigten,* pp. 323ff, points out that it is the resurrection (Auferstehung), i.e., the appearance of Jesus as the Risen One and not the cross and the awakening from the dead (Auferweckung) as reconciliation that is the basis of New Testament eschatology. 'It is not the reconciliation which took place in the cross and the *awakening* but *the resurrection* understood as the dawning confirmation of the completed atonement which is the real anticipation of redemption . . . the *resurrection* and not the *awakening* is the anticipation of the *parousia*.' (Ibid., p. 323.)

23. *C.D.,* IV/1, p. 324.

24. *The Glory of God and the Transfiguration of Christ,* London, 1949, pp. 34-35.

25. *St. Paul's Epistle to the Thessalonians,* p. 147 (Ramsey, ibid., p. 34).

26. Op. cit., pp. 34-35.

27. *Eschatology* (Scottish Journal of Theology Occasional Papers, No. 2), p. 71.

28. *Grundfragen der Dogmatik,* p. 113. Cf. also W. Kreck, *Die Zukunft des Gekommenen,* p. 87f.

29. These writers are but representatives of others who are of the same opinion.

30. Op. cit., vol. 2, p. 321.

31. For further treatment of the resurrection see particularly *C.D.,* IV/2, pp. 298ff, and *C.D.,* III/2, p. 441ff.

32. *C.D.,* IV/3, 1, p. 291.

33. Ibid., p. 292.

34. Ibid., p. 351.

35. Ibid., pp. 349-360. Cf. *C.D.,* III/2, pp. 468, 487, 491. Accordingly he is not represented by the Christian community (as is the tendency in Roman Catholicism) nor absorbed in the *kerygma* (Bultmann). See *C.D.,* IV/3, 1, p. 349.

36. Ibid., p. 351.

37. *C.D.,* III/2, p. 468.

38. *C.D.,* IV/3, 1, pp. 351, 352.

39. Ibid., p. 361.

40. Ibid., p. 362. As well as a day of glory as his day, it is that of the Church and so is 'a repetition of the humiliation of the Lord' (*Credo,* p. 121).

41. Ibid., p. 327.

42. *C.D.,* IV/2, pp. 656-657.

43. See *Credo,* pp. 120-121; *C.D.,* IV/3, 1, p. 331.

44. This was to have been the title of Barth's fifth and final volume of the *Church Dogmatics.*

45. *C.D.,* III/2, p. 487. Cf. *C.D.,* IV/3, 1, pp. 293 and 301. However Barth can and does apply these terms also to the resurrection and the Holy Spirit. See ibid., pp. 305, 307. *C.D.,* III/2, p. 488. But they are more often and specifically referred to the final appearing. It is the fact of the unity and totality of the whole that makes this interchange of the various terms possible.

46. Since Barth speaks of the eschatological perspective as universal in scope, do we end up with *apokatastasis*, the redemption of all? Many

have accused Barth of this but it is scarcely the conclusion to be drawn and is certainly not the one he ever specifically makes. However, since the emphasis is so much and so rightly on God's Yes to man, we must view the possibility of universal salvation or redemption with genuine expectation and hope. Why should we not at least have such hope? Does not the very thrust of the overwhelming love and grace of God impel us in this direction even if we cannot definitely say that it will be so? Cf. *C.D.*, IV/3, 1, pp. 477–478. See also for a good discussion of this subject J. D. Bettis, 'Is Karl Barth a Universalist?' *SJT*, vol. 20, no. 4, December 1967, pp. 422–436.

47. *C.D.*, IV/1, pp. 324–329.
48. Ibid., p. 325. Cf. W. Kreck, *Grundfragen der Dogmatik*, p. 104.
49. Ibid. Some of its forms Barth states: (*a*) Our indirect connexion with Christ, (*b*) the isolation of the community in a world estranged from him, (*c*) the hiddenness of the basis of Christian life in Christ invisible, (*d*) the deadness of the sphere in which the life of the resurrection is focussed, i.e., this world and fallen humanity.
50. Ibid., p. 324.
51. Ibid.
52. Ibid., p. 327. Cf. W. Kreck, *Die Zukunft des Gekommenen*, pp. 68, 90–91.
53. Ibid.
54. Ibid., p. 328.
55. Ibid.
56. Ibid., p. 327.
57. Ibid., pp. 326–327.
58. *C.D.*, III/2, p. 485. [Italics mine. J.T.]
59. *Credo*, pp. 119–120.
60. *C.D.*, III/2, p. 489. Cf. *Dogmatics in Outline*, p. 134f, where Barth speaks of this as an 'unveiling', i.e., a making visible of what is known by faith but which is not as yet a matter of sight. See also W. Kreck, *Die Zukunft des Gekommenen*, p. 100.
61. Ibid, p. 490.
62. *Credo*, pp. 122–126, for the following.
63. *C.D.*, IV/1, pp. 211–283.
64. *Credo*, pp. 123–124.
65. Ibid., p. 124.
66. Ibid.
67. Ibid., p. 125.
68. *C.D.*, III/2, p. 486. [Italics mine. J.T.]
69. *Credo*, p. 122.
70. *C.D.*, III/2, p. 487.
71. *C.D.*, IV/3, 1, p. 351.
72. *C.D.*, III/2, p. 487. *C.D.*, IV/3, 1, pp. 301–2, 315, 345.
73. *Eschatology* (Scottish Journal of Theology Occasional Papers, No. 2), p. 15. Manson deduces from this that the scene of the *eschaton* will be 'the world in which man's life is lived and in which Christ died and rose' (ibid.). But of course a world redeemed and so changed into the form of 'the Age of Glory' (ibid.).

74. *C.D.,* IV/3, 1, p. 315; *C.D.,* III/2, p. 487.
75. *C.D.,* III/2, p. 487.
76. Ibid., pp. 489–490.
77. Op. cit., p. 323.
78. *C.D.,* III/2, p. 497. This is against the views of A. Schweitzer, *The Quest of the Historical Jesus. From Reimarus to Wrede,* English translation, London, 1910. Barth states that the New Testament itself does not teach the 'non-arrival' of the *parousia.* Had this been so then this would have been the content of its testimony and indeed that of Jesus himself. (*C.D.,* III/2, p. 509.)

Barth also strongly criticizes the view of Roman Catholicism that the *parousia* is anticipated in the being and structures of the Church. This means that the Church shares in the work of the Holy Spirit, does not await a 'Second' Coming, nor in any real sense expect the reality of a last judgment since 'the future at the end of time will simply be the confirmation of its own present and distinctive perfection' (*C.D.,* III/2, p. 511). This is, as Barth says, the ' "de-eschatologising" of Christianity with a vengeance' (ibid.).

79. Ibid., p. 490.
80. Ibid., p. 491.
81. F. W. Camfield, 'Man in his Time', *SJT,* vol. 3, no. 2, June 1950, p. 133.
82. *C.D.,* III/4, p. 582. Cf. O'Grady, op. cit., vol. 2, p. 322. 'Jesus proclaimed that his kingdom was "at hand", imminent, to come within his own generation. But he also proclaimed it as coming at the end of the world, and imminent in the sense that the time of his final coming is known only to the Father, and therefore can take place at any moment.'
83. Cf. the significant phrase of P. T. Forsyth, 'A Circumambient Eternity'. Cf. *C.D.,* IV/1, p. 327. 'He "encloses us before and behind" (Ps. 139: 5), and therefore altogether and in eternity. That we are in him is true unreservedly and without any loophole for escape.'
84. *C.D.,* III/4, pp. 580–584.
85. Ibid., p. 582.
86. Ibid., p. 583.

INDEX OF NAMES

INDEX OF SUBJECTS